THINK BIG, START SMALL, MOVE FAST

A BLUEPRINT FOR TRANSFORMATION FROM THE
MAYO CLINIC CENTER FOR INNOVATION

NICHOLAS LARUSSO
BARBARA SPURRIER
GIANRICO FARRUGIA

New York   Chicago   San Francisco   Athens   London   Madrid
Mexico City   Milan   New Delhi   Singapore   Sydney   Toronto

1 2 3 4 5 6 7 8 9 0   DOC/DOC   1 2 0 9 8 7 6 5 4

ISBN   978-0-07-183866-5
MHID   0-07-183866-X

e-ISBN   978-0-07-183867-2
e-MHID   0-07-183867-8

Library of Congress Cataloging-in-Publication Data

LaRusso, Nicholas, author.
  Think big, start small, move fast : a blueprint for transformation from the
Mayo Clinic Center for Innovation / by Nicholas LaRusso, Barbara Spurrier,
and Gianrico Farrugia.
     p. ; cm.
  ISBN 978-0-07-183866-5 (alk. paper) — ISBN 0-07-183866-X (alk. paper)
  I. Spurrier, Barbara, author. II. Farrugia, G. (Gianrico), author. III. Title.
  [DNLM: 1. Mayo Clinic. 2. Hospitals, General—Minnesota. 3. Hospital
Administration—Minnesota. 4. Organizational Innovation—Minnesota.
WX 28 AM6]
  RA981.M6
  362.1109776—dc23   2014016207

This book is dedicated to Mayo Clinic for making the world a better and healthier place.

CONTENTS

ACKNOWLEDGMENTS

We would like to thank Mayo Clinic's patients who inspire us daily to transform the delivery of health care and Mayo Clinic's staff who make sure the needs of our patients come first. This book is only possible because of all the wonderful staff at the Center for Innovation, past and present. We owe a big debt of gratitude to our writer, Peter Sander, who put up with three highly opinionated authors and magically translated our thoughts onto paper. We are so grateful to McGraw-Hill Education and our editor, Mary Glenn, for her collegiality and support through the entire process and to Jane Palmieri, our editing manager, for her expertise.

While we have had the privilege of launching and leading the Mayo Clinic Center for Innovation and of documenting and describing in this book how the CFI began, evolved, and functions, it would have been impossible to write this without many colleagues at Mayo Clinic and from other organizations who helped us in this endeavor. We are grateful to all of them, too numerous to mention in the space allotted. But there are a number of individuals we need to call out in particular, including:

Ron Amodeo
Alfred Anderson
Kenna Atherton
Marcos Bari
Jo Bernau
Jeff Bolton
Dr. Michael Brennan
CFI External Advisory Council members: Tim Brown, the late William Drentell, Jim Hackett, Larry Keeley, Frank Moss, Rebecca Onie, David Pratt, Stan Richards, Terry West

Conference Board Council on Innovation, especially Randall
Ledford, James Lichtenberg, Michelle Proctor
CPC Innovation Work Group and in particular Jeff Myers,
Brent Phillips
Dr. Rajeev Chaudhry
Matt Dacy
Linda Downie
Donny Dreyer
Dr. Richard Ehman
Scott Eising
Dr. Bruce Evans
Dr. Glenn Forbes
Dr. Mike Harper
Randall Jones
Julie Koch
Kari Koenigs
Jeff Korsmo
Dr. Paul Limburg
Jerry Malagrino
Dr. John Noseworthy
Dr. Kerry Olsen
Dr. Sandhya Pruthi
Fran Ripple
Jim Rogers III
Lorna Ross
Our much missed colleague Nan Sawyer
Jeff Sigrist
Craig Smoldt
Dr. Douglas Wood
Naomi Woychick
Monica Sveen Ziebell

Dedications

In memory of my parents, Kathryn and Frank, who taught
me to strive for excellence in everything I do; to my four children, Elizabeth, Nicholas, Matthew, and Michael, from whom
I learn about love and life every day; to Lee and Loren, who

have brought new joy and happiness to my life; to the Jesuits, who educated me; and to Mayo Clinic, for providing me with the opportunity of having an impact and making a positive difference in people's lives.

—Nicholas LaRusso

To my husband and best friend, Mike Fox, and to my sons, Charlie, Sam, and Jack Fox, for inspiration, always love, and not letting me take myself too seriously; to my sister, Lauren, and brother, Greg, and their families and to my father and mother-in-law, Gene and Claire, and all my family and dear friends for your encouragement; to Laura Westlund and Marcia McMullen for your professional advice and support; to the CFI, the most talented and passionate team of people I have known and who really want to change the world; and in memory of my dear mother and father, Inger and Burt Spurrier, who taught me love and kindness and that anything is possible.

—Barbara Spurrier

To my infinitely tolerant and supportive wife, Geraldine, and to our two wonderful sons, Luca and Stefan, who make us proud parents; to my mother and late father who pushed me to always aspire to do more; to my brother, sister, my in-laws, and their families for their much appreciated support; to Kristy Zodrow for always keeping me organized; and to my extended work family who make work rewarding, fun, and inspiring.

—Gianrico Farrugia

INTRODUCTION

The rubber-gloved phlebotomist clutches the needle in her hand. The child squirms. Everyone knows what's about to happen.

Blood will be drawn—an experience that happens thousands of times daily. Grownups can handle it, though some better than others. But we're guessing it probably isn't your favorite experience either.

But for most children, it's a crisis. It's scary and uncomfortable. Vein search, needle probe, the jab, the blood, the whole idea of the thing. No matter how many times the child endures it, always the same experience, always the same outcome. We're doing well if the child doesn't tense up, cry elephant tears, faint halfway through, and pout for hours afterward.

How can well-meaning grownups be such vampires, so cruel? Couldn't anything be done to make the thing more pleasant? Or if not pleasant, at least less scary and yucky? Easier for the child? Easier for the phlebotomist, the doctor, the nurse, and the other grownups in the room? Easier and less time-consuming for all?

Enter the Mayo Clinic Pediatric Phlebotomy Chair (Figure I.1).

The chair, designed by a team led by Mayo pediatric endocrinologist Aida Lteif, M.D., has a "Buzzy" on it, which looks like a bumblebee and vibrates when the child touches it. That distracts the child, much as your dentist might distract you with a slight tap on your teeth or cheek as he inserts the novocaine needle. The chair has a built-in iPad, iPod, and projector screen to display pictures, videos, games, and other distractions aimed at 1- to 15-year olds. Even the kids' own stuff if they want. And the chair has easy-to-access levers and pedals to help the children recline should they feel faint.

"We know that distraction works, so the idea is for kids to come in and sit in the chair and rather than focus on the blood draw, they'll focus on what the chair has to offer them," explains Dr. Lteif.

FIGURE I.1. PEDIATRIC PHLEBOTOMY CHAIR

Transforming the Experience

Think about the Pediatric Phlebotomy Chair. As an innovation, how would you describe it?

Did it change the world of medicine? Did it affect the clinical outcome of the blood draw? Will there be a headline in the *New York Times* or a story on the *PBS News Hour* about a new revolution in medicine? A new cure or wonder drug? A new noninvasive option to surgery?

No. The Pediatric Phlebotomy Chair did not change medicine. It changed how medicine was *delivered*. *It changed the patient experience.*

Why is that so important?

Because, in a nutshell, we intend to transform health and health care. And we intend to do that by transforming the patient experience.

The Elephant in the (Waiting) Room

Everybody is aware of it. Health care has mushroomed over the past 30 years into a $3 *trillion* annual problem in the United States. A problem not far from gobbling up 20 percent of the U.S. economy. We have the most expensive health care system in the world. And what do we get for that lavish price? We do provide cutting-edge care—in fact, arguably the best care—for highly complex conditions.

Remarkable innovations in diagnosis and treatment of disease have come from our health care system. However, as overall health care outcomes go, 36 countries rank better than the United States, according to T. R. Reid, *Washington Post* correspondent and author of *The Healing of America: The Global Quest for Better, Cheaper, and Fairer Health Care*. The United States came in last when ranked against Australia, Canada, the Netherlands, New Zealand, the United Kingdom, and Germany, according to the Commonwealth Fund, a private foundation "working toward a high performance health system."

So what are we going to do about it?

Reframe, Then Solve

Albert Einstein once said, "If I had an hour to solve a problem, I'd spend 55 minutes thinking about the problem and 5 minutes thinking about the solution."

Indeed, at Mayo Clinic, we do feel a responsibility to lead a global transformation of health care. But isn't it a huge challenge in a very complex industry? A "giant hairball"? Where do we start? How do we transform an industry, or at the very least, how do we transform our enterprise to take the lead?

At Mayo, we got started. Aside from many modernizations already done or well under way and a legacy of innovation for 150 years, we did a couple of big things that may serve as a good model for any organization trying to achieve large-scale innovation in a complex space.

First, we reframed the problem to be about the *health and the health care experience*. It goes beyond clinical and technical "break-fix" health care to include care *before*, *during*, and *after* the health care event. It's about the whole cycle, from end to end. It is not just the episodic care occurring inside the clinic itself.

As we like to say, it is "Health and health care" delivered "here, there, and everywhere."

By focusing on this larger definition of the health experience, we think we can transform the bigger picture of global health. It's an ambitious objective, but we've reframed the problem and created a vision around it. Throughout this book, we'll see how that vision is put into play and how the same principles can be applied to any large enterprise.

Second, we created the Mayo Clinic Center for Innovation (CFI). The CFI is a formal and embedded—not isolated or outsourced—interdisciplinary group of 60 people working hand in hand with Mayo Clinic medical practices and outside partners and dedicated to the greater Mayo Clinic vision of *an unparalleled experience*. We state our mission quite clearly:

> To transform the delivery and experience of health and health care.

Think Big, Start Small, Move Fast is all about developing a transformative vision and managing a portfolio of platforms, programs, and projects, large and small, to deliver on that vision. It's about applying the principles of *transformative innovation* to the patient experience. It is about how the Mayo Clinic Center for Innovation makes it all happen in a complex and challenging environment.

Disruption—with a Small "d"

So how does our Pediatric Phlebotomy Chair fit into this picture? Did it *transform* health care? Did it solve the $3 trillion problem?

By itself, no. It's an example of one of many innovations—and really, an example of the innovative *spirit*—that we feel will ultimately disrupt the health care system. That spirit and approach will transform it from a 20th century model of care to a new, evolved 21st century model of care that really works.

Did we say "disrupt?" Indeed, we did. That deserves an explanation.

You've probably read about, or heard about, the idea that innovation can be either *sustaining* or *disruptive.* By the "street" definition, *disruptive innovations* change the world, or at least significant portions of it. Disruptive innovations change markets and commerce forever, as the automobile affected passenger rail service in the first half of the 20th century, as ATMs have affected banking, and as the Internet has affected everything for the past 25 years.

Then there's the concept of "disruptive" put forth by the innovation expert and Harvard professor Clayton Christensen, who suggests that disruptive innovation brings products and services that are faster, cheaper, and simpler and thus more available to all, with the clear examples of the PC disrupting computer markets in the 1980s and Henry Ford disrupting automobile markets with inexpensive, mass-produced cars in the 1920s. Dr. Christensen also describes "sustaining" innovation as evolving a product or service essentially to keep up—that is, to refine it for the next iteration of expectations in the marketplace.

Is our Pediatric Phlebotomy Chair a disruptive innovation within either of these definitions? Probably not. Although it did transform a patient experience, it's hardly a game changer—and really, that's by design. Tearing down everything and starting over is not an option in health care. Patient lives are at stake, as is a system vital to sustaining human life in general. We can't blow it all up and start over, and we can't leave it to patients and physicians to work out the bugs. Yet we do have to dramatically alter the way health care is experienced, and that requires lots of innovations, some small and some not so small, but all targeting a complete redesign of the patient experience, each attacking the problem from a different angle. We refer to these as *transformative innovations.*

What Does It Mean to Transform?

When we say "transform," we really *do* mean both "disrupt" and "sustain" together. Our vision calls for a 21st century model of care substantially different from and much evolved from the 20th century model. But do we need a Hurricane Sandy–like event to make it happen? Do we want the health care system to collapse under its own weight? Under the burden of delivering the $200 billion worth of annual care for Alzheimer patients alone? Storm clouds—like Medicare cutbacks—dominate the horizon and signal trouble.

We know a reset is necessary, but we cannot wait for a metaphorical hurricane to demolish what we have, and we do not want the chaos that it would bring. As a consequence, one of Mayo Clinic's approaches to better health is to *transform* health and health care by going after the health care experience, and we will do it a step at a time. Tim Brown, the president and CEO of IDEO and the author of *Change by Design*, puts it this way: "Complex systems don't get solved by a few people in a room. They get solved incrementally, layer by layer, by implementing sequential and layered designs that connect to deliver a better whole." In our case, we are layering our designs toward a better and more effective patient experience and toward a greater vision of a transformed health (not just health *care*) system.

We will take apart the definition of *transformative innovation* in Chapter 2. It is disruptive—with the word spelled with a small "d." It is ultimately and unabashedly patient (that is *customer*) centered. It is *layered*, and it is *iterative*. It has impact on the customer *irrespective of scale*. It is a series of layers that, like laminated plywood, come together to give form and strength to the whole above and beyond basic material and dimensional strength. It brings together diverse disciplines, and it merges the discipline of design with the scientific method to deliver the result.

Health and Health Care, Here, There, and Everywhere

Consider eConsults, another Mayo Clinic Center for Innovation success story. The eConsults platform is a series of electronic tools connecting patients (and sometimes their local physicians) wherever they are with Mayo Clinic physicians. Patients no longer have to physically travel to a Mayo Clinic site. Instead, these tools enable individuals to stay in contact with a health provider via video, text, a smartphone app, or similar devices. Over time, the patient—and physician—experiences are transformed.

Such a vision becomes clearer when you consider another success story still in the CFI lab. It's called OB Nest. With OB Nest, expecting mothers can use electronic tools to connect with care providers at all stages of the pregnancy. No more waiting for appointments, rushed travel to clinics, long waiting room waits, or wasted visits. Mothers can get answers to questions that come up day and night. They are activated and *empowered in their own health*. It fits and works with our mobile society. When delivery or other care events occur, physicians know more about what the mothers experienced along the way. No more one-size-fits-all care delivered in a clinical setting only. Ultimately, it should cost less for the patient and the provider—less infrastructure, fewer staff members, and *less highly skilled* staff members will have to be in place to deliver transformed—and better—care. It's a win-win-win—for the patient, provider, and payer.

Such "here, there, and everywhere" solutions are built around today's new connectivity tools—but they don't stop there. We embrace the future of nanotechnology and the monitors and implantable devices that might come to be—all connected to such a network. We embrace the advent of user-friendly monitoring and imaging tools that will give us on a regular basis remote access to an ultrasound image, patient weight, or even skin color and appearance.

These technologies can be deployed for preventative health, for health episodes or care events, and postepisodic care. They can be deployed not just for young mothers but also for elderly individuals who require more monitoring in assisted living facilities—or even in their own homes. They can be wired not only to provide access and contact to health professionals but to the family members and professional caregivers that want to—literally—keep their fingers on the pulse of their loved ones.

Health and health care, here, there, and everywhere.

Four Platforms of Transformation

Toward this transformative vision, there are some 40 projects going on within, or connected with, the Mayo Clinic Center for Innovation at any given time. One fundamental aspect of transformative innovation is to tackle problems from many angles simultaneously, using CFI as the coordinating core rather than charging forward with one big concept at a time. Now doesn't that sound like a giant hairball in and of itself? How do we manage such an assortment of projects? Moreover, what is the "connective tissue," the laminate "glue," that binds these layers together with a common vision and toward a common goal?

Organization is part of the story. Over time, we have organized ourselves into four major *platforms*, or areas of strategic focus, that we describe throughout the book. Three of the four, as we'll see, are devoted to health care delivery; the fourth supports the other three and, further, the task of innovation itself both within CFI and in the greater organization. Within each of these four platforms we have *programs*, and within these programs, we have *projects*.

These are our four platforms:

> ▶ *Mayo Practice.* This platform targets practice redesign of the health care episode, and it works toward optimizing processes and the patient experience during the care event. Project Mars is just as the name suggests: What would the ideal medical practice look like if started from scratch on Planet Mars? Physical and technology design are both in play here. We also deploy the Multidisciplinary Design Outpatient Lab where physicians and care team members see real patients in a prototype environment, and together they co-create new processes and workflows to improve the experience and efficiency of the practice.

> ▶ *Connected Care.* Connected Care delivers both health and episodic care "here" and especially "there" and "everywhere." Programs include eHealth, which connects patients, and sometimes their local care providers, to Mayo physicians using video and other conferencing technologies, providing high levels of care often without patients leaving their homes. The mHealth

program uses mobile technologies to maintain health and provide care for specific diseases such as asthma. New practice models, such as the OB Nest already mentioned and a diabetes program, are working to move the center of gravity away from the physician's office and give the person, the patient, the tools he or she needs to manage his or her health care.

▶ *Health and Well-Being.* This broad platform is targeted toward the "health" (as opposed to "health care") part of the cycle. Programs include a broad Community Health program designed to improve ongoing health with coaching and monitoring tools to help individuals stay healthy and avoid the health episode cycle. The Thriving in Place program emphasizes connected health for seniors, helping them stay in their homes, safe and connected. The Healthy Aging and Independent Living (HAIL) Lab, embedded in an assisted living facility, is a centerpiece of this design effort.

You can see a flow here: care starts with Health and Well-Being, continues with contact through Connected Care, then segues to Mayo Practice when a patient must visit a facility, finally returning to Health and Well-Being and Connected Care. Together these platforms connect to deliver the vision of "Health and health care, here, there, and everywhere." Then, to enable these programs, and just as importantly, to keep innovation continuously in front of Mayo leaders and staff, we have a fourth platform:

▶ *Innovation Accelerator.* To strengthen the spirit of innovation and to keep moving forward, a successful innovation group must become part of the fabric of the larger organization. The Innovation Accelerator *transfuses* innovation techniques and successes throughout the organization with a broad set of communications, educational tools, and idea collectors, as well as a speaker series and a major annual innovation conference called TRANSFORM Through the CoDE (for Connect, Design, Enable, a CFI way of work) program, CFI provides seed funding, and it incubates ideas that originate in the medical practices—the Pediatric Phlebotomy Chair was one such project. Through the Innovation Accelerator platform, the greater Mayo organization acquires the new ideas and the "muscle memory" to keep innovating toward the transformative vision.

Think Big, Start Small, Move Fast

Transforming to a new-and-improved 21st century model of care experience is what we're all about at CFI. We don't seek new miracle clinical cures for medical ailments. That is also essential, but there are other parts of the organization working on those—including hundreds of physicians and medical researchers within Mayo Clinic. Instead, we strive to integrate design, knowledge, and technology to deliver a better experience for the patient.

The Pediatric Phlebotomy Chair was a relatively small project. It was conceived within the Mayo Clinic practice and brought to life via our Innovation Accelerator platform. This innovation and others like it have come from a disciplined, patient-centric, experience-focused innovation organization—an organization that functions within a much larger and complex health care enterprise to deliver on such ideas. We use these small steps to lead to a bigger vision of transformation. We've learned how to partner within our organization, and *outside* of our organization, to make things happen.

It's all part of what we, at the Center for Innovation, call Think Big, Start Small, Move Fast. We're so dedicated to that principle that we trademarked the phrase.

Who Should Read *Think Big, Start Small, Move Fast?*

Our mission is to help you realize transformative innovation in *your* organization based on our Center for Innovation experience. Our book is aimed at complex organizations that must create compelling customer experiences to become or stay competitive. Those experiences can relate to delivering a service directly or to delivering a service wrapped around a product.

You may or may not need to transform your industry, as we believe we do. As a strategic objective, you may merely be looking to reinvent your enterprise. But as the folks at Apple have shown us, transforming your industry may be the best way to transform your enterprise. Apple transformed the digital industry with digital music and tablets, and thus it moved from being a bit player in computers to a market leader in a transformed industry.

This book is for key individuals and management teams both within and outside the health care industry. It's for those working in complex organizations that can't quite seem to bring transformative innovations to market. It's for those trying to get their complex organization to pursue innovation in a methodical way, with some structure and discipline but not with so much that transformative innovations become stifled or lose their impact.

Your Authors: Who We Are and What We Do

So, let's switch gears to share a bit about us. We are two physicians and a professional health care leader, all employed by Mayo Clinic. Two docs and a leader who together have almost 80 years of combined experience practicing our trades within Mayo.

During our careers, we developed a passion for our profession—that's hard *not* to do when working for an organization like Mayo. But our experiences and passions led us beyond our practices into a keen interest in the patient experience and, most important, into a formal innovation effort focused on that experience. After years of innovating within our own organizational silos, our passions gave rise to the Center for Innovation as a distinct Mayo Clinic entity in 2008, and we haven't slowed down since. We've initiated, incubated, and collaborated on some 275 completed innovation projects, and, as mentioned above, we have 40 more in the works.

Here are our bios.

Nicholas LaRusso, M.D.

Dr. LaRusso is the founding medical director of the Mayo Clinic Center for Innovation, and he is the Charles H. Weinman Endowed Professor of Medicine and Biochemistry and Molecular Biology and a Distinguished Investigator of Mayo Clinic. A practicing hepatologist and the former chair of the Department of Medicine, he has also held positions as editor of the journal *Gastroenterology* and as president of both the American Association for the Study of Liver Disease and the American Gastroenterology Association.

He is the author of more than 500 publications, the principal investigator of three National Institutes of Health (NIH) grants, and the recipient of a Method to Extend Research in Time (MERIT) Award, the highest accolade for scientists from the NIH. He is a highly sought after speaker and panelist on innovation as well as on his own basic research.

Barbara Spurrier, MHA

Ms. Spurrier is the founding administrative director of the Mayo Clinic Center for Innovation, a role that she still holds. With 25 years of experience in health care strategy and operations from four organizations, Ms. Spurrier lectures frequently on innovation.

She has served on a number of boards including the Medical Group Management Association, and she has served as the president of its Academic Practice Assembly. She completed her Leadership Quality Blackbelt Certification from the University of Minnesota's Juran Institute, and she is a Certified Medical Practice Executive.

Gianrico Farrugia, M.D.

Dr. Farrugia is the Carlson and Nelson Endowed Director of the Mayo Clinic Center for Individualized Medicine and the associate director of the Mayo Clinic Center for Innovation. He is a practicing gastroenterologist, a laboratory-based researcher funded by the National Institutes of Health, and a professor of medicine and physiology at Mayo Clinic.

Dr. Farrugia is the editor of the journal *Neurogastroenterology and Motility* and the president-elect of the American Neurogastroenterology and Motility Society. He has helped launch several companies. He has published more than 250 articles, and he speaks widely on individualized medicine and innovation.

How We Organized *Think Big, Start Small, Move Fast*

Our book is divided into three parts, as described below.

Part I: The Needs of the Patient Come First

Part I sets the stage, describing *who we are*, *what we do*, and *why we do it* in three chapters. Chapter 1 gives a brief overview of Mayo Clinic as an institution—its history, values, culture, and form.

Chapter 2 explores the imperatives and challenges facing innovation in the health care industry and service industries in general, and it offers a deeper explanation of transformative innovation.

Chapter 3 covers the Center for Innovation as a distinct unit within Mayo Clinic—its inception, evolution, makeup, role, and philosophy.

Part II: Think Big, Start Small, Move Fast

The four chapters of Part II explain how we *do* it and how we *manage* it. Chapter 4 describes the general model, which we call the Fusion Innovation Model. This is the model we use to assess and frame customer needs and to imagine, build, test, and implement transformative innovations.

We don't stop there. Chapters 5 and 6 explain the all-important communication and education processes to connect with the rest of the organization (we call this *transfusion*)—to build the culture of innovation, capture innovative ideas from the practices, and disseminate news and information about current projects and completed work.

Finally, Chapter 7 describes how we've evolved the leadership model and style into a "village" approach to effectively build and nurture the innovation portfolio.

Part III: The Mayo Clinic Model in Action

How does it all really work? In Chapter 8, we take you on a tour of CFI projects in action, starting with Project Mars, a Mayo Practice project conceived within CFI to use a clean slate and new technologies to develop the medical practice of the future. Chapter 8 continues with a description of eConsults within the Connected Care platform, which applies some of the same new technologies to enable remote patient access to physician consultations.

Next, we explore Optimized Care Teams, a project that touches both of the first two under Health and Well-Being as a way to reexamine the composition of the care team to match the right players with the right health circumstances and to change the approach to delivering care. We wrap up that chapter with an overview of the Mayo Clinic App, another outcome of the CoDE incubator in the manner of the Pediatric Phlebotomy Chair.

Finally, in Chapter 9, we bring it all together into a short wrap-up of how to best take what we've learned and experienced and apply it to your organization.

Now we invite you to join our team to find out how Think Big, Start Small, Move Fast has transformed innovation at Mayo Clinic—and how it will transform health and health care in the 21st century and how it may help you transform your own organization.

PART I

THE NEEDS OF THE PATIENT COME FIRST

CHAPTER ONE

An Experience of Civility

I first came to Mayo Clinic in the summer of 2001 because I was wheezing doing a Prairie Home Companion *show, getting on and off stage, because, as it turned out, I had sprung a leak in a mitral valve. So I came to Mayo, and it took the internist about five minutes to make the diagnosis, and the choice was fairly simple . . . uh, either Dr. Orsulak will operate and sew up your mitral valve, or else you will sit in a sunny corner of your kitchen and wait for God to harvest his flowers.*

Right off, you may recognize the storyteller. It's none other than Garrison Keillor, host of Minnesota Public Radio's well-known show heard weekly for some 40 years on most National Public Radio affiliates. At the 2012 Mayo Clinic Center for Innovation TRANSFORM symposium, Keillor got a chance to tell us about his Mayo Clinic experiences. Pretty amazing stories these turned out to be, especially since the half-hour keynote was completely unscripted and unrehearsed. Experiences—memorable experiences these were—from the mind and from the heart. Let's listen in:

The operation turned out well. . . . Besides repairing the mitral valve, it also gave me an experience. . . . It gave me a crucial experience . . . in the kindness of extremely competent people. You were brought into the operating room, you were naked, you've been shaved in embarrassing ways. You were wrapped in a sheet. You were lifted off the gurney onto this glass and steel table in this dim, very chilly room, strange lights, and masked people. . . . It's out of a science fiction movie. You're laid down there, and they adjust you, and in this unreal world, to have a human being touch you with some feeling . . . just put a hand on your bare shoulder . . . means the world, means that we are people. . . . You are a person, I am a person, and you recognize that I am. Someone asks you how you are doing and means it. . . . It means the world to you. The humanity . . . the humanity . . . and kindness . . . the way in which things are done. . . . And then you disappear into the fog . . . and the fog breaks hours later, and you find yourself in a recovery room, and these angelic beings appear out of the mist . . . and they speak with Minnesota accents . . . and they remove this 12-inch drainage pipe from your mouth, and they tell you that you're alive . . . and you are grateful for that . . . and 11 years later, I still am.

This is an amazing experience for an adult person to have . . . to experience competence and kindness . . . all wrapped up in one piece. . . . It's what I love about Mayo Clinic. . . . It has international expertise and small town manners in my own experience with the place.

When I came down to Mayo for my prostate biopsy, what those two men did for me (aside from telling me I don't have prostate cancer) . . . I'll never forget. It's an embarrassing thing. It's uncomfortable. As the doctor's assistant said, it's like having nine hornets up your butt . . .

But they went at it like a Vaudeville team, like an old time comedy team . . . the Russian urologist and his assistant . . . and . . . the jokes were almost funny . . . and the conversation and the bi-play. . . . And now we've got four more, and now we've got three more, and now two, and one, and now you're done. And when you were done, you shook hands with them, and you said thank you, and you meant it. Aside from its medical value, this was such an experience of civility.

An experience of civility.

There's a lot of meaning wrapped up in that phrase. And also in the phrase "international expertise with small town manners." And, continuing, "to have a human being touch you with some feeling, . . . to put a hand on your bare shoulder." And "great competence put at your service by people who recognize your humanity."

You get the main idea. There's something pretty special here. Excellence not just in health care but also in the health care *experience*. Excellence in an experience beyond the medical outcome, excellence that draws patients from around the world to Mayo, and has done so for 150 years.

So just what is Mayo Clinic? If you're like most Americans and many around the world, you recognize the name and the brand, and you likely associate it with world-class medical care for some of the most challenging illnesses we might confront in our lives. But as you learned in the Introduction, our book isn't just about health care, and it isn't about the status quo. It's about how to innovate in a complex environment. We use the way Mayo Clinic delivers health care today, and how that delivery will be transformed in the future, as a guiding example. The roots of the Mayo legacy—how our organization earned its renown, and how it goes about improving and achieving excellence every single time a patient comes in contact with Mayo, anytime and anywhere in the world—make up a key part of our story.

How did Mayo Clinic come to be such an "experience in civility"? As with any great organization, particularly a successful one like Mayo, its roots define its culture, and its culture defines its achievements. So a sketch, a glimpse, a short movie about just what Mayo Clinic is, its history, its culture, its values, its ethos, and how it all came to be a setting for today's and tomorrow's transformative innovation in health and health care—this is a logical place to start.

"The Care Begins When You Arrive at the Door"

You walk down Third Avenue SW in Rochester, Minnesota, and look around. It's a notably clean and traditional-looking town of about 110,000 residents approximately 90 minutes south of the Twin Cities of Minneapolis and St. Paul. Tallish buildings and parking garages surround you. People are looking for parking spaces, people are walking around the streets, and people are being pushed in wheelchairs. You stare straight ahead at the Gonda Building, the 20-story world headquarters, the integrated practice centerpiece of Mayo Clinic (Figure 1.1).

You're curious, and you walk inside. You see more people in wheelchairs, many being assisted by family members. You see the concerned looks on their faces. About a thousand patients come through these doors every day.

It's a beautiful lobby with a pleasing, contemporary, tasteful design, like a fine hotel. All designed by world-renowned architect Cesar Pelli, who gave us the title quote for this section, and by Ellerbe Becket. It was funded in a large part by the family of Leslie Gonda, an American entrepreneur and Holocaust survivor. The lobby is adorned with a massive glass sculpture by Pacific Northwest artist Dale Chihuly—a sculpture beautiful in its own right but also indicative of the sorts of gifts given regularly to Mayo by grateful patients.

FIGURE 1.1. MAYO CLINIC GONDA BUILDING

You walk through this attractive and calming space. And what's that you hear? Piano music accompanying a small choir. Nice. You go out the back entrance—east—toward Second Avenue SW. There's a small town square known as the Peace Plaza with attractive shops and—today—a street festival with fancy crafts, great food, and tasteful live music thanks to a collaboration known as Destination Medical Center, an economic development cooperative with Mayo Clinic, the city of Rochester, the state of Minnesota, and other partners. There are stately older buildings that were designed with great purpose in mind in the 1920s, on both sides of the square. We'll return to those buildings shortly. The modern 18-story Mayo Building is attached to Gonda to the south. Mayo Clinic Hospital, Methodist campus flanks it to the north.

You see a young couple in an embrace—an embrace of all-out love and passion. She is standing gingerly on a leg prosthesis, with eyes closed, and is smiling intently as they hug. She is one of the thousands who come every year to Mayo Clinic for a definitive answer. She comes with the hope of receiving medical care that might save her life and salvage her connection with her loved ones. To think about what they have to deal with brings tears, even to the eyes of a stranger. But it's perfectly clear that Mayo Clinic, the city of Rochester, and countless others are pulling out all the stops to make their visit as comforting, pleasant, and, really, joyful as possible—for that couple and any loved ones who might be with them.

It's an experience in civility, and it happens every day.

Mayo Clinic: The Snapshot

Mayo Clinic is the *first* and *largest* integrated, not-for-profit medical group practice in the world. Today's Mayo Clinic employs more than 4,000 physicians and medical scientists and 54,000 allied health staff.

Mayo Clinic is headquartered in Rochester, with additional full service facilities in Arizona and Florida. Mayo Clinic also operates a Mayo Clinic Health System network of about 70 hospitals and clinics across Minnesota, Wisconsin, and Iowa. More than three-quarters of the employees are located in Rochester and the surrounding health system, and the remainder are in Arizona and Florida. There are also about 3,400 students and residents associated with the Mayo Medical School, the Mayo Graduate School, and the Mayo School of Graduate Medical Education, which fulfill the education mission of Mayo Clinic.

Beyond these Mayo-owned facilities, a new Mayo Clinic Care Network has been formed that offers health care systems the benefits of Mayo Clinic knowledge and expertise without having to travel to a Mayo Clinic facility. Mayo Clinic provides these like-minded organizations care delivery offerings and information-sharing tools through a partnership agreement. The network recognizes that people prefer to get their health care as close to home as possible, and it serves to extend and expand the Mayo brand beyond the traditional Mayo geography and bricks-and-mortar facilities. Currently there are 29 such organizations in the network across the United States and beyond. The Mayo Clinic Care Network will most assuredly expand as the health care industry wrestles with accountable care, affordability, and access.

Mayo Clinic treats more than 1 million unique patients each year. The vast majority, 85 percent, are treated on an outpatient basis, many staying in Rochester, Scottsdale, or Jacksonville for days or weeks of successive outpatient treatments. They take up residence at one of the many local hotels that offer special accommodations and weekly rates for patients and their families. Shuttle services ply the streets continuously between these accommodations, the outpatient center, and the two affiliated hospitals.

The physical presence of Mayo Clinic in Rochester is impressive, with a complex of downtown-style city buildings occupying several city blocks. In Rochester, Mayo Clinic occupies 30 buildings in all and some 15 million square feet, about 3.5 times the size of the gigantic Mall of America just south of the nearby Twin Cities.

Today's Mayo Clinic operates primarily as a "destination" medical center, gathering in patients from across the United States and 150 countries across the globe for highly specialized treatments for a wide assortment of diseases. Increasingly,

Mayo has broadened its footprint by expanding into more local and regional geographies, and as we'll see, it is also reaching out in a big way through innovations and technologies that allow remote patient visits with diagnosis, treatment, and monitoring. Mayo has also moved squarely into health and wellness, embracing a holistic shift from just sickness or health care to helping people optimize their well-being over their lifespan—the difference between "health" and "health care" as noted in the Introduction. Increasingly, Mayo physicians collaborate with local physicians and staff to deliver health and health care, both in Mayo locations and, through partnerships, to non-Mayo locations. In this way, the Mayo brand is gradually growing beyond the idea of destination medicine.

Much goes on at Mayo Clinic beyond the medical practice itself. However, to quote John Noseworthy, M.D., Mayo Clinic president and CEO, "the practice is the main thing." The three shields of Mayo, which have existed from the beginning, are Patient Care, Research, and Education (Figure 1.2).

In addition to the patient care and education shields already described, Mayo Clinic under its research shield conducts extensive studies in clinical care, including new diagnostics, medications, devices, tools, and procedures.

FIGURE 1.2. THREE SHIELDS OF MAYO: PATIENT CARE, RESEARCH, AND EDUCATION

Almost 9,000 active research studies were conducted in 2012 by about 3,300 research-dedicated personnel on a budget of $633 million resulting in 4,000 publications. This does *not* include the patient experience research and innovation conducted by the Mayo Clinic Center for Innovation, the central subject of this book.

Interestingly, Mayo Clinic physicians are paid a fixed salary that is not linked to patient volume or income from fee-for-service payments. This model was put in place to ensure that the needs of the patient would always come first and to minimize any financial motivation to see patients in large numbers or perform unnecessary procedures. It adds an incentive to spend more quality time with individuals, as well as to devote more time to collaborate with other personnel for patient care and, importantly, for innovation.

Mayo Clinic: The History and the Heritage

As big and impressive as Mayo Clinic is today, both as a facility and as a brand, it is just as instructive to look at Mayo Clinic's past. In that story we can find many historical and cultural clues descending directly from its founders to form its values, which have shaped today's approach to medicine. That past has also shaped today's approach to innovation and the patient experience.

Early Beginnings, and a Twister of Fate

It all started rather inconspicuously with the birth of William Worrall Mayo in northern England in 1819 to an English family of Flemish descent. As with many successful innovators, his parents, who were of modest means, insisted on a good education. Among other things, this led to private tutorage from none other than chemist John Dalton, considered a father of modern chemistry and physical science and one of the first to scientifically describe atoms and the periodic table. William Worrall Mayo's passion for science was set for life by his exposure to Dalton. Not a bad place to begin.

Mayo immigrated to the United States in 1846 at age 27. And like many other immigrants, he migrated westward seeking opportunity where it could be found, gaining experience in many trades including pharmacy, tailoring, farming, publishing, and ultimately, medicine. He enrolled at the Indiana Medical College in La Porte, Indiana, and he graduated in 1850. He set up to practice medicine and pursue medical knowledge with a microscope, one of the first to do so in a medical practice. He kept detailed clinical notes, and he was known for the persistent comment, "Left open for further thought and research," that accompanied many of his observations. For Dr. Mayo, status quo didn't cut it.

In 1851 he married Louise Abigail Wright, who would become his devoted spouse and medical companion for the next 60 years.

As a consequence of malaria and related fevers, common at this time, he went west by riverboat to the fresher climes of Minnesota, and he settled there and started practicing medicine. Louise eventually followed.

When the Civil War broke out, he applied to become an army surgeon for a Minnesota regiment, but for reasons unknown, his application was denied. In hindsight, that was fortuitous, for shortly thereafter he landed a position as the examining surgeon supporting federal troops involved in the nearby Indian wars, still quite active at the time. The headquarters of the conscription board was in Rochester.

New job in hand, Dr. Mayo ("Worrall," or "W.W.," as he is fondly called by Mayo employees) and Louise settled down in 1864 and had four children—two girls and two boys. And not surprisingly, Dr. Mayo took his two sons, William ("Will") and Charles ("Charlie"), under his wing to teach them science at a very early age. They went on his rounds, helped in the office, sometimes even with surgery, and read a lot of good books like *Gray's Anatomy* and Paget's *Lectures on Surgical Pathology*. There was lots of encouragement from Mom too. Many years later Charlie described her as "a real good doctor herself."

And not surprisingly, both boys went to medical school—William to the University of Michigan, Charlie to Northwestern University. Both graduated in the 1880s.

Meanwhile, on a hot August afternoon in 1883, a massive tornado leveled a good part of Rochester, killing 24 and seriously injuring 40. Dr. W. W. Mayo, his sons, who were home for the summer, and other volunteers set up a make-shift hospital. Needing more help, Dr. Mayo called on Mother Alfred Moes and her Sisters of St. Francis, who were teachers, not nurses, to assist in round-the-clock patient care.

A partnership was formed, and eventually from it a new permanent hospital, Saint Marys, opened in 1887, now called Mayo Clinic Hospital Rochester, Saint Marys campus. It has been in operation ever since. It is one of the earliest examples of collaboration between doctors and administrative staff on the design and operation of a medical facility.

The two boys formally joined the practice in 1889. By now all three Mayos were gaining a reputation for surgical accomplishments at Saint Marys.

My Brother and I

In the late 1800s, the practice of medicine was still in its early stages. Most medical practices were simple storefronts staffed by an individual physician with varying degrees of professional training. That physician learned and delivered all forms of medicine. There were no "specialists" to call on. Physicians learned by reading, by doing, and by watching each other perform. The age of science-based, research-based medicine was just at its beginnings.

The Mayo brothers and their father continued to practice together, an unusual construct in those days. They traveled extensively, in the United States and abroad, to acquire new knowledge. They shared their observations and knowledge, and they were dedicated to a "team" approach to delivering better patient care and, in so doing, advancing medical science. Soon, other doctors started arriving from long distances to observe their practice—and patients began coming from afar as well.

The teamwork became a guiding mantra. As Dr. W. W. Mayo put it: "No one is big enough to be independent of others." They shared medical knowledge, took interest in each other's professional growth, and even shared a bank account. In later years, Drs. Will and Charlie would simply refer to themselves collectively as "my brother and I" when giving talks, accepting awards, or discussing matters with a patient.

Teamwork—mutual respect and the sharing of diverse skills for a common good—is the essence of Mayo Clinic. Biographer Helen Clapesattle later called it a "spirit of cooperative individualism."

The Needs of the Patient Come First

The Mayo founders believed that the combined wisdom of one's peers is greater than that of any one person. They went out of their way to be inclusive, way before "crowdsourcing" became a popular term. An integrated team of compassionate, multidisciplinary physicians, scientists, and allied health professionals who are focused on the needs of patients is a core principle and value of today's Mayo Clinic. At the time the clinic was founded, however, it was a revolutionary idea and way to practice medicine.

Dr. William Mayo put it quite clearly in a 1910 commencement address:

> *As we grow in learning, we more justly appreciate our dependence upon each other. The sum-total of medical knowledge is now so great and wide-spreading that it would be futile for one man to attempt to acquire, or for any one man to assume that he has, even a good working knowledge of any large part of the whole. The very necessities of the case are driving practitioners into cooperation. The best interest of the patient is the only interest to be considered, and in order that the sick may have the benefit of advancing knowledge, union of forces is necessary.*

In these words you can clearly identify the teamwork approach. But another guiding light shone down from this address, to become the core philosophy and value of Mayo Clinic: "The best interest of the patient is the only interest to be considered."

Over the years, the wording has been consolidated into Mayo Clinic's primary value, heard daily from any employee across the organization: "The needs of the patient come first."

Practice Makes Perfect: The Integrated Practice Comes Together

The practice grew. In the early 1890s Drs. Will and Charlie began inviting more partners to provide services to complement their own surgical practice. In 1892, Dr. Augustus Stinchfield, a well-known Minnesota practitioner, joined the Mayos as their first partner. At about that time, Dr. W. W. Mayo, now 73, retired. Two years later, Dr. Christopher Graham, a brother-in-law and recent medical graduate, joined the growing practice as the second partner. By 1908, eight more professionals—four physicians, a medical illustrator, a professional administrator, a medical librarian, and a secretary—had joined the practice.

The Mayo brothers were building a true interdisciplinary team, recognizing the value of nonphysicians as core members of the team, on equal footing to physicians. We will come back to this point in Chapter 3, when we describe the approach taken in building the Center for Innovation. In 1894, the brothers made a decision to dedicate half their income in perpetuity in the "service of humanity" to what ultimately became the Mayo Foundation. "We try to take up the medical surgical education of selected and promising men where the state leaves off. My interest and my brother's interest is in the service of humanity. . . . If I can train 50 or 500 pairs of hands, I have helped hand the torch."

Dr. W. W. Mayo passed away in 1911, and by then, the practice had continued to grow both in size and in reputation. The Mayo "Red" Building was built in 1914 to house it, adjacent to what is now the Peace Plaza. It was subsequently torn down in 1989 to make room for the Harold W. Siebens Medical Education Building. As with many other Mayo buildings, many important artifacts from the original site were preserved.

In 1919, the original founders decided to convert the Mayo practice to a not-for-profit entity dedicated not only to medical practice but also to research and education. That entity came to be known as Mayo Clinic. And with that, the foundation was laid not only for Mayo's reputation for excellence but also for it to be an innovation-focused enterprise that would be driven to advance the science and the delivery of health care. That enterprise was integrated and staffed by professionals of broad disciplines and skills, a theme we will see again and again as we explore the mission and approach of the Center for Innovation.

Early Innovations and the Birth of the Modern Medical Practice

All eight new partners to join the Mayo practice between 1892 and 1908 made notable contributions to research and diagnostics, as well as to the administration of a collaborative, patient-oriented practice. The Mayo brothers were primarily surgeons, but they could see that these other areas were also important. Two of these new partners deserve special mention in Mayo's journey to become—and really, define—the modern medical practice: Dr. Henry Plummer and Harry Harwick.

Dr. Henry Plummer

Dr. Henry Stanley Plummer became a full practice partner in 1901, and he was a primary driver of Mayo Clinic's early success. He designed many of the systems that are now used universally around the world today, such as a shared, individual dossier-style medical record and an interconnecting telephone system.

Up until that time, medical records were kept by the physician for that physician's own personal use; they were not shared among physicians, nor was there any kind of common format. Medical records were physician centered, not patient centered, until this new innovation appeared.

Dr. Plummer was also the first to adopt, understand, and use an X-ray machine in the practice, then a new technology. He created new diagnostic procedures, and he devised new ways for physicians and other personnel to interact and to share medical information. He was the first to truly incorporate medical specialization into what became known as the *integrated group practice.*

Later, he was the chief design collaborator with architect Franklin Ellerbe in the design of a then-modern medical building that would eventually become known as the Plummer Building. The Plummer Building, a Gothic-inspired structure that would look quite at home on Manhattan's Fifth Avenue, was completed in 1927. At the time the tallest building in the state, it has been preserved largely as a museum and monument to the early Mayo practice, innovation, and culture. It is one of the two stately older buildings found just east of the Gonda Building on Second Avenue (the other is the Kahler Grand Hotel, an elegant grand lady completed in 1921 and surviving to this day mainly for the convenience of Mayo patients). The Plummer Building is topped by a distinctive tower that contains a 56-bell carillon dedicated, as Dr. Will said, "to the American soldier, in grateful memory of heroic actions on land and sea to which America owes her liberty, peace, and prosperity." Music is played from it several times a week, which can be heard throughout downtown.

Primarily for his creation of the modern medical record and his collaboration on the design of the model collaborative medical practice facility, Dr. Plummer is widely held by today's physicians to be the architect of the modern medical practice. He was an innovator before the term came into common use, and he established the pattern for much that was yet to come in today's Mayo Clinic and its Center for Innovation.

Harry Harwick

From the first days after his 21st birthday in 1908 to his retirement as chief executive officer of the Mayo board in 1952, Harry Harwick was dedicated to developing the administrative foundation of the Mayo Clinic practice. He and Dr. William Mayo conceived the idea of the not-for-profit Mayo Clinic years before it was formed. Like everything else, from specialized medicine to medical records to X-rays, dedicated administration was a new thing to modern American medical practice. Harwick introduced new accounting systems, and he generally worked "to free the physician from the daily burdens of business affairs." These efforts were modeled in a wide variety of professions beyond medicine, and they became a model for integrating sound business methods with professional practice. Again, this became an important part of Mayo's DNA.

The 150-Year-Old Brand: Growing into Today's Mayo Clinic

The deaths of brothers Drs. William and Charlie Mayo occurred within two months of each other in 1939. But Mayo Clinic continued to flourish through the years because by then, the rich heritage and core values were already well established in the organization. The size, reputation, brand image, and quest for innovation have continued to grow through the present.

A Growing List of Innovations

Starting in the early days of Dr. W. W. Mayo's quest for new and better ideas back in the 1850s, Mayo Clinic has become recognized for a long list of innovations shaping clinical medicine and medical practice. Some of the leading-edge medical practice innovations, like common medical records, have already been noted, and they have been developed further since. Among the thousands of other innovations since the early days, the more recognizable ones include these:

1905: First method of freezing tissue during surgery as a means of diagnosing cancer

1915: First program in graduate medical education

1919: First not-for-profit practice aligned with medical education and research

1920: First index to grade tumors

1935: First hospital-based blood bank

1940s: First aero-medical unit to transform aviation

1950: Nobel Prize for discovery of cortisone

1955: First series of operations with heart-lung bypass machine

1969: First FDA-approved hip joint replacement

1973: First CT scanner in North America

2001: In response to the September 11 terrorist attacks, development of a rapid diagnosis procedure to detect anthrax poisoning

2002: First multisite comprehensive cancer center in the United States

Mayo Clinic's 150-year history is beautifully shared in this short film, which is narrated by Tom Brokaw, noted journalist and member of the Mayo Clinic Board of Trustees: http://www.youtube.com/watch?v=3w6z7IbeJj4.

The Early Days of Telemedicine

Mayo Clinic has been known for its medical innovations from the very beginning. But as you can see from the list above, and the early innovations of Dr. Plummer and others, the term *innovation* has covered a lot of ground for some time at Mayo.

Consider telemedicine—which seems like such a straightforward idea now, with today's telecommunications technologies. Indeed, it has become one of the central themes, or *platforms*, of the Center for Innovation, known to us today as "Connected Care." But the idea of teleconnected medicine, like many others, has humble roots in early experimentation and design.

The idea got started in the 1960s and 1970s. Physicians and other health care professionals in Canada, Australia, the United States, and other countries with remote and scattered populations explored the use of radio, telephone, microwave, two-way television, computer, and satellite technologies to link isolated, rural areas to urban medical practices.

Mayo Clinic climbed on board in 1967 locally in Rochester with the first remote data transmission, by telephone lines, of electrocardiographic (ECG) signals from Saint Marys and Rochester Methodist Hospitals to a local clinic laboratory. In 1971 the idea went global when two Mayo Clinic cardiologists based in Rochester received ECGs from a hospital in Sydney, Australia, with the transmission involving telephone cable and satellite technologies.

In 1978, Mayo participated in its first two-way live, intercontinental exchange. During the 45-minute live telecast, Mayo staff in a studio in the Plummer Building interacted with staff of a Sydney hospital. In 1984, the Telecommunications Task Force was formed at Mayo to exploit new communication technologies that would allow remote practice sites to operate interdependently. In 1986, a

5,000-pound satellite dish was hoisted by helicopter to the top of the Mayo Building.

Today, such data interconnectivity is routine. But imagine for a minute what has become possible with the Internet, tablets, and smartphones. These technologies, of course, have become standard design components for the 21st century model of care. At the Center for Innovation, we do not use technology just because it's there. We use it to make "fast, friendly, and effective" health care available through personal technology, which has been and remains a strategic priority and a reality for us.

The Footprint Expands

Through the 1980s and 1990s, Mayo Clinic took the idea of "healing body, mind, and spirit" on the road through an expansion campaign. The following facilities were built or integrated during this period:

- ▶ *Saint Marys and Rochester Methodist Hospitals—1986.* The first step was right at home in Rochester. These two hospitals had operated for a long time under a close partnership. In 1986 they were formally absorbed into the Mayo Foundation and Mayo system. They now operate as one with their outpatient facilities and clinical staff, and in 2014 they were respectively renamed as Mayo Clinic Hospital, Saint Marys and Methodist campuses to highlight their integration.
- ▶ *Mayo Clinic Jacksonville—1986.* A new facility was built in 1986 on 140 acres of Florida woodlands. Today there are five buildings used by over 90,000 patients annually.
- ▶ *Mayo Clinic Scottsdale—1987.* A second new practice was established in this Phoenix suburb. Today it hosts 100,000 patients a year, and it is tied to two new research facilities and a second Mayo campus in Phoenix.
- ▶ *Mayo Clinic Health System local clinics—1992.* Mayo Clinic expanded beyond its traditional destination medical center role by buying or building a network of 70 smaller clinics and hospitals, which are located mainly in the upper Midwest.

> ▶ *Gonda Building—2001.* Built as a state-of-the-art facility, the Gonda Building taken together with the interconnected Mayo and Charlton Buildings is the largest medical facility of its kind in the world. The impressive structure is designed for the kind of teamwork and collaborative practice Mayo specializes in, and it is home to the Mayo Clinic Center for Innovation.

The Spirit of the Clinic

In a 1919 address to the Mayo Alumni Association, Dr. William Mayo, ever the spokesman for the actions, visions, and values of Mayo Clinic, offered his views of what made Mayo Clinic successful:

> *In view of the large number of sick who come here to be cared for, it would be natural to attribute the cause of their coming to work well done, but since good work is being done everywhere, there must be another and deeper reason. Perhaps this other reason may be best summed up in one phrase, "the Spirit of the Clinic," which incorporates the desire to aid those who are suffering, the desire to advance in medical education by research, by diligent observation, and by the application of knowledge gained from others, and, most important of all, the desire to pass on to others the scientific candle this spirit has lighted.*

Later that same year, he articulated four conditions he felt were essential to the future of Mayo Clinic:

1. Continuing pursuit of the ideal of service and not profit
2. Continuing primary and sincere concern for the care and welfare of each individual patient
3. Continuing interest by every member of the staff in the professional progress of every other member
4. Continuing the advancement of the science and delivery of medicine

You can clearly appreciate these values in the early evolution of the clinic as well as in its activities and "vibe" today.

But in 1978, Dr. Emmerson Ward, the chair of the Mayo Clinic Board of Governors, added another tenet that ultimately gave rise to the spirit of this book:

5. A willingness to change in response to the changing needs of society

Later, in 1984, two more conditions were added by administrator Robert Roesler:

6. Continuing effort toward excellence in everything that is done
7. Continuing conduct of all affairs with absolute integrity

Focus on the customer (the patient), teamwork, service, integrity, excellence, and market-directed change—this captures the spirit of Mayo Clinic, and it describes a unique environment in which patient-centered, transformative innovation is a natural consequence.

Today's Mayo Experience

Leonard Berry and Kent Seltman summed up what Mayo Clinic has become in their 2008 book *Management Lessons from Mayo Clinic*: it has evolved to become a "'modern-traditional' enterprise that aligns strategy with value, innovation with tradition, talent with teamwork, and science with art."

If you talked to anyone at today's Mayo Clinic, including the patients who have been under its care, you would probably hear the Mayo experience and its delivery summed up something like this:

Mayo physicians understand that medicine is far too complex for any one person to know; therefore, a collaborative, team approach works better. Care is overseen by a single physician team leader who manages the patient experience from start to finish—no handoffs, no delays, no confusion or miscommunication. That physician is paid on a salary and is guided by a commitment to the highest professional standards, so there is no incentive to see larger numbers of patients; quality supersedes quantity. On the other hand, modern systems and processes allow patients to have multiple medical evaluations and tests on the same day; it is often possible to have same or next day surgery or other procedures. Our destination facilities are designed for comfort and efficiency, to "heal body, mind and spirit"; that said, when possible, consultations, updates, and evaluations are done remotely. In short, the needs of the patient come first, but we also don't forget about the families. It is a holistic experience consistently delivered with the utmost respect and compassion.

As Keillor's keynote story suggested, it broadly qualifies as an "experience of civility."

The Value of Deep Values

They've been in place for 150 years, but without doubt the basic values, structures, and systems put in place by the Mayo brothers, their father, and other early contributors are still highly relevant today. Customer focus, teamwork, service, integrity, excellence, and patient- and market-directed change are all still very much part of Mayo Clinic. Employees are loyal, hardworking, open to change, and driven by values, and they do what's right when they see something that needs to be done.

The deep personal and universal commitment to the organization's values appears consistently throughout Mayo Clinic; it is "woven into the fabric." As former CEO Dr. Glenn Forbes put it: "If you've communicated a value but you haven't driven it into the policy, into the decision making, into the allocation of resources, and ultimately into the culture of the organization, then it's just words." Put another way, core values are core values, not just training items.

When these values put the customer first and embrace collaboration and a "willingness to change," you have the right ingredients for transformative innovation. You have the right "innovation DNA" as innovation guru, president, and cofounder of Doblin and director at Deloitte Consulting LLP Larry Keeley would put it.

Moving into the 21st Century

In the sidebar that follows are the Mayo principles that have collectively come to be known as the *Mayo Model of Care*. This set of articulated principles has been evolving since the end of the 19th century. As forces of the present and the future coalesce, it is more important than ever that Mayo transforms the model into a 21st century version. That is the overriding mission and vision of today's Mayo Clinic, and it is the specific mission and task of the Mayo Clinic Center for Innovation.

For starters, in this century we must move beyond the long-standing "The care starts when you walk in the front door" model. That model has served us well, but the present and future demand more. The delivery model of the 21st century starts *before* the front door; it starts with the patients' health and wellness. It starts *before* the front door in the patients' interactions with their primary care providers and in their remote interactions with their community and their local care providers. It continues *during* the care event and, when needed, through the treatment of complex diseases. It continues *after* the care event to ensure healing and care plan progress.

"Health" and "health care" mean you're always connected to help and care—always in health as well as in sickness. The "experience of civility" is continuous. It is continuously *connected*. It really is Connected Care. Mayo Clinic of the future will serve individual and family health and health care needs here, there, and everywhere, through both bricks-and-mortar and virtual delivery assets and protocols. All of this will become the Mayo model of care of the 21st century: "Health and health care, here, there, and everywhere, continuously connected." This will happen, as we will describe in the next chapter, against a backdrop of change and *as part of* the new cost consciousness. As the Mayo Clinic Center for Innovation leads the way to define this model and turn it into reality, you can follow along to understand the challenges and how the Center for Innovation has risen to the task to define the pieces and put them together into the 21st century vision and model of care.

Finding *Your* Organization's Innovative Spirit

Why did we share this sketch? How can you use this discussion to generate, stimulate, and steward transformative innovation in your organization?

Clearly, your organization isn't the same as ours. You don't have the same founders; you may not have the same issues that confront us in the health care industry. But regardless of your enterprise, regardless of your enterprise model, you probably do share the challenge of how to innovate in a complex environment. A visit to the "model of care" you deploy for *your* customers will likely nourish the mission and deployment of your innovation enterprise especially if viewed in the light of the Mayo Model of Care.

The Mayo Model of Care

The fundamental elements of today's established Mayo Model of Care include 14 tenets, of which 7 are directed toward "Patient Care" and 7 concern "The Mayo Environment." These tenets are not only useful in understanding today's Mayo Clinic but also in understanding the nature of an environment that is conducive to the types of innovations we will discuss throughout the book.

Patient Care

- A team approach that relies on a variety of medical specialists working together to provide the highest-quality care
- An unhurried examination of each and every patient with time to listen to him or her
- The physicians taking personal responsibility for directing patient care in partnership with the patient's local physician
- The highest-quality care delivered with compassion and trust
- Respect for the patient, family, and the patient's local physician
- A comprehensive evaluation with timely, efficient assessment and treatment
- The availability of the most advanced, innovative diagnostic and therapeutic technologies and techniques

The Mayo Environment

- Highest-quality staff, mentored in the culture of Mayo and valued for their contributions
- Valued professional allied health staff with a strong work ethic, special expertise, and devotion to Mayo
- A scholarly environment of research and education
- Physician leadership
- Integrated medical records with common support services for all outpatients and inpatients
- Professional compensation that allows a focus on quality, not quantity
- Unique professional dress, decorum, and facilities

Innovation the Mayo Clinic Way: Developing Your Own Model of Care

The goal is not only to innovate but to innovate *faster*. The more aligned you are with your roots, your vision, and your culture—your own model of care, of the past and for the present and the future—the more likely it is that you will make progress:

- *Find your cultural hooks.* What was it about your history, your founding, your original products or services, and the delivery methods for those products or services that was unique and distinctive in your early days? What themes, slogans, or philosophies guided the early formation of your enterprise and your brand? "A car in every garage," "Think different," "We bring good things to life," and "Better living through chemistry" are examples. What did your organization say about itself? What *would* it have said about itself in its early days? Can you capture the essence of your culture in a statement or short paragraph?
- *Look for other historical clues.* Slogans and visible marketing messages are useful, but you can also look back at unique and formative decisions that were made about your products,

how they were positioned, and how they were delivered to customers. Mayo Clinic has always emphasized innovation, both on the clinical side and in the delivery of care. We invented the integrated destination medical practice, and we made the investments to make it more successful. Likewise, your organization made early choices about what it would be and how it would get there. The exercise here is to observe how those choices were made, what innovations were involved and how they came about, and how that formula might be applied today.

▶ *What made your founders tick?* Every organization has founders, and all founders had visions and methods for getting things done—methods that may have been watered down, changed, or evolved as the organization grew and matured. Going back to what those original founders thought and did—and why—is an important exercise. The Mayo founders' footprints are quite clear in this regard, and they established a clear pattern for the future. What about yours?

▶ *What makes your organization tick today?* Just as your founders had a vision, how does your organization see itself today? What do you (or your leaders) really think drives success today? Innovative products? Lowest cost? Best customer relationships? At Mayo, we see ourselves driving a transformation in health care through the innovative optimization of the care experience—that's what makes us tick.

▶ *Apply these hooks and clues to your innovation effort.* Your history, your vision, your guiding purpose, and your culture will drive the kinds of innovation you strive for, and they will help define how you will get there. Innovation that doesn't support your vision, and that isn't in turn supported by your culture, is unlikely to succeed.

CHAPTER TWO

A Willingness to Change

The Imperative for Transformative Innovation in Health Care

> *You must be the change you wish to see*
> *in the world.*
>
> **—MAHATMA GANDHI**

The needs of the patient come first.

We live that. The core value of Mayo Clinic arches over the gateway to our ethos. We see it every day, our patients see it every day, and it guides our every action, our every behavior, and our being. We deliver on it.

So why are we so concerned about innovation? What is it we are trying to change or move forward to? What's wrong with the status quo? Why do we *need* a 21st century model of care?

Even with the recent major changes laid out in the Affordable Care Act (more completely, the Patient Protection and Affordable Care Act of 2010), most outsiders still perceive today's health care industry as complex and hard to change.

More and more, they perceive an industry that needs to become simpler and more affordable, but yet, there are few alternatives. When you're sick, you need health care, and yes, it's expensive and complex. But for about three-quarters of us, it's paid for by someone else, so there are other things to worry about. Compared to many industries, "demand" is relatively fixed and relatively insensitive to cost. Although medical tourism exists and is growing, it still accounts for only a very small fraction of health care. No competitor is going to steal your business overnight. So if you're in the health care business, what's there to worry about?

At Mayo, we see it differently.

At Mayo, we see major threats—and major opportunities—in the health care space. First, there's the *macro problem*—the "giant hairball," as author Gordon MacKenzie would describe it: the necessary transformation of health care to a simpler, more cost effective system that provides better health outcomes for everyone. We are proud that Mayo Clinic offers cutting-edge medical treatment and does it at a cost that over time is less than other major medical institutions. But we'll be the first to agree that the current model is too expensive, can be very inefficient and wasteful, and often doesn't deliver a fast, friendly, and effective patient experience. We must evolve toward a 21st century model of care that costs less, that delivers outcomes commensurate with the cost, and that is intuitive and easy to interact with. Put simply, if the United States is to have the most expensive health system in the world, it should also be the best.

NPR's John Hockenberry, who among his many pursuits makes an annual pilgrimage to Rochester to moderate the Mayo Clinic TRANSFORM symposium hosted by the Center for Innovation, puts it this way: "It's easier to have a debate on Syria than on the future of health care. . . . We tend to embrace such symbolic issues and leave the harder ones for later" (Figure 2.1).

Suffice it to say, the macro health care problem is daunting. Yet we believe that through innovating toward a 21st century Mayo model of care, we can contribute to long-term systemic improvement.

FIGURE 2.1.   JOHN HOCKENBERRY MODERATING THE ANNUAL MAYO CLINIC TRANSFORM SYMPOSIUM

But there are also significant *micro,* or enterprise-level, *issues* lying at our doorstep. As a large, "best in class" health care institution, one might think that Mayo Clinic is insulated from most of the challenges facing other medical institutions, but we are not immune. The forces of technology, competition, and mobility, to name just a few, are coming home to roost, causing us to question whether our current business model can continue. Can a destination health care model thrive? As the alternatives to the traditional fee-for-service model continue to surface and be tested, does our current model of care still work? How will the Affordable Care Act influence patient behavior? As Medicare cutbacks threaten our financial stability, can we continue to offer our signature patient-centered care?

We're a not-for-profit institution. But still, if we don't generate a small profit to fund our three-shield mission of patient care, education, and research, we perish. As Sister Generose Gervais, a larger-than-life part of the history of Saint Marys Hospital and the Franciscan alliance with Mayo Clinic, once said, "No money, no mission."

As Starbucks CEO Howard Schultz recently put it, "Any business that embraces the status quo as an operating principle is going to be on a death march." Former GE CEO Jack Welch said it this way: "If the rate of change on the outside exceeds the rate of change on the inside, the end is near." We recognize that even if the big picture of health care doesn't change much over the next few decades (and we think it must), our approach to health care—our care model—needs to evolve, and it needs to evolve quickly and decisively.

Doblin president and cofounder and Deloitte LLP director Larry Keeley explains in his book *The Ten Types of Innovation*: "Innovations that change industries can seem like they come out of nowhere. In fact, you can see the early warning signals that reveal when big changes are needed—and then seize on them."

Those early warning signals are coming in—loud and clear.

In this chapter, we'll examine some of the forces of change—the early warning signs—we're working to address. You may not have a "health care problem" in your industry. But if you're part of any complex modern organization, it's virtually certain that you face many of the same enterprise-level forces of change that we do. Times are changing fast. Even if there's no imperative to transform your industry, there may be one to transform your enterprise. As we noted in the Introduction, sometimes transforming your industry is the best way to transform your company. In our case, transforming our enterprise is likely the clearest path to transforming our industry. That's what we've done from the beginning, going back to the early 20th century transformations into an integrated medical practice model under the leadership of Dr. Plummer. After describing the forces of change confronting Mayo, we'll take another tack to identify some of the opposing forces that typically make change in complex organizations difficult. Then we'll come back to our definition of *transformative innovation*—and how we use that model to deal with the opposing forces that make change difficult.

The Giant Hairball: Challenges to the Health Care Industry

This book isn't about the national "health care problem," nor is it directly cast toward solutions for that problem. There is plenty to read on that topic, and the extensive debate would be hard to keep up with in book form anyway.

Instead, as you'll recall, this book is about innovation in complex enterprises in complex industries.

Still, it would be incomplete to ignore the greater health care problem. Obviously, much of what drives the needs of Mayo Clinic as an enterprise, arises from it. Ultimately, if we're on target, achieving new levels of health care delivery excellence at Mayo Clinic will put a dent in the larger health care universe.

At the Center of the Storm: Health Care Costs

While not getting overly immersed in this, it's important to touch on some of the facts and figures from U.S. health care today, all of which provide background and context for our thinking and our model of care vision.

According to a report released in early 2013 by the Commonwealth Fund, health care "constitutes 18 percent of GDP, up from 14 percent in 2000 and 5 percent in 1960." The report predicts a 21 percent share by 2023. Continuing: "The U.S. spends twice as much on health care per capita and 50 percent more as a share of GDP, as other industrialized nations do." And yet, "we fail to reap the benefits of longer lives, lower infant mortality, universal access, and quality of care realized by many other high-income countries, . . . and there is broad evidence that much of the excess spending is wasteful." These are big numbers—daunting enough to sap the growth of entire swaths of the economy and lead to economic dislocations (for example, the transfer of jobs to other countries) that would be otherwise unjustified, leading to further economic malaise.

Washington Post columnist T. R. Reid, author of *The Healing of America: The Global Quest for Better, Cheaper, and Fairer Health Care*, noted that an average Japanese citizen sees a physician 16 times a year, compared to 3.5 times a year for a U.S. citizen—and yet Japan's health care costs per capita are less than half. In a comparative examination of health care systems, Reid notes that the United States has four different systems in play: private payer/private provider (typical employer-sponsored health plans, about 50 percent of the population); public payer/private provider (Medicare model, 16 percent); public payer/public provider (Veterans Administration model, 6 percent); and the rest, out of pocket (15 percent). The remaining 19 percent are unclassified or a mix of the above. He points out that the United States is unlike every other country because it maintains so many separate systems for separate classes of people, driving both complexity and considerable inequity depending on who you are in the system. Most other countries have settled on one dominant model.

According to research published by the Kaiser Family Foundation, while health insurance cost increases have indeed moderated in recent years, the cost of family coverage has still increased 80 percent over the past 10 years—about three times as fast as wages (31 percent) and inflation (27 percent). Furthermore, employees, though covered, are being tapped for almost 28 percent of the cost of that coverage— an average sum of about $4,500 of their own money toward family coverage that costs on average just over $16,000 per year. This and other trends toward defined-contribution health plans noted below are gradually exposing consumers directly to more of the cost—and thus more of the choice— of health care.

Forces Driving Change: Cost Plus

Obviously, much of the current crisis is driven by cost, but there are other "tangles" in this giant hairball, making major change a far greater task. Pressures to manage cost have been growing and are starting to be legislated. The Affordable Care Act formalizes some of the mandates to reduce cost, first by aiming to reduce or eliminate the out-of-pocket payer segment through mandatory coverage, then by streamlining and reducing Medicare costs and setting up insurance exchanges to reduce some of the friction in the private payer/private provider market. Some will lose and some will gain as these initiatives gain traction. We won't dive too deeply into the merits and pitfalls of the Affordable Care Act, but clearly it's a watershed event in the definition of the 21st century model of care for *all* providers and payers.

It's worth taking a look at the biggest external forces and where the current state of health care has brought us. Among them are the following:

▶ *Cost pressures are increasing.* As health care costs escalated relentlessly, first Medicare, then private insurers, and then the people buying that insurance, largely employers, started to revolt against the burden. Pressures were put on providers, even on individual physicians, to reduce costs. In many cases, Medicare reimbursed providers at a level 20 to 50 percent below the cost of providing care, and those efforts continue not only through lower reimbursements but also through an increased emphasis on limiting utilization—that is, admission, length of stay, and discharge planning. Meanwhile, physicians and providers do not want to exclude Medicare patients, nor do they want to compromise on the quality of care given to them.

▶ *Consumers are footing more of the bills, and they want more choices.* As Sam Ho, M.D., chief medical officer of UnitedHealthcare, puts it, "Health care is the last sector of society to be consumer driven." Pressure from consumers will eventually cause providers to become more accountable and to pull back on costs. Today, for the majority of U.S. citizens, someone else pays the tab. As time goes on, however, consumers will be increasingly driven into the loop. To some extent, that has already occurred as consumers covered by employers foot more of the bill through copays, coinsurance, and other accompanying out-of-pocket payments. The trend is also being driven forward by the Affordable Care Act and the approach taken by many employers in complying with it, which is to get away from paying all the costs and *taking all the risks* associated with employee health care, as described next.

▶ *Companies are moving away from defined-benefit health coverage.* Companies have already largely transitioned away from paying all the costs and taking all the risks associated with employee retirement benefits—and the model is starting to be applied to health coverage. As a first step, noted above, employees must pay for an increasing share of their coverage. The second and more aggressive step is the transition modeled after the *defined-benefit retirement plan* (pensions, typically) conversion to *defined-contribution plans*, where the company pays a fixed sum and the employee/retiree takes the risks and responsibilities for making the money last. Today, as the transition begins to be made, leading companies are giving a fixed health care benefit and turning their employees loose to shop for coverage on the new insurance exchanges set up under the Affordable Care Act. Within this model, participants are more likely to choose a less expensive, higher-deductible plan—and thus, they are more exposed to the actual costs and choices of care. Walgreens is among the first to adopt this new model for its 160,000 current employees. IBM, Time Warner, and others have recently dropped guaranteed health insurance for retirees in favor of a fixed stipend model. Shopping for insurance will turn participants into consumers who will be sensitive to choices and demand transparency of cost data, again driving us to become more efficient.

▶ *The Medicare landscape is changing.* Initiatives begun years ago to cut Medicare reimbursements have been strengthened under the current legislation. The Affordable Care Act mandates a $716 billion cut over ten years (2013–2022) in total Medicare costs. Admissions and discharges are receiving much greater scrutiny, and special auditor teams are "taking back" Medicare payments in the millions. Medicare is also trying to reduce readmissions by assessing penalties to hospitals with "excess" readmission rates. Further, the Affordable Care Act places more emphasis on the patient experience, and Medicare reimbursements can be reduced if hospitals fail to provide a sufficient level of patient satisfaction. At Mayo, we lose almost a billion dollars annually on Medicare; that's a lot for a $9 billion a year enterprise. We must become more efficient, and we must make sure our services align for Medicare and non-Medicare patients. These forces will drive transformation. Consider, for instance, how the new penalties for readmissions might drive physicians and provider organizations back to doing house calls or e-versions of house calls. In this context, one can start to visualize a more mobile medical force, with more technology, and more nonphysician care providers—this could all make a big difference.

▶ *Accountable care organizations are growing in number.* The so-called *accountable care organizations* (ACOs), piloted as part of the Affordable Care Act, have driven providers away from fee-for-service systems to payment systems that are tied to patient health outcomes, with upper limits—*capitation*—for many kinds of services. Savings for Medicare under this model are split between Medicare and the providers. Capitation drives providers toward reducing costs both for the most "well" patients and for the sickest patients in their base. Those reductions are achieved through providing more continuous and proactive care to reduce the cost and frequency of adverse events, by providing care by less expensive professionals like nurse practitioners and physician assistants, and by making other delivery model changes. As of 2013 about 500 provider organizations use the accountable care model.

▶ *The administrative complexity is increasing.* Physicians and provider organizations are becoming overwhelmed by administrative chores. We have become an increasingly litigious society. Furthermore, new regulations concerning patient privacy, byzantine private and government insurance reimbursement systems, and the complexity of a highly specialized medical system all mean that doctors are spending increasing amounts of time filling out forms and giving instructions to patients and colleagues. The widespread implementation of the electronic medical record has helped, but not by much, and achieving administrative and process efficiency remains a huge challenge.

▶ *The population is aging, and the burden of chronic disease is growing.* In the meantime, people are surviving longer with chronic diseases, as evidenced by the $200 billion spent in the U.S. economy on Alzheimer care alone. Obesity affects larger percentages of the population—and requires more and more expensive care as more people become obese and live longer. People are living longer and getting more expensive to care for as time goes on. Preventative care and wellness are becoming increasingly important.

▶ *The infrastructure is outdated.* Although some process improvements like electronic medical records have taken hold, the basic "legacy" service infrastructure has changed little since the 1950s. Patients get sick and go see a doctor. That is disruptive in their busy lives, time-consuming, inconvenient, and often not necessary in light of connected care alternatives. It becomes an order of magnitude more complex and less efficient if it's a complex disease—networks of specialists, providers, payers, and administrators make complex care a daunting task. While other "service" industries have modernized their processes, that has largely not happened in health care.

▶ *Acceptance of the normalization of deviance.* As a result of all of the preceding forces, there might be what Dr. Eric Manheimer at New York's Bellevue Hospital calls "a normalization of deviance," where failures, cost overruns, high costs, and mediocre performance become accepted as the norm. It's similar to the familiar models of government bureaucracy. The health care industry, which has been able to pass on its overruns and errors for years, must enter a new age.

As you can see, this is a fairly daunting—really, disrupting—list of challenges we face from the outside, a major storm to weather. But, as if these aren't enough, we also face many challenges at the enterprise level driven by structural changes in the health care provider market.

Challenges at the Enterprise Level: Mayo Clinic Must Compete Too

Aside from the needs-of-the-patient focus and the drive to "advance the science" and to educate the next generation of health care providers, Mayo has some real threats and opportunities in our sights, including these:

▶ *Competition.* Yes, you read that right. As strong and revered as the Mayo brand is today as the "Supreme Court of medical opinion," as a 1961 market research study described it, there is new and emerging competition. Thousands of Mayo patients come from outside the United States, and new state-of-the-art medical centers in those countries are giving residents less reason to make the trip. Hospitals are merging into larger health systems with greater brand awareness. Tenet Healthcare is one large example; organizations like Dignity Health on the West Coast and BJC Healthcare in St. Louis are but a few of the many regional or local smaller examples. The Cleveland Clinic is advancing its brand beyond its traditional core of cardiac care. The upshot: we must keep moving to continue our brand prominence as the most trusted medical center in the world.

▶ *Evolution away from the destination model.* We just noted the forces challenging international destination care. Beyond that, responding to a busier, more mobile society and enabled by advances in technology, there's greater opportunity in the expansion of local care delivered *anywhere, anytime, beyond the bricks and mortar.* Although complex surgeries and other remedies still warrant the trip, many consultations will no longer require a pilgrimage to Rochester or one of our other destination locations. Surgeries and procedures will increasingly be delivered in remote ways such as with robotics. With our extensive destination location investments, this evolution could be perceived as a major threat. But we also see it as an opportunity for Mayo to extend its knowledge and expertise, not by building expensive facilities everywhere but by partnering and backing other care providers through Connected Care technologies. As an example, Mayo Clinic has established a Mayo Clinic Care Network extending Mayo Clinic's knowledge and expertise to physicians and providers in like-minded organizations that share a common commitment to improving the delivery of health care in their communities through high-quality, data-driven, evidence-based medical care. Through this network, organizations such as NorthShore University Health System in Chicago retain their complete autonomy while having direct access to Mayo Clinic's expertise.

The partnership and brand extension benefit both the local organizations and Mayo Clinic. So this transformation is hardly a threat; it's more of an opportunity to extend our reach and our brand.

▶ *Trend toward data-driven solutions in service industries.* Translation: "Big Data" and all of the analytic tools around it. Progressive health care organizations will drive toward *predictive modeling*, which might help deliver better, more predictive, more targeted, more cost effective care and eliminate the waste around it. A number of service industries, including police, schools, and airlines, have already been moving in this direction, toward data-driven methods in which they closely monitor their processes for anomalies. The result has been more efficient systems with fewer errors. "Separating the signal from the noise," as Vidant Health Network CEO David Herman, M.D., puts it, is hardly a threat at all. It is a huge opportunity.

▶ *Everybody's getting involved.* With these often-confused seas of change, it should be no surprise that health care organizations of all types and sizes are getting on the innovation bandwagon. More and more providers and payers are putting innovation teams in place and defining internal entities like Mercy's Center for Innovative Care or Kaiser Permanente's Garfield Innovation Center. When participants in the 2013 Mayo Clinic Center for Innovation TRANSFORM symposium were asked in an informal poll "Do you have a design team or some other innovation-centered body in your organization?" some 61 percent said yes. In some ways we see this as an affirmation of our early, and at the time unique, efforts to incorporate design and design thinking into how we frame and solve problems in our practice—as we'll learn more about in the next few chapters. No doubt, there is a lot on our plate, and much of it can be perceived either as a threat or as an opportunity. They're threats if you're complacent and allow the confused seas of change to swamp your boat. They're opportunities if you think things through, allocate the resources, put your raincoats on, and set sail aggressively through the storm. By setting sail aggressively, we can *transform* these threats into opportunities through optimizing the delivery model as we move toward a 21st century model of care.

Bottom line: "a willingness to change" has become more important than ever.

Dialing Up Change as the Mobile Industry Is Doing It

The opportunity to change is even greater when you consider the impact of emerging technologies. Paul Jacobs, Ph.D., chairman and CEO of Qualcomm, describes his own industry challenges and opportunities this way: "Mobile is the biggest platform ever created—with now over 6 billion users." With such a large user base, according to Jacobs, it's more important than ever to look out 5 to 10 years to try to see where the industry is headed.

As he sees it, health care has a similarly sized user base—and really, it should take a similar approach, looking into the future. The opportunity for convergence of mobile technology and health care is huge. For example, doctors in India use mobile technologies and imaging to diagnose and monitor skin care maladies—for $1 per encounter instead of $10 previously. Imagine a future with fully integrated mobile technologies, wearable devices that act as always-on, always-connected patient monitors, and even embedded nanotechnology-driven medical devices all connected on a mobile network.

Jacobs suggests—and we agree—that health care is not unlike the mobile revolution, both in size and scope and of the forward-thinking required to lead change. Certainly, one way or another, most of the world's population is touched by mobile.

When you look at today's global and enterprise-level health care challenges, thinkers like Jacobs are invaluable. They can see 10 years ahead to what the industry will be like—and try to steer their ships and the underlying technologies toward that vision. Right now, no single health care leader or organization has stepped up in the way that Qualcomm has in the mobile industry, but we feel Mayo Clinic and the Center for Innovation can take this leadership role. Beyond learning from the mobile model, we can also *use* these mobile technologies and their future vision in our designs and design thinking.

Continued

So it's worth ringing up the mobile model, both here and now and for the future—all in the interest of *health and health care, here, there, and everywhere, continuous, and co-created by the patient, the provider, and the payer.*

Clearing the Way for Big Change

Larry Keeley puts it this way: When "in the course of human events" it becomes necessary to have a revolution, you're better off to just do it. Revolutions are part of the landscape in military history, technology, and education—but not so much in health care. Moving toward a 21st century model of care will require improving both the *pattern* of progress and the *velocity* of progress. To all in the industry: it's "our job to reinvent the mechanics and economics of health care delivery." He's not surprised that efforts to improve today's situation seem more complex than ever and perhaps even futile. We're "climbing the confusion curve," as he sees it. But that's not all bad, for that happens before things become elegant and simple. We've seen that in a lot of other business environments.

As an industry, we feel we've been climbing the confusion curve forever. However, the Affordable Care Act has introduced an additional layer of change and confusion (albeit well intended) into the ongoing efforts to standardize health care in the long run and to achieve cost savings through process efficiencies beginning with Medicare. We would hope that, if writing this book 5 to 10 years from now, a lot of change would already be behind us and we'd be discussing opportunities to fine-tune, not so much to revolutionize, the system.

But that's not where we are now. Change has been happening, some driven by the Affordable Care Act, and some driven by other forces already in progress before it came along. In response, our first step, an important one, was to cast aside organizational impediments in the way of pursuing the vision—that action led to the formation of the Center for Innovation in the first place. Recognizing and dealing with organizational barriers in complex environments is not unlike clearing a storm drain before a heavy rain—not a bad thing to do anytime but best before something big happens.

A Pattern of Resistance: Why Large, Complex Organizations Can't Innovate

As an important summary and helpful lesson for the many readers who participate in complex organizations in complex industries (like ours), we'll switch gears a bit. The new gear takes us to identify the resistance to innovation, to deliberately calling out some of the forces and factors that make innovation difficult in complex settings. We've identified 15 factors that typically get in the way—both from our own experiences and observations elsewhere. As more of a checklist than a full course, here they are—you've probably experienced many of them yourself. The idea here is to assess your own organization and context with this list—that is, to assess where you are and where you're starting from. Our list is presented in no particular order:

1. *The problem is not clear, or the vision or strategy is either unclear or out of alignment.* What defines success? Our favorite Yogi Berra quote resonates: "If you don't know where you're going, you won't get there." What is your future? What defines your success? It's good to have achievable goals (program and project outcomes), but if they don't point to a transformation or at least a rapid evolution, you'll be left behind even if you are able to bring some innovations to market.

2. *The organization is too focused on its core or its inner products.* We see this often—organizations that are too focused on what they already do and that are overly centered on physical products. They fail to see the larger context and possible innovation frontiers that lie everywhere from customer service to supply chain to internal organizational matters that can also deliver better value and better experiences. Remember that the product is just part of what you do. We'll come back to this idea as we reexamine Larry Keeley's "Ten Types of Innovation" model in Chapter 4.

3. *The organization fails to "get" the customers.* My, we see this so often! You can think you know the customer, and you can spend a lot of time thinking about customers—but do you really *get* them? Common ills are these:

   a. *Leaving it to someone else.* Do you personally do the research and spend time with customers? Or do you outsource it to someone else outside the enterprise? Apple, famously, did not spend a dime on outside customer research, except to design their retail stores.

   b. *Not seeing the customers' intentions or their latent or tacit needs, only their stated ones.* Listening to what they say isn't enough. Reviewing patient satisfaction surveys isn't enough. You must get to a deeper, more holistic understanding of your customers' needs. We'll return to this in Chapter 4.

   c. *Yielding to groupthink.* Do your team members, especially those on the line, get to freely express their thoughts and observations about their customers' reactions to your products or services? Or do organizational dynamics and hierarchies suppress customer insights? Be careful if all of your team members have the same backgrounds and same organizational roles—and thus the same biases in how they interpret customer feedback.

4. *There is a risk-averse culture.* Does your organization encourage—or suppress—taking prudent risks?

   a. *Are people admonished for thinking differently or failing?* Does the reward system encourage—or at least, accept— failure? Most organizations now proudly declare that they "embrace failure" and that they want to "fail fast." Yet very few if any have translated that into action. In your organization, are failures really viewed as positives in performance reviews or in board meetings?

   b. *How strong or omnipresent are the "organizational antibodies"?* Do certain individuals or groups find it easier to find someone else's failure or to resist change than to contribute to change? Do the organization's leaders as a whole adopt a find-the-fault mentality with everything they see?

5. *Day-to-day rules the day—the organization's leaders are too absorbed in short-term performance.* Is the enterprise culture or leadership so engrossed in meeting short-term numbers and objectives that they can't see clearly or act toward the big picture? This can manifest itself in four ways:
   a. There is insufficient time or resources dedicated to innovation.
   b. There is no tolerance of "skunk works" or anything not exactly aligned to the plan.
   c. Transformative innovation is not part of the leadership message.
   d. Transformative innovation is not part of the organizational scorecard.

6. *The organization is trying to maintain the status quo, and it is resisting any transformative or disruptive innovations—even when they are "sure things" backed up by sound research.* This pitfall is typically a combination of the last two: (a) the organization is too risk averse and short-term focused, and (b) individuals on teams are looking for short-term obvious rewards because they must do so to survive. Here, the "arrogance of success" can enter the picture as well—the feeling that the organization is already at the top of its game (for example, as happened with Kodak and Blockbuster), so why bother to change anything?

7. *Innovation is not centered or embedded within the "main" organization.* Too many times, innovation teams and labs are set aside, off in separate facilities, not tuned in or acting in concert with the main business. They don't involve individuals and business units that deliver product or sit in front of the customers.

8. *There is poor internal communication of innovation efforts.* As they say, if you wink in the dark, nobody will know you winked. Are employees—and leaders—at all levels tuned into the transformation? Visions, innovations, innovative accomplishments, and the innovative *spirit* must all be front and center throughout the enterprise. We call this *diffusion* into the organization; it is the centerpiece topic of Chapters 5 and 6.

9. *The organization's focus is on the process, not the results.* This is the bane (one of them, anyway) of large, complex enterprises—and frequently the innovative entities within them. They must first follow the process or methodology, whatever it is. That becomes an end in and of itself. Process becomes more important than result. Ask yourself: Does the process serve the innovation (good)? Or does the innovation serve the process, often becoming a mere checklist item in a business plan (not so good)?

10. *The organization's pyramid is upside down.* If innovation is driven only by the organization's leadership, one very important component is left out—the day-to-day customer experience. Organization leaders are not normally in daily contact with customers. The result: innovation can become internally focused on factors that benefit the organization but may not benefit the customer experience. When it comes to innovation, the frontline folks should top the organization's pyramid!

11. *Innovation teams, when they exist, aren't diverse enough.* You have an innovation team—but they're all engineers. They're steeped in the technology and know all about your products. But you fail to bring in the insights, the global perspective, the "gestalt" of the real world, the problem-solving abilities that, for instance, a fashion designer or architect (we have both) would add to a team. We'll cover this in the next chapter.

12. *Your organization has a poor understanding of key industry trends.* Similarly, you and your team are aware of what you hear from your own people, your own sales force, or your own designers. But how "clued in" are you to industry and world trends? Make sure to formally "infuse" people with current trends; designate "trendwatchers." More about this in Chapter 6.

13. *Innovations are described in two-dimensional designs and documents—not in working prototypes and examples.* Many designers do the research and science on paper or computer screens, with the result that they miss the nuances and customer usability insights that would come sooner in the process if there were a working prototype. Whether designing a product or process, your design team should have "real" ways to noodle with something before settling on a design. Chapter 5 elaborates.

14. *Innovation investments occur and resources are made available only in good times—not bad.* Especially in the for-profit world, we've found that innovative discovery is funded only, or it is better funded, when times are good, and it can be among the first things cut when things are bad within or outside the enterprise. This is upside down: the greatest innovation efforts, especially transformative innovation, should occur when the road gets rough.

15. *There is too little—or too much—collaboration.* The "ill" of too little collaboration is straightforward—people feel left out, and many of them, especially those on the front lines, can't contribute their experiences or insights. However, some organizations—like ours—are built on collaboration, and sometimes we take on too many collaborators! Mayo has been described as an "organization of 2,000 VPs," meaning large numbers get involved in everything and can potentially bog it down. The secret is to set up the right, and right number of, hooks into the organization and communicate accordingly.

This checklist is presented as a tool for self-assessment. If you work in a complex organization, undoubtedly you've run into and will have to overcome some of these barriers. We did, and much of the rest of this book describes how we overcame them. Innovating in complex organizations means getting the context and setting right first—otherwise innovation energies get absorbed and reversed by the frictions inherent in the organization. Your first task is to recognize those frictions and then move toward putting a culture and process in place that works.

Innovation the Mayo Clinic Way: Transformative Innovation in Complex Enterprises

We believe that removing barriers and adopting a transformative innovation model is a vital part of building a successful innovation culture. In this context, transformative innovation is both a goal and a process, the idea being to transform an enterprise, even an industry, with a strategic "layering" of high-potency improvements.

To help you toward this goal, we bring you back to the definition and key attributes of transformative innovation as we see it. The concept and its definition have worked for us. First, the characteristics:

▶ *The innovation is customer focused.* Innovation starts with the customer and, in our case, the customer experience; there's no credit for any other answer.

▶ *The approach is iterative, incremental, and scalable.* We don't just strive for one "boil the ocean" change—which usually gets bogged down by its own size. We seek a sequence of layered innovations—all achievable, directed toward an evolving vision, all with successes and learnings, aligned with a prevailing strategy.

▶ *The innovation is an assembly of existing technologies and ideas.* We'll invent a new technology if we have to, but it's distracting and it consumes resources. Where we can, we'll assemble and adapt existing and emerging technologies, like apps and telecommunications technologies, to our needs.

▶ *The innovation development process merges diverse disciplines—in our case strong design and scientific discipline.* We're designers and scientists, and we adhere to a rigorous scientific discipline, which means forming hypotheses, testing, prototyping, modifying, learning, concluding, and documenting our exercises. We are a true lab, merging a rigorous laboratory approach with design thinking and design research principles.

▶ *The innovation emerged from end-to-end thinking.* Any time we conceive a project, it must fit the big picture or emerge from it. Projects that don't fit the vision of the greater health care delivery goal don't fly.

▶ *The innovation turns negative experiences into positive ones.* It isn't always the case, but frequently transformative innovations "transform" a negative experience into a positive one, which allows the customer or patient to think more positively about the product or service while simultaneously becoming used to the idea of further improvements. Think about electric starters or automatic transmissions for cars, or ATM machines in banks—these innovations helped transform their industries by transforming the negatives of these experiences into positives.

▶ *The innovation is fully "transfused" so as to eliminate the organization's inertia and "antibodies."* True transformative innovation doesn't happen in a vacuum. Instead, it gets the organizational support and dedication that it deserves and needs to carry on. It becomes a common goal and a way of life for everyone in the organization, a well-lit sign both at the entrance to the lab and the greater organization. Team members are truly excited to see a product come to market. A solid two-way, formal communication effort supports the task and gets all members of the organization, from the leadership to the rank and file, on board.

With these ideas in mind, we present a comprehensive definition of *transformative innovation*, as we use the term at Mayo Clinic:

Transformative innovation is an evolutionary form of innovation built on an undivided focus on the customer and customer experience. It uses design discipline and scientific methods to integrate and deploy new and existing technologies to improve experiences and efficiencies, and it is often associated with discovering and turning negative experiences into positive ones.

Transformational innovation is innovation that has an impact on the customer irrespective of scale. A transformational innovation substantially changes an experience. It does not matter if the substantial change affects a person, a group of people, or a whole organization. It is transformational irrespective of scale. We use this definition to guide every decision we make in the Mayo Clinic Center for Innovation. We constantly ask: Will our actions have the potential to profoundly impact the experience and delivery of health and health care?

This definition, and its component characteristics, has worked well for us. It keeps us on track and thinking toward the future 21st century model of care.

Working within this model, we can remove some of the barriers to innovation, and we can look at how to make it all happen, first organizationally by building a Center for Innovation (described in Chapter 3), then strategically and tactically (described in Part II).

Transforming Your Way to Disruption— by Automobile

We'll be the first to admit—we're good, but we won't transform health care all by ourselves. It's too big. There are too many players, challenges, and pieces to the puzzle.

That said, we've seen multiple, layered transformations lead to disruption in other important industries. They happen, and they happen without any single individual leader or leader organization in charge.

Consider the 20th century automobile phenomenon. The automobile disrupted transportation, and by doing so, it disrupted commerce, social structure, and, really, the very course of civilization. But was that disruption part of any single leader's or organization's transformative vision? No, not explicitly. Henry Ford's vision and innovations came close, but even in that case, a series of transformative innovations outside of Ford's sphere made his own possible and made them work.

And we'd add that a great number of those transformations happened around the customer experience. When that experience finally landed where it needed to be—after changing a large laundry list of negative experiences into positive ones—the foundation was laid for disruption.

Consider some of the key innovations: the automatic transmission, the electric starter, the rearview mirror. Were they disruptive by themselves? Did they single-handedly change how people traveled? No. But add windshield wipers, turn signals, air-conditioning, smooth roads, a network of gas stations, and a bunch of other innovations—and now you have a series of transformations that finally did disrupt scheduled transport as the primary means of human movement. Each of these transformations had value on its own, but each of them also served as a building block for a larger transformation of the industry.

Such transformations have happened in other industries. Consider the iPod. Apple integrated several existing technologies to arrive at the iPod device, then hit on a major transformation with iTunes, making the customer experience "work" for millions of users. Now digital music is integrated with your smartphone apps, and your smartphone is integrated with your car. With iPod and iTunes, the personal recorded music world clearly didn't just "evolve." It was built upon a series of transformative innovations, driven by a grander vision and brought forward into a new and disrupted reality. Known technologies were integrated with new design thinking to disrupt the way music is delivered and to transform the listening experience. In Apple's case, the company and industry were led by one extraordinary individual, Steve Jobs, but transformation being brought about by one person, rather than many, is the exception, not the rule.

We at Mayo seek the building blocks to transform the health care industry, as well as to transform our own enterprise. Rather like the modern automobile, we think that we'll all come to drive the 21st century model of care.

CHAPTER THREE

Building a New Innovation Ecosystem

The Mayo Clinic Center for Innovation

Inspired by the past. Innovating for the future.

**—WALL PLAQUE AT THE ENTRY TO THE MAYO CLINIC
CENTER FOR INNOVATION**

As we move forward into the 21st century, the need for transformative innovation in health care has never been greater. As Chapter 2 described, the cost and complexity of the current system have approached a tipping point, and the necessary transformations in the complex landscape of providers and payers are disruptive even to the most established players like Mayo Clinic.

As an organization, we saw this coming years ago.

Why? In part, for most of its history, innovation in health care has been largely centered on the development of clinical solutions—better treatments and more advanced technologies, instruments, equipment, and procedures. The vast majority of this innovation today occurs through publicly and privately funded efforts in universities and university hospitals. As noted in Chapter 1, we're also quite involved in this innovation space; research is one of the three Mayo shields of practice, education, and research.

But most of this research is about pure medicine. It's about treatments, healing, reversing disease, and dealing with symptoms rather than the patient experience and the processes supporting it. Most of the research targets "sickness," not "wellness," leaving a big part of our health experience unaddressed. Are we critical of such innovation? Hardly. It's vital to the progress and quality of health care delivered in a clinical setting. We've seen some amazing things happen over the years.

Indeed, in the 150-year-old Mayo Clinic story of serving humanity and advancing medical science, we have had many impressive accomplishments including developing methods of freezing tissue to diagnose cancer during surgery; designing and using the first integrated patient medical record; developing an index with which to grade tumors; developing the first hospital-based blood bank; discovering cortisone, for which we were awarded the Nobel Prize; making the first FDA-approved hip joint replacement; installing and using the first CT scanner in North America; and developing a method for the rapid diagnosis of anthrax poisoning, which was needed in the aftermath of the September 11 and subsequent terrorist attacks.

But as the new millennium unfolded, we increasingly recognized a growing gap: no other research organization was focused on the design or effectiveness of the patient care experience. As we saw in Chapter 2, Mayo Clinic has understood the importance of the patient experience from the early days of Dr. Plummer and the integrated practice, so this research was a natural fit for us. We were indeed inspired by the past, and we saw a tremendous opportunity left on the table. We felt that if we created a dedicated focus to lead the way in the transformation to a 21st century model of care, we could also guide the continued success of Mayo Clinic. That *focal point* would dedicate itself exclusively to the experience and delivery of health and health care, and it would apply scientific and design principles normally reserved for clinical research to that experience. It would have to garner resources and organizational buy-in to succeed. As such, it would have to be formally established and embedded in the organization. It would have to apply a structured and well-understood methodology. It would have to do this all in a credible way, with credible leaders and support from high-level Mayo leadership to flourish.

Today, this *organizational focal point* exists and prospers as the Mayo Clinic Center for Innovation (CFI). In this chapter, we will take you through the history and the guiding principles of CFI—how it evolved, how it overcame its challenges, how it approaches innovation, how it sits in the larger ecosystem of Mayo Clinic, and how it is likely relevant to your organization.

Meeting the Challenges

In 2001, coauthor, CFI cofounder, and formerly chair of the Department of Medicine Dr. Nicholas LaRusso pondered the establishment of an innovative franchise within Mayo Clinic to target the patient experience. At the time, he and his colleagues knew they had a lot of hurdles to clear.

There were the usual ones—hurdles like securing management buy-in, funding, and staffing and deciding how much to invest and ensuring a return on that investment. No matter what industry or what enterprise we sit in, don't we all have these challenges when organizing a transformative innovation effort? Mayo Clinic was and is no different. It's a big, complex organization with budget constraints and pressing deadlines and a talented staff dedicated to delivering what they are good at, day in and day out.

But in addition to those challenges, we had others to overcome. One, which may or may not apply to your organization, was the ongoing tension between the ethos and mindset of a physician and medical organization and the transformative innovation that we really had to achieve. For physicians, there's a natural tension between medical exactitude—failure can mean death—and the back-of-mind knowledge that we should—and must—innovate. Further, especially as Mayo physicians, we have our traditions and a built-in conservatism to err on the side of patient health, safety, and well-being and to stay within ourselves, with what we know and can do. But mustn't we also uphold the tradition of Mayo Clinic as clinical and medical practice innovators?

So how do we conceive and evolve an innovation organization in such an environment? How do we gain traction, and how do we do it quickly? We'll admit—our evolution wasn't so rapid. It has taken us about 11 years to get where we are now. We'd expect that to disappoint most of you trying to deliver aggressive and transformative change in your organization. We thought big and we started small, and we moved fast in specific areas, but health care is huge so we didn't move very fast in the beginning. Probably not as fast as you want to in your organization.

And that's why we want to share this recipe with you. We built the Center for Innovation very carefully with a sequence of iterative steps. We declared our focus and our vision. We got support from high-level leadership. We got an adequate, multiyear commitment of resources. We recognized early on that environments matter, and we created a visible physical presence conducive to innovation. We deployed credible leadership. We created a process focused on results, not on process, bureaucracy, and committees—specifically to avoid the 15 barriers to innovation called out in the previous chapter.

Not all of these steps worked perfectly. But if you follow our recipe, you should get there faster than we did. We proceeded visibly and inclusively, with stakeholders who understood and live these conflicts. We started with, but quickly moved forward from, a "skunk works" model, where innovations fly under the radar until they're good enough to fly into the radar—because "conflicted" participants and especially management teams tend to fear under-the-radar programs. We chose to get and stay "front and center" with the organization.

We paid careful attention to the methods we used and to communicating our progress and successes (and our failures) to the rest of the organization. We viewed our role as not only to develop and implement innovations centered on the patient experience and health care delivery but also to inoculate the organization with *innovation thinking*—the competence and confidence to innovate on its own.

If you learn from our story and our success, we know that you can create a successful, embedded, credible, experience-driven innovation center within your organization. We feel that what we're about to share will help you match our success but will take only a fraction of the time. That sounds good, but the bad news is that you will have to match some of the commitments made at Mayo—and that might not be so easy.

Much of the rest of our story is about how to get an innovation practice started with the resources, credibility, and leadership necessary to make it work, to make it successful. Anybody can start a skunk works. It's harder to start an innovation team that works and gains rapid traction in a complex organization. Here we'll place less emphasis on the facts and stories of our success and more on the "secret sauce" of how and why it works.

A Short History of CFI

The story of the Mayo Clinic Center for Innovation starts in the Department of Medicine (DOM), the largest physician group within Mayo Clinic, under the leadership of Nick LaRusso, M.D., the department chair, and his administrative partner, Barbara Spurrier (also a coauthor of this book). Their team included, in particular, Michael Brennan, M.D., the associate chair of the DOM Outpatient Practice, and Douglas Wood, M.D., who was, at the time, the vice chair of the DOM and who is currently the medical director of the Center for Innovation. The DOM recognized a need for patient-centered innovation beyond the clinical innovations already being championed by Mayo's Research arm. This innovation effort evolved in stages.

At the outset, in 2001, "to promote innovation" became one of six stated objectives in the DOM's strategic plan. That objective called for the creation of a formal and dedicated design lab known as the See, Plan, Act, Refine, Communicate (SPARC) Lab. SPARC and other department initiatives were combined into a formal DOM program known as the Program in Innovative Health Care Delivery. SPARC was the showcase and flagship, and it turned in some of the early successes of applying a design thinking mindset and an innovation discipline. In the summer of 2008, the program was formalized in the broader organization, with the formation and launch of the CFI we know today.

Here are some highlights of the story.

An Early SPARC

In the early days, coauthor Nick LaRusso discussed the challenges facing Mayo and the patient experience with a small group of colleagues. They wondered, specifically, if the care delivery process could be subjected to methodical study, just as clinical care had been studied and advanced for some time. Some of the earliest discussions occurred between Nick and Michael Brennan, usually during their long runs together or afterward over a few pints of Guinness (usually provided by Dr. Brennan, a Dublin-born Irishman).

They saw the connection between what they were trying to do and what others outside the medical community, particularly in service industries, were attempting. That led to engagements and ultimately collaborations with outside specialists and consultants, most notably the design and innovation consulting team of IDEO but also HGA Architects and Engineers and Steelcase, the large office furniture company. Those relationships still exist today, and in particular CFI remains closely engaged with Jim Hackett, now former CEO of Steelcase, and Tim Brown, president and CEO of IDEO and author of *Change by Design*.

The core idea at the time and to this day was to evolve a design discipline, a design-centered way of thinking, into a health care organization. We'll cover design thinking more in Chapters 4 and 5, but for now it's enough to say that it incorporates a thorough and contextual analysis of true customer needs and an open-ended but disciplined approach to delivering innovations to benefit that customer.

FIGURE 3.1.   EARLY SPARC LAB

The DOM leadership team set up what they then referred to as a "skunk works" laboratory called SPARC (Figure 3.1). Started in 2002, the lab was staffed with four people, and it opened operations in a specifically designed and constructed practice space within the Mayo Building. It was at this time that coauthor Barbara Spurrier, then senior administrator for the DOM, entered the mix.

In its first years of existence, SPARC looked at patient flow, including how patients used waiting areas and exam rooms, how they interacted with providers, and how technology was deployed (Figure 3.2). The resulting innovations took on a redesign of patient exam rooms—expanding their size, doing

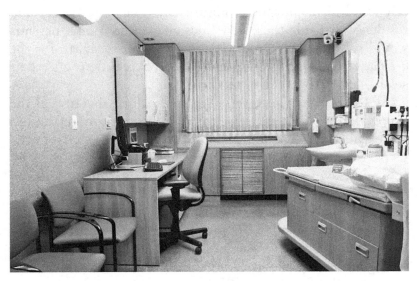

FIGURE 3.2.   REDESIGNED EXAMINATION ROOM: BEFORE

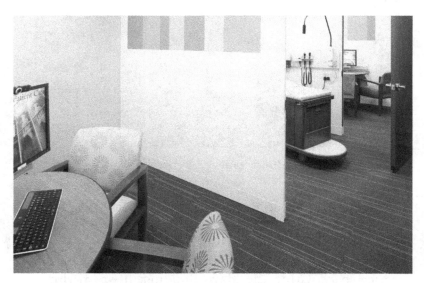

FIGURE 3.3. REDESIGNED EXAMINATION "JACK AND JILL ROOM": AFTER

away with sharp corners, and setting up computer swivel monitors so that both the physician and the patient could look at them from where they sat. They divided these *Jack and Jill rooms* into dressing, exam, and conference areas, set up properly for all three purposes (Figure 3.3). The hypothesis—and result—was that in these newly designed exam rooms, patients would feel more involved with their own care. Ditto for the *decision aid documents* explaining medical regimens and their steps—for example, diabetes care.

SPARC's early successes owed to the formalization of the innovation process, and especially of design thinking, and to the early credibility of leadership, coming directly from the Department of Medicine. Other physicians, seeing the success and the organization's commitment, became "friends of SPARC," and they became involved in early SPARC projects. Likewise, the formalization of effort led to a gift from an outside benefactor, which obviously helped move the concept forward more rapidly. The internal processes, combined with strong leadership and early organizational hooks, and emerging external influence were the secrets to early success.

At first we operated under the radar as does a typical skunk works, but even then the project had many of the seeds, including top organizational leadership and commitment, of a more formal program. The term *skunk works* originated from Lockheed Martin. A skunk works operation is created, and often self-created, with a high degree of autonomy, resources, and time usually off the books (with no formal staffing or budget), outside the bureaucratic realm (and often off the premises). It sometimes works on secret projects. Our project had some of those seeds too, but we quickly realized that to gain the organization's commitment and support, particularly from the medical practices, our work would have to have a more formal and visible effort.

Maybe we were a skunk works, maybe we weren't. We simply were trying new things and needed a protected environment in which to do so, and the DOM offered that cover. But we saw that better things would lie ahead, including buy-in from Mayo leadership and practicing physicians, if we became more visible.

We feel that the CFI that emerged is a hybrid—combining some of the best characteristics of a skunk works (a degree of autonomy, absence of strict hierarchy, minimal to no bureaucracy, and nontraditional processes) with the best features of a formal, embedded, fully staffed, highly visible, and "public" internal enterprise. It was the world's first embedded design group to be integrated into a live medical practice, and it remains so today.

A Center for Innovation Is Born

SPARC was successful on two fronts. First, it brought useful and credible innovations in spatial design, patient processes, and patient communications to life. But second, and probably more important, it demonstrated the concept of an embedded design lab, with its patient-centered, design-enabled innovations, to the Mayo practice and culture.

The "C" in SPARC stands for "Communicate," and that too became a big part of the success story. SPARC projects and successes were presented in various parts of the organization, brochures were printed, and a website was built to help followers track its activity. Physicians were brought in to see and participate in design prototypes, and they could also conceive and initiate projects within SPARC. These communication efforts played well with Nick LaRusso's credibility within Mayo as chair of the DOM, and as time went on, SPARC caught the attention of the institution's leadership and individuals outside the DOM.

Really, SPARC was a design prototype for the more formal patient-centered innovation organization that was to emerge. In 2007, discussions commenced with the Rochester board of governors and Mayo's CEO and president at the time, Glenn Forbes, M.D., about a more formal, enterprise-wide, institution-wide effort that ultimately became known as the Center for Innovation. Dr. Forbes was a huge believer in the DOM's Program in Innovative Health Care Delivery, and he encouraged the Mayo leadership to recast this effort as a broader organizational capability.

Barbara Spurrier joined the team as Nick's administrative partner, as did coauthor Dr. Gianrico Farrugia, who was then leading an innovation effort for the Mayo Clinic Clinical Practice Committee. The advent of the CFI within the greater Mayo Clinic organization was announced at the first TRANSFORM symposium in September 2007—a Department of Medicine–sponsored internal/external showcase of innovation in the health care experience. The infrastructure was created, and the SPARC Lab was integrated into the formal launch of the Center for Innovation in June 2008.

As we move through this chapter, you'll see what makes CFI unique among innovation groups and labs in other complex organizations, and what makes it work in the Mayo organization. It starts with the vision, which we will cover extensively, and the staffing, which we will also cover. You'll see the uniqueness and clarity of our operating purpose, philosophy, and principles. You'll see how we partner with key individuals and groups, both inside and outside of Mayo. And last but not least, you'll see how we operate as a committed, embedded, public, visible, design-centered, and change-oriented enterprise.

What the Experts Say

If you've read our book sequentially thus far, you've become acquainted with innovation expert Larry Keeley in the Introduction. Keeley is the president and cofounder of Doblin, Inc., an innovation strategy firm known for pioneering innovation systems. It is now a unit of Deloitte Consulting LLP. Keeley has been recognized by *Bloomberg Businessweek* as "one of seven innovation gurus who are changing the field." He brings enormous insight about innovation in large organizations, and he had this to say about CFI:

> *I think the Center for Innovation at Mayo Clinic has been quite brilliant about trying to dragoon enough of the critical mass of the leaders of different business units and different practice areas so that they've created a credible momentum around the idea that Mayo Clinic has a point of view about innovation, Mayo Clinic has a signature set of processes around innovation, Mayo Clinic has a commitment to innovation.*

Dragooning support. Credible momentum. A point of view about innovation. A signature set of processes and a commitment. Powerful stuff.

The CFI Way: Philosophy and Guiding Principles

Like most other innovation teams in large, complex organizations, the Mayo Clinic Center for Innovation faced many challenges from its inception. In Chapter 2, we laid out 15 reasons why large organizations can't innovate or, at least, have a hard time doing so. We've also described throughout the inherent conflict between design-based innovative thinking and the conservative, risk-averse culture of the physicians we work with. Combine all this with the Mayo organizational "pinstripes"—its reputation, its committee-based approach to shared decision making, its pride in past and current success, and frankly, the "arrogance" of its success—and you have a difficult mix to work with as an innovation center.

Unless, of course, you lay the proper groundwork.

In the early days, we carefully considered—and really, thrashed around a bit with—form, structure, vision, and guiding principles for CFI. We wanted to create a *culture* and competency in which innovation could thrive, to position the CFI as a catalyst and igniter of innovation across the organization. We worked with the experts, who gave us insight into what works and what doesn't. We visited with other health care and medical organizations, including Memorial Hospital in South Bend and Medtronic, and an assortment of innovation leaders from other industries including IBM, Procter & Gamble, Cargill, 3M, Steelcase, and IDEO. We read practically every book available on innovation, and we tested ideas with our constituents. We observed the successes and failures of our early efforts with SPARC and other initiatives. Finally, we created and fine-tuned (and we continue to iterate) a set of guiding principles. We share these eight principles, which evolved through experience, here and in Figure 3.4 to light the way (and there are more throughout the book):

1. *Build a discipline of innovation.* The key word is "discipline." Build it, live it, champion it throughout the organization.
2. *Recruit a diverse team.* Designers, project managers, and others from outside the world of medicine—for example, engineers, architects, product designers, and anthropologists—bring diverse backgrounds and thought processes. Combine them with scientists and organizational experts, and mix well and often.

Lessons Learned About Innovation

- Build a discipline of innovation.
- Recruit a diverse team.
- Embrace creativity and design thinking.
- Environments matter.
- Co-create with your customers and stakeholders.
- Organize around Big Idea platforms.
- Collaborate inside and outside.
- Consistently share your vision, process, and results.

FIGURE 3.4. CENTER FOR INNOVATION GUIDING PRINCIPLES

3. *Embrace creativity and design thinking.* A customer orientation, experiments and prototypes, arts and sciences all converge. Failures are expected and tolerated.
4. *Environments matter.* Create open, Silicon Valley–style lab experimentation spaces that simulate real spaces. This fosters realism, collaboration, creativity.
5. *Co-create with your customers and stakeholders.* Involve practices at all levels in your projects. Provide platforms with which to incubate and accelerate your customers' and stakeholders' ideas, not just yours.
6. *Organize around Big Idea platforms.* All projects must fit the big picture and vision. Articulate and organize around the smallest number of big ideas.
7. *Collaborate inside and outside.* Bring in appropriate players from the practices, and also encourage outside participation, partnership, and sponsorship where it makes sense. No detached ivory tower labs here, please!
8. *Consistently share your vision, process, and results.* Communicate the vision and "transfuse" the principles and tools of innovation into the organization. Be visible, and be easy and useful to work with. This is the subject of Chapter 6.

These eight items comprise an evolving cultural blueprint that defines our ethos and permeates every action inside CFI. Every CFI team member gets it and lives it. It's a signature by which we survive and thrive inside the Mayo community and, increasingly, in the outside world.

The CFI Way: Think Big, Start Small, Move Fast

Cannon Falls, Minnesota, is a small, quintessentially Midwestern town about halfway between Rochester and the Twin Cities. Its claims to fame are that (1) it is the site where Barack Obama kicked off his 2012 presidential campaign, (2) it is home to the Pachyderm Studio, a music recording studio used by Nirvana, among others, and (3) it is the site of Mayo Clinic's first remote test of the eConsults platform, our evolving electronic pathway enabling remote physician-physician and physician-patient communications.

You probably haven't heard of Cannon Falls, and we introduce it only to make a point. That point connects to another signature part of our operating culture, one that has risen in stature to become a trademarked operating philosophy and even to become a department motto and subbrand (Figure 3.5). It's our book title as well: Think Big, Start Small, Move Fast.

Okay, so General Electric has "We bring good things to life," and Coca-Cola has, "Things go better with Coke" and a stable full of others. What's so special about a subbrand? A jingle? An "elevator pitch"? We're not about to film TV commercials, so what's the big deal?

The big deal is that, as part of our design and execution discipline, we always frame our activities with this concept. We "think big"—about things that really matter and lead to "putting a dent" in the health care universe. We "start small"—by not trying to do everything at once with a large-scale or complex implementation, hence our choice of a small, Mayo-operated clinic in Cannon Falls and an independent breast cancer clinic in Anchorage, Alaska, to try out our eConsults ideas. We "move fast"—to learn from our prototypes, sell into the organization based on those prototypes, and proceed toward larger-scale, iterative, staged implementations.

The importance of this framework is perhaps better illustrated if we look at what would happen if we *didn't* use it:

▶ If we didn't "think big," we would never transform the health care industry. Our projects, while successful, wouldn't amount to enough to garner attention or continued support. We would likely expend too much energy on trivial issues.

▶ If we didn't "start small," our projects would be too big and complex, implementation would be slow and uncertain at best

FIGURE 3.5. THE CFI OPERATING PHILOSOPHY

and likely would never happen, and we wouldn't be able to learn or demonstrate as we go. Programs would ultimately take too long and probably deliver suboptimal results. Innovation is as much about execution as it is about ideation.

▶ If we didn't "move fast," the greater organization would lose interest. Our *own players* would lose interest too—innovators like to see their innovations come to market. Ultimately we would lose the opportunity to lead the transformation.

As a consequence, all of our projects must fit into the big picture of innovation that matters but be constructed small enough (or with small enough pieces) to get to a fast implementation or at least a rich prototype. We try to implement at least a major prototype within six months of a project launch. We'll come back to these concepts throughout Part II of this book.

The CFI Way: Structuring for Success

When you think about establishing an innovation competency and an internal innovation capability within a large organization, it's natural not to think too much about structure in the beginning. You think about ideas, scope, funding, staffing, spaces, *culture*—but not so much about the *structure* of the endeavor. For many, structure might seem contrary to the idea of letting ideas flow, and it might seem to be something that will sort itself out over time. We disagree.

The Importance of Structure

If innovation is a discipline, as we believe it is, then creating a structure is important from the very beginning. How do you structure the vision into neat compartments so that you can address them effectively? How do you structure projects into those compartments so that they aren't off track or even contrary to the vision? Structure is important for any innovation investment, particularly in light of Think Big, Start Small, Move Fast. In fact, we don't think you can really achieve Think Big, Start Small, Move Fast *without* an effective working structure.

And what do we mean by *structure*? Structure isn't about organization charts. *Structure* in this case refers to the *organization of work*. How do we align our programs and projects to accomplish the major goals, or platforms, of our transformative vision? How do we align other organizational resources to support these efforts and to "transfuse" our visions, our accomplishments, and the higher-level innovation competency into the rest of the organization? That's what we mean by *structure*.

Organizing our work and our duties helps in three major ways:

▶ We build the right team with the right individuals.
▶ Individuals within the unit see how activities fit together.
▶ Others outside the group see the vision and fit, and they can see how to work with us.

Perhaps the most important consequence is the last—having a visible structure allows all of our constituents and partners to see what we're doing and how it supports the greater vision. The structure becomes a major part of any presentation of our capabilities and accomplishments.

The CFI Organization of Work: Platforms, Cores, and Labs

The best way to illustrate "structure" is to show our own, one that has evolved over time. Figure 3.6 shows the essence of the Mayo Clinic Center for Innovation through its structure. There is a guiding vision toward which all of this is aimed—to transform the health care paradigm into an "Always be there for me" continuous presence, both as part of ongoing "health" and the effective delivery of care during "health events" that health care is known for today. In other words, we play both in sickness *and in* health. That vision is described more fully in the next section.

Isn't the cart before the horse? Normally, wouldn't we present the vision, *then* the structure required to execute on the vision? We're trying a different approach—one that worked for us—in that the structure may explain the vision more effectively than vice versa. The point is, they both play together, and in fact, much iteration may be required to get

Organization of Work

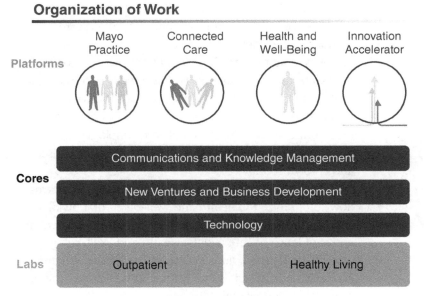

FIGURE 3.6. CFI ORGANIZATION OF WORK

both the vision and the structure right. Sometimes, structure will help define the vision. We think you'll see this more clearly as you go through this and the next section.

Highlights of our structure include the following:

▶ *CFI Platforms.* CFI is organized around *four platforms,* or *strategic opportunity areas for transformation*: Mayo Practice, Connected Care, Health and Well-Being, and the Innovation Accelerator.

   ● *Mayo Practice.* The Mayo Practice platform includes initiatives designed to improve the bricks-and-mortar facility-based patient care, in the outpatient or hospital setting. These initiatives include but aren't limited to pre-visit, visit and post-visit processes, spatial design, information gathering and recording systems, and care instruction and learning tools. Parenthetically, the progress made as a result of the initiatives within this CFI platform will not be limited to the Mayo practice, but ultimately could be emulated by other care delivery organizations.

- *Connected Care.* Connected Care initiatives are, as the name implies, a series of tools enabling patient care without a physical presence in a facility, that is, outside of our bricks and mortar. Connected Care projects connect physicians and other care providers directly with patients, or they may connect local physicians with Mayo physicians for an advanced consultation. Connected Care projects incorporate networking and mobile technologies, and they may be directed toward general care or to specific diseases and chronic conditions.

- *Health and Well-Being.* Health and Well-Being concerns how to optimize the health and *well-being* of individuals and families. Well-Being pertains both to ongoing health and avoidance of care events. Health and Well-Being projects engage individuals to optimize their health and increase their capacity to make decisions that maintain or increase functional status.

- *Innovation Accelerator.* The Innovation Accelerator platform includes programs to educate, incubate, and provide visibility to innovation across the Mayo organization. The platform includes an Internet-based tool to crowdsource ideas with Mayo Clinic employees and an incubator called CoDE (Connect, Design, Enable), which acts like an internal venture capital firm to select, fund, and assist with about 10 ideas per year originating in the practice. Also in this platform, the annual international TRANSFORM symposium provides both internal and external lift and visibility to CFI activities. We'll cover the Innovation Accelerator platform in more detail in Chapter 6.

▶ *Cores.* These include skill sets and services that support our programs and connect them with other parts of the organization or to the outside. Services like information technology, communications, and business development are brought in from their host areas within Mayo. Resources officially report to their local home area, which helps to create a distributed internal network, but these resources serve and are embedded in the CFI group.

▶ *Labs.* These are the physical lab spaces where we experiment and prototype our new models. In addition to the administrative home of the CFI, we also have a separate Multidisciplinary Design Outpatient Lab, which has been constructed to simulate real outpatient environments and handle real patients as our prototypes require. We also operate the Healthy Aging and Independent Living Lab, a fully functional lab simulating a real living environment for seniors located in our Charter House, which is a continuing care retirement community (CCRC) owned and operated by Mayo. A new Healthy Living Lab is scheduled to open in early 2015, and it will be focused on testing and prototyping health and well-being services and products in the home and office environments.

These descriptions may seem a bit minimalist at this point, but we will come back to these platforms, cores, and labs throughout the book.

Our platforms help us organize our work, but again they wouldn't be complete without a structure to manage our work. To do that, within each of the four platforms we define *programs* and *projects*:

▶ *Programs.* These are major strategic efforts within the platform usually aligned to a certain care segment or technology base for the activity. Programs include related projects managed in a coordinated way to achieve greater benefit and efficiency than managing them individually. Within Connected Care, we have the eHealth (network communications) and mHealth (mobile) and condition-specific programs like our connected support platform (OB Nest) for pregnant mothers-to-be and our support program for diabetes. Health and Well-Being programs include Thriving in Place projects for the elderly, Student Well-Being for Learning and Life, and community projects designed to improve health and coordinate resources in the community. The Mayo Practice platform has a large program called the Mars Outpatient Practice Redesign that looks at significantly enhancing efficiency and reducing cost in the specialty practice. The Innovation Accelerator includes the dynamic CoDE program with a continually changing portfolio.

▶ *Projects.* Finally, we get to the list of 100-plus projects that fit under the programs just outlined. These projects are tactical, temporary, and may or may not be active at any given time. They are all in various stages of completion, and they may go inactive for periods of time as resources and testing schedules dictate. The project list includes the practice-originated CoDE projects awarded and supported each year. This structure for projects was far from finalized when we established CFI. It has evolved as our vision has evolved, as project ideas have flowed in, as the needs of the business have changed, and as we have grown. Indeed, the current structure is Version 2.0 of the CFI, and the current projects are enumerated in Appendix B. The listing of all Mayo Clinic Practice Partner Departments since the CFI's inception is presented in Appendix A.

Our platform, lab, and core structures have all grown as we've become a more mainstream Mayo entity. Our platforms have become more defined and clear—we started with five in 2008, and now we have four, each with a robust portfolio of programs and specific projects and metrics. Based on our experience, we recommend establishing a structure as soon as possible to start an innovation function, to be evolved as need be.

The CFI Way: Vision for Success

Now, at last, we arrive at the guiding vision for the Center for Innovation, and really, the guiding vision for the overall transformation of health care into a 21st century model of care. All the history, structure, and context you've read so far have led to this vision; this vision in turn guides everything we do.

The vision can be stated most succinctly: "Always be there for me." Now that may be a bit too high level to grasp or to put into action, but it really speaks to a long-term relationship between the individual and the organization, a relationship that transcends that of being a series of transactions and events to becoming a lifelong partnership. If that seems odd, just think about the companies and industries that work hard just to have a relationship with their customers that extend beyond fixing a product when it breaks, like the relationships we see in the auto industry.

Vision: Always be there for me.

We think we can provide a better experience and better health outcomes—with more patient comfort and lower cost—if we have a continuous relationship with the customer, enhanced by technology and powered by a Mayo team. It is no longer "get sick, go to the doctor." The new model is continuous care, available in a "fast, friendly, and effective" manner at all points of contact.

At a slightly more detailed level, we also express our vision as "Health and health care, here, there, and everywhere." It is about health, not just fixing health problems. It is about ongoing health and maintenance, and it can be delivered anywhere—on a mobile device or remotely by a care team in a real-time consultation from multiple locations. With current and future technologies, we can render a majority of bricks-and-mortar office visits obsolete, instead connecting health and care to individuals where they live and work.

All of our platforms, programs, and projects go to support the idea of broadening health care beyond the acute care event, getting what we can out of the hospital and doctor's office, and transforming what does require a doctor's office or other facility into a better experience. It all leads to our mission:

The Mission:
Transform the delivery and experience of health and
health care.

From Only Here to Here, There, and Everywhere

Okay, that's nice, but how do we get there? How do we execute an orderly transition, a transition from today's facility-centered, break-fix medical treatment paradigm? We've thought that one through too.

The chart in Figure 3.7 maps the evolution of the 21st century model of care over time—not coincidentally, through the three major CFI delivery platforms: Mayo Practice, Connected Care, and Health and Well-Being.

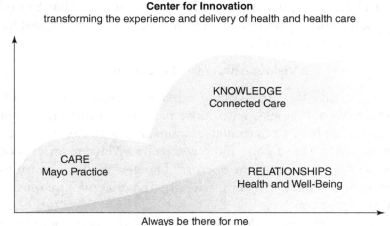

FIGURE 3.7. CFI VISION: THE 21ST CENTURY MODEL OF CARE

The *x* axis, of course, is time. We see a gradual but persistent evolution into the 21st century model. That evolution takes us beyond health care to just plain health. It also moves the center of gravity away from the physician's office and hospital to the patients in their homes and communities.

Initially, we improve the patient experience within the Mayo Practice. Improved outpatient facilities and workflows, hospital experiences, patient knowledge, and a better balance of staff make the process more "fast, friendly, and effective" to those who visit the doctor. It is today's care model, remixed and enhanced. As time goes on, we build our Connected Care capabilities, enabling us to connect through technology with patients at any point in the maintenance and care cycle. As these technologies are developed, refined, and diffused, the Mayo Practice "here" remains part of the transformation, but more of the care is delivered through technology, thus, "there" and "everywhere." Finally, we develop the well-being and healthy living concepts that transcend care over time; with Connected Care, many of these too can be delivered "there" and "everywhere."

The net result? We get to the right balance of health and health care. We like to refer to it as "changing the rhythm of care." This is the essence of the transformation to the 21st century model of care.

And when will this happen? We are currently targeting 2018 as the year to reach this balance.

A Shift to the Left

As another way to illustrate this multidimensional transformation, we often refer to our "Shift Left diagram," presented in Figure 3.8. The chart, like the one in Figure 3.7, shows a gradual transformation toward health and wellness management, using Connected Care tools, and away from traditional health care delivery at medical facilities. The shift improves the quality of life while reducing the total cost of care.

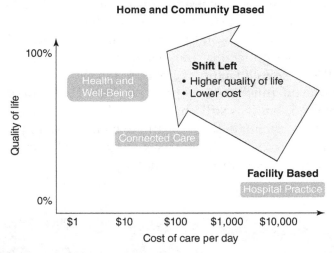

FIGURE 3.8.   A SHIFT TO THE LEFT

The CFI Way: Spaces for Success

Now we move from the conceptual aspects of building the Center for Innovation to the more "real" ones—in this case, the facilities and labs of CFI. We believed from the beginning that "innovation needs a special place."

While many innovation efforts, particularly those of the skunk works variety, make do with the spaces they have—often some bit of unused space in an existing facility, or even leased space somewhere outside the operative mainstream of the enterprise—we felt from the beginning that it was important to have the right kind of space in the right location.

Dating back to our SPARC roots, we believed that our space needed to have the look and feel of a design center and that it needed to be deeply embedded and as central as possible to the practices and the individuals for and with whom we innovate. By "design center look and feel," we wanted open, contemporary, and collaborative spaces that fostered creativity and led to the sort of team building and informal networking we feel are vital to the exchange and development of ideas. "Watercooler" discussions were, and still are, very important to us.

Gonda 16

Our original space was designed with the help of IDEO and Steelcase, the latter providing much of the furniture for our original SPARC Lab and what became our central Gonda 16th-floor design facility and headquarters (Figure 3.9). The 10,000-square-foot facility is embedded in the geographic center of Mayo Clinic's medical practice. The office arrangement has evolved, but it is still characterized by open offices with adjacent and facing desks to facilitate collaboration, plenty of conference rooms with large tables and glass walls, and the latest in computer and display technology.

FIGURE 3.9.   GONDA 16 CFI HEADQUARTERS

If you walk into today's Gonda 16 facility, you'll see the "writing on the wall" in the form of whiteboards and writing on the glass walls and windows echoing various conversations among the team members. The open spaces, glass walls, Post-it Notes, and project summary posters facilitate collaboration and transparency between projects. Team members can see each other's work—literally—and they feel involved with each other. There's room to display and work on prototypes, and prototyped technology solutions like Connected Care projects are easy to see and experience.

We call it "space that doesn't get in the way" of our innovators, and it is space that does not form a barrier between us and our stakeholders and practice constituents. The "front stage" of the space is open to any Mayo Clinic employees to use, even if they are not working with CFI, simply to allow them to experience the space and conjure a "thinking differently" mindset. Our space is important, but it is by no means exclusive to our use, and it has become popular as a Mayo Clinic showcase, and it forms a key part of the fabric of our existence.

Multidisciplinary Design for the Outpatient and HAIL Labs

In addition to design space, it is also important to have spaces to research the patient experience and to prototype new models. It has to be done in spaces that are as realistic as possible for the patients and that are set up for proper observation of old and new behaviors. For this research we have two dedicated labs, and we make use of other settings as well.

The Outpatient Lab, known formally as the "Multidisciplinary Design Outpatient Lab," is located on the 12th floor of the Gonda Building (Figure 3.10). Furniture and walls are movable, wall décor is magnetized to allow changes in look and feel, and the technologies are flexible and can be set up to simulate real interactions while allowing data collection by observers. All aspects of a clinical visit can be simulated with real patients, from waiting room to check-in to exam room activities.

As noted earlier, CFI also operates a senior living lab known as the Healthy Aging and Independent Living, or HAIL, Lab

FIGURE 3.10. GONDA 12 OUTPATIENT LAB

(Figure 3.11). The lab, operated in partnership with the Robert and Arlene Kogod Center on Aging, is physically located in the Charter House, a continuing care retirement community of 400 residents, which is adjacent to the main Mayo campus in Rochester. The lab is configured as a set of retirement community apartments, each with a full living room, bedroom, bath, and kitchen as well as central dining facilities and a nursing station. It is set up to test and prototype "aging-in-place" programs within the Health and Well-Being platform, and it has been used by outside organizations for various research projects.

In addition to the prototype lab spaces, we routinely go to the patients for observation and ethnographic understanding.

FIGURE 3.11. HEALTHY AGING AND INDEPENDENT LIVING (HAIL) LAB

For example, if we are researching the inpatient experience, we hang out with patients and their loved ones in the hospital and even transition with them to their homes to understand the whole experience. A designer and anthropologist might embed themselves for months in a Minnesota town to understand health from the perspective of community residents. Or designers might embed themselves on a college campus, as they did at Arizona State University, to understand the needs of students as they try to manage significant stress and optimize their health.

The CFI Way: Staffing for Success

The Center for Innovation is a dedicated, multidisciplinary, embedded team sitting right at the intersection of design and medicine. As such, we have staffed the organization with a diverse set of individuals from inside and outside the health care industry, individuals who bring a broad set of skills and motivation to our design and program management. People who join our group like new ideas and change and are uncomfortable with the status quo. They can tolerate ambiguity and the messiness of innovation, and they can synthesize the lessons of the outside world with the realities of medicine to produce results.

Over time we have grown the group from its early SPARC days of 4 people to a team of 60 with the following distribution:

- Service designers (14)
- Innovation coordinators (5)
- Administrative assistants (4)
- Clinical assistants (4)
- Project managers (13)
- Platform managers (4)
- Technology analysts and programmers (5)
- Physician leaders (5)
- Business development manager (1)
- Medical and administrative directors (2)
- Operations manager (1)
- Design strategist (1)

▶ Financial analyst (1)
▶ Others (not dedicated) from nursing, legal, systems and procedures, media support services, and human resources

Job Description: Service Designer II

Position Overview

As a member of the Center for Innovation, the designer consults internally with the departments, divisions, and committees across the clinic looking to innovate the delivery of Mayo's health care services. The designer uses the human-centered and participatory methods of "design thinking" to identify unmet patient, provider, and institutional needs and creates new service concepts or business strategies to better meet those needs. These methods include conducting observational research, interviews, and workshops; undertaking internal and external research activities; generating conceptual frameworks and formulating insights related to the synthesis of the research data; and communicating findings and concepts to project sponsors in a clear and compelling visual manner. Most projects will be cross-functional in nature, involving split or shared responsibility and problem solving with disciplines and personnel from other areas. The designer is an integral team member who works both independently and collaboratively through each phase of the project with other designers and project participants.

Minimum Education and/ or Experience Required

Master's degree in interaction, graphic, or industrial design; communication; or other related field; and four years of experience managing design projects, teams, or other creative endeavors. Or a bachelor's degree in interaction, graphic, or industrial design; communication; or other related field; and eight years of experience managing design projects, teams, or other creative endeavors. Demonstrated knowledge of "design thinking" and/or design research tools and methods. Must develop and maintain an understanding of major operating systems and overall policies, procedures, and objectives of the institution. Excellent interpersonal skills to include presentation, negotiation, persuasion, and team facilitation, and excellent written communications skills.

The designer must have the ability to independently manage a varied workload of projects with multiple priorities. Must be able to prioritize work and outline the nature of the problem and the overall urgency. Must be capable of consulting, designing and conducting studies, and developing and implementing solutions for issues with significant financial and operational impact to the organization. Because the work is complicated by being performed in an environment of multiple high-priority projects and sometimes resistance to change, strong time management skills and sound judgment are required.

Additional Experience and/or Qualifications

Creative problem-solving skills. A curious mind and an enthusiastic work ethic. Experience in design planning and design research methods. A passion for enriching the design process with meaningful research. Comfort with ambiguity and complex problems. Ability to work effectively with a wide variety of professionals and disciplines. Demonstrated project management experience with an ability to lead complex projects effectively. Ability to make rough interactive prototypes. Proficient with InDesign, Photoshop, Illustrator, Flash, and/or Dreamweaver. Ability to articulate the meaning of the design work to colleagues and clients through formal and informal presentations. Serves as a mentor for new employees, interns, and trainees. In-depth understanding of core institutional processes, clinical practices, and support areas. Works similarly to an independent consultant with own set of clients.

We also have embedded core resources, including a business development manager, IT specialists, communications staff members, project managers, graphic designers, and media specialists. And of course, the group includes health care team members such as nurses, physicians, nurse practitioners, physician assistants, and clinical assistants.

As mentioned, we pride ourselves on our diversity of skills and experiences. Our people are unique in many ways when compared to Mayo Clinic employees—they are younger, more are women, and they tend to be on more mobile career tracks. About 50 percent of our personnel come from outside the health care industry. We brought in such diverse talents as an architect, an anthropologist, a fashion designer, an ethnographer, and a former IBM peripheral manufacturing engineer. We feel strongly that these different disciplines add to our capability to frame and solve problems and to create truly human-scale experiences.

It's also worth mentioning the cultural ethos of our team. While the job roles and department structures are carefully defined, we do operate in a looser, more informal, "water-cooler" kind of way than do a lot of other organizations and even the departments in the rest of the Mayo Clinic organization. We limit the hierarchical structure and bureaucracy, and we offer autonomy and flexibility to our individuals wherever possible. Everyone is on a first-name basis; our workspaces are open, and our communications are open and informal whenever possible. Our space is comfortable—both for our own workers and for those in the greater organization or outside who choose to visit. The emphasis is on collaboration and tasks, not structure and formalities.

The CFI Way: Partnering, Networking, and Outreach

In nearly any business enterprise, partnerships serve to expand the resource and knowledge base available to accomplish the task. The exchange of ideas and the sharing of resources typically allow both partners to accomplish more than they could without the partnership. It's all about finding "win-win" partnerships to accelerate the pace and strategically share resources, intellectual property, and/or branding.

We at Mayo have embraced the notion of partnering particularly with our larger innovation programs. We know that we have brand value to offer, and in some cases, we can offer innovations and solutions that our partners can use or even eventually license, which brings in a revenue stream for Mayo.

Partners can help with funding, intellectual property, and experience of their own, and in some cases, they may provide settings to test and advance our programs.

Our partners come from the commercial, nonprofit, institutional, and academic sectors, mainly in the United States but some from overseas. In some cases, we form collaborations with a specific enterprise, as we did with Cisco for the eConsult program. In others, we form consortiums of partners who offer different resources and expertise, as we did with the HAIL Lab program. The HAIL Consortium is currently a group of four partners from different industries bringing in diverse resources and experiences:

- Best Buy, the electronics retailer, a founding partner
- Good Samaritan Society, with senior services and facilities in 240 communities across the United States
- UnitedHealthcare, the largest health insurance carrier in the United States
- General Mills, one of the world's largest food companies

In the HAIL example, the consortium connects frequently to establish the HAIL strategic direction and determine the experiments and investments, leading to customer insights that help all the organizations accelerate their product and service innovation and commercialization. The consortium meets formally twice a year to review results and identify future strategies.

Innovation Whisperers: The External Advisory Council

In addition to oversight from the Internal Advisory Council (IAC) composed of senior clinical and administrative leaders and patients, the External Advisory Council (EAC) was created when CFI was formed. This diverse group of thought leaders in their fields of design, technology, advertising, business, and health care meet twice a year, with frequent consultations as needed between meetings.

The EAC helps us look to the outside for effective partnerships and alliances. Currently the EAC has nine members, including Larry

Continued

Keeley; IDEO CEO Tim Brown; UCLA Innovation Center director Dr. Molly Coye; Steelcase former CEO Jim Hackett; Steelcase research director Terry West; Richards Group president Stan Richards; and Rebecca Onie, founder and CEO of Health Leads, a nonprofit agency involved in health care solutions for low-income families; and others who prefer anonymity. Until his recent passing, Yale faculty fellow William Drenttel was a vibrant and active founding member of the EAC, and his wisdom will be sorely missed.

The EAC provides strategic direction, external innovation expertise and experience, external connections, and a sounding board for ideas, programs, and strategies. The council members act as mentors, and they can provide "air cover" with inside and outside entities to help articulate strategies and get traction.

The EAC has been invaluable to CFI's evolution. We recommend forming an advisory group made up of people outside the organization for any innovation entity that is working within a complex organization or industry.

The CFI Way: The Fusion Innovation Method

At this point it's time to mark the transition from the *why* and *who* to the *how*. How does the Mayo Clinic Center for Innovation approach the complex task of bringing about transformative innovation? Now that we understand the 21st century model of care, and some of the internal and external roadblocks to innovation, and how we set up CFI to address those roadblocks, how do we actually get there?

Part II of our book explains the how-tos, while Part III goes into greater depth with examples and recipes to help you emulate our success. As a way to get started, here we present the building blocks to what we ultimately call the Fusion Innovation Model, depicted in Figure 3.12, as part of the Mayo Model of Innovation.

Now—deliberately so—there isn't a lot of rocket science in this innovation model. But it provides a guiding context and a balance among disciplines that we feel are necessary for success. For example, we don't want to go overboard with

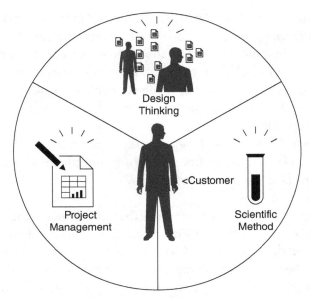

FIGURE 3.12.   FUSION INNOVATION MODEL

technology. Technology can often be a "solution looking for a problem," a panacea that is shiny and compelling but if not handled properly and in the greater context of innovation, can waste a lot of time and energy. Technology should *support* a strategy. It is not strategy in and of itself. We view technology as a necessary but not sufficient enabler for transforming the experience and delivery of health care.

So technology is a given, a necessary enabler for what we do—you can't have technology without a strategy, and generally you can't have a strategy without some enabling technology. The customer, of course, is at the center of everything we do—and more often than not, the patient is the primary customer in mind. That said, customers can also be providers, staff members, payers, and other players in the system.

That leaves three critical elements in our innovation model:

▷ *Design thinking.* We'll expand on this in the next chapter, but *design thinking* means using a deep understanding of the customer to frame a problem and then applying a methodical creativity to generating insights to solve it.

▶ *Scientific method.* The scientific method in this context is a rational, rigorous, data-driven, structured approach based on hypothesis, experimentation, and logical conclusions. Success must be demonstrated through a series of design and test cycles before taking an idea to market. Following these steps is especially important for our physician constituents in the practices.

▶ *Project management.* Finally, a rigorous project management discipline involving strong leadership and communication is critical to the success of the innovation model.

So now we're at the point where the rubber meets the road. In the largest sense, our innovations apply technology and process to do something important for the customer. But—how do we get from here to there? What do the customers need? What new technology or process should we provide? How can we make sure that the approach we take truly solves the problem? How can we be sure to build it in such a way that it works and fits our overall vision? How can we make sure it's delivered on time?

That's where the three elements in Figure 3.12—design thinking, scientific method, and project management—really come together. In fact, as we'll see, in our view they're inseparable.

As a consequence, we've "fused" these three elements into a combined approach to delivering innovation that we call the Fusion Innovation Model. We recognize that good ideas aren't worth much if the organization can't move them forward. The Fusion Innovation Model centers on the customer, but it deploys a rigorously balanced discipline of design thinking, scientific method, and project management to turn them into reality. This balance helps us stay on course to provide the best results for every project and to deliver those results to the organization. Chapter 4 covers the Fusion Innovation Model.

Innovation the Mayo Clinic Way: Creating an Innovation Ecosystem

We don't offer summaries at the end of every chapter, but we thought here it would be wise to wrap up some of the key ideas of CFI (and for establishing *your* own CFI) as a jumping-off point into the more process related material that follows. These are some of the highlights:

- ▶ *Embedded, physically and metaphorically.* Tight connections need to exist between the CFI and the operating parts of the business—in our case, between CFI and the Department of Medicine, for example.
- ▶ *Credible leaders from the start.* The head of the Mayo CFI was the top leader from the largest department within Mayo, and all leaders had significant institutional credibility.
- ▶ *Clear-eyed view of purpose.* Without purpose, you have no program, and without a program, you have no innovation. State your purpose and principles, and make them everyone's guiding light.
- ▶ *Design thinking.* Structure creativity toward achieving a deep understanding of the customers' needs.
- ▶ *Diverse team members.* The CFI team was drawn from a wide and deep mix of designers and operations experts with outside training and credentials.
- ▶ *Establish a guiding EAC.* This is not just a steering committee. It is a group of people who can add expertise and alliances. Note that "E" stands for "external," not "executive."
- ▶ *Inoculating the organization.* Transfuse the seeds of innovation throughout the organization by providing resources, communications, and a point of view about innovation.
- ▶ *Structure.* Establish a working structure aligned to the CFI vision in the beginning, and then evolve it as necessary, building the organization and its communications around that vision. Structure is important.
- ▶ *Strategic partnerships.* Never underestimate who might want to partner with you and what they might have to offer. Partnerships can provide anything from funding to expertise to filing cabinets.
- ▶ *Balance.* Don't overdose in panaceas—for example, technology ("Let's put everything on the Internet") or project management.
- ▶ *Fun!* Innovation, when done right, can be very fulfilling, engaging, and exciting. Take a tour of our CFI, and you'll see what we mean.

PART II

THINK BIG, START SMALL, MOVE FAST

CHAPTER FOUR

Fusing Design Thinking with Scientific Rigor

The Fusion Innovation Model

*If I asked my customers what they wanted,
they'd have told me "A faster horse."*
—HENRY FORD

The Ford "faster horse" quote is an old standard in the annals of innovation, and it is by no means new to any of you familiar with innovation literature. We bring it to you not so much as a revelation but as a way to frame our thoughts and to introduce the *how* component of our innovation story—the Mayo Clinic Center for Innovation approach and model for making innovation happen.

Of course, the main idea embedded in the quote is that, if we think in narrow terms, we're unlikely to succeed in identifying what the customer really needs. As a result, our innovation will be off track from the beginning; any innovation that ignores true, deep, or "latent" customer needs will usually fail—becoming downgraded to a shiny new idea or gimmick or gadget or product that fails to create customer value.

We know that even if we ask the *patient*-customer what he or she needs, we're still exposed to the risk that we'll miss badly with our innovations. Why? Because in many cases, customers can't tell us what they really need. Put differently, they tend to frame their answers in what already exists or is known to be available—in the oft used quote, a faster horse.

At CFI, we look beyond these immediate and obvious needs. We must, because the process of health care delivery is too complex and it has too many moving parts and technical complexities for most customers to really be able to articulate what they need, particularly within a framework of what is possible. Furthermore, most customers have lived with our current health care delivery standards for a long time; as a result, their expectations have been lowered, and their vision of what's possible has been limited. It therefore falls to us to envision and reach a level of health care delivery well beyond what our patient-customers expect.

Health care brings with it additional complexity. Retaining a singular, unwavering focus on *patient*-customer needs is critically important but also not enough: it will not get the job of reinventing health care delivery done. Why? In part because we work in a large organization of physicians and health care providers in a demanding field that defaults to tradition and considers unacceptable anything that puts the delivery of its product at risk. Beyond that, we also work at the behest of a network of payers, secondary providers, government agencies, and others, all of whom have a stake in what we do.

Furthermore, change is good—but only if we've demonstrated that we know what we're doing and that we've considered the alternatives. Patients' lives are at stake, after all. Satisfying or even delighting in the short term doesn't count if we're compromising long-term health outcomes. Furthermore, as we've mentioned, the world is training its collective green eyeshades on the cost of health care. Bottom line: we must satisfy our customers—*all* of them.

So in this complex context, early on, we had to define *how* we innovate. How do we deliver an exceptional customer experience, while still satisfying risk-averse internal constituencies that demand scientific rigor to move forward? How do we keep every project we bring to the table from succumbing to the "organizational antibodies" that tear it apart and reject it, never to see the light of day?

From the Beginning

We pondered this carefully right from the start. We needed a method and process flexible and open-minded enough to get to transformative innovation, yet structured enough to meet the demands of a traditional medical practice and beyond to a vast and well-entrenched global field of medicine.

We started our SPARC Lab, engaged with consultants, and visited leading innovators like IBM, 3M, Procter & Gamble, and Cargill who were in similarly complex industries to learn and observe what was the same and what was different about their situations. We synthesized from these visits and our own early experiences. It all led to this: to get to true customer-driven transformative innovation, we needed a process that was simultaneously rigorous about understanding customer needs while being flexible in how those solutions would be delivered. And those solutions had to clear the bar of scientific rigor and testing before bringing them to market. We couldn't tie ourselves down with unnecessary inertia and bureaucracy.

We needed a process that could Think Big, Start Small, Move Fast.

The truth is that, really, rather than a strictly defined process, we sought a *model* for innovation. The model would be deeply customer driven and highly creative, yet scientific and structured enough to provide rigor and cover the organizational bases. Make it too loose, and nobody would buy in; we would create cool ideas that would never make it to market. Make it too tight, and little would happen, or at best, we would be tied down to incremental, process-driven innovation confined to tweaking the known.

From all of this we arrived at something we call the Fusion Innovation Model. The Fusion Innovation Model "fuses" the important methods of design thinking, scientific method, and project management into a thought process under which we all operate. It also *suggests* a process flow to execute a program, but it doesn't *specify* it. We think, live, and breathe by the *spirit* of the fusion innovation method, not by the "letter" of a defined process. The resulting balance and flexibility are more *organic*, giving our designers, project managers, and physicians the freedom to discover, design, and deliver transformative innovation while avoiding the tentacles of bureaucracy.

The Fusion Innovation Model allows us to Think Big, Start Small, Move Fast.

This chapter is devoted to presenting and illustrating the key principles that underlie the Fusion Innovation Model—design thinking, scientific method, and project management. We will also take a short tour of the generalized flow we use to move a project forward. In Chapters 5 and 6, we'll add on the "transfusion" components—how we nourish fusion innovation and keep its activities connected and relevant to the organization. Finally, in Chapter 7 we'll describe how we've evolved our leadership model to manage our innovation in practice.

Forming the Fusion Innovation Model

From an organization like Mayo Clinic, most of you would likely expect a deeply detailed, structured innovation process that bases everything on data and mandates numerous meetings and lengthy structured project reports. Most of you in large organizations probably experience this type of process.

The reasons would be clear. Innovators must be held accountable for what they do. Everybody wants tested, proven ideas, ideas that have passed muster with all stakeholders, no surprises. Everyone wants a good return on their investments, a healthy ROI, especially when there's a lot of investment at stake. Nobody wants a rogue team to deliver a biased or unmarketable innovation or to make a costly mistake. In short, innovation brings tension to an organization.

Beyond general tensions around investment and change, innovation also calls out many more issues to balance in any innovation method or model an organization deploys:

▶ *Intuition versus science.* Intuition, without proof, can be wrong; science without intuition can miss opportunities and take too long.

▶ *Speed versus precision.* Speed without enough precision leads to unacceptable errors, putting lives at risk; precision without speed misses opportunities. The wrong thing done right is still the wrong thing.

▶ *Structure versus freedom.* Structure brings certainty to the methods; freedom allows open thinking encircling *more* opportunities, and it reduces inertia.

▶ *Customer-driven versus process-driven innovation.* Customer-driven innovation more likely transforms the marketplace; process-driven innovation may miss transformative nuggets. In many organizations, the process *becomes* the customer. Innovation serving a process and not a customer is far less likely to succeed, and it is more likely to consume resources.

▶ *Known versus unknown.* We sought a model that would take us into the unknown—really, that would turn as much "unknown" into "known" as possible but that would not get stuck on what we already knew.

▶ *Risk versus certainty.* Certainty is nice, but it takes too long, and it can be constraining. Obviously we can't accept too much risk when lives are at stake, but when they are not, we're willing to tolerate a lot of risk to move forward.

▶ *Creativity versus business constraints.* Simply, good ideas may be too expensive to deliver. But if we always let business constraints squelch good ideas, our efforts in the end will suffer. There are times when a lack of an obvious business model should not stop a radical innovation. The trick is to know when and how many of those times your organization can live with.

▶ *Creativity versus efficiency.* A relentless emphasis on efficiency can make an enterprise less creative; such an enterprise settles for routines, not progress or action. We can become very efficient at doing the wrong thing.

▶ *Discrete versus continuous.* Process-focused organizations tend to view most activities, including innovation, as a series of discrete, sequenced steps. Start a task, do the task, finish a task, review it, and start the next, always in order, always

in the *same* order. Emphasis is placed on the "start" and
"end" of the task versus what is happening *during* the task.
In contrast, the "continuous" approach has reviews and
checkpoints, but it may do several things simultaneously—or
it may return to an earlier stage (as below) to discover and
develop something new.

▶ *Iterative versus linear.* Similar to the above: a flexible process
allows the physicians, designers, and project managers to
explore or experiment with something found from an earlier
discovery. An innovation may proceed through the same
"steps" several times. Sequence is less important than true
discovery; innovators have more freedom to "go where the
project takes them."

These tensions may seem obvious. Yet in our observations
of innovation in complex organizations, the tendency is to
become more structured and process driven over time even
if it does not start that way. In some cases, the customer is
barely noted on the list of objectives. We saw this in several
companies we visited where they have fallen into the trap of
measuring success almost exclusively in terms of the number of patents generated. To be fair, patents are essential for
many organizations, but, without doubt, some of those patents edged toward serving a process rather than actually being
delivered to market. In large organizations, a planned and
repeated reevaluation of the model is required to correct the
drift toward process over creativity.

At Mayo, in developing our innovation model, we strived
to become anything but a patent mill, anything but an organization in which "the innovation served the process" rather
than the process serving the innovation. In forming this idea,
our early discussion with 3M was particularly enlightening.
We visited 3M's headquarters in St. Paul to learn how to position innovation within a complex enterprise. 3M had just
undergone a transition from CEO James McNerney (originally from GE) to George Buckley. McNerney had merged
innovation with quality improvement, and he had placed a
"relentless emphasis on efficiency." Buckley saw it differently,
and he sought to restore the culture toward growth, especially

important in today's "idea-based, design-obsessed economy." The 3M team noted that process and quality improvement "demands precision, consistency, and repetition," while innovation needs "variation, failure, and serendipity."

As a consequence of these discussions and observations, we began to resolve the "tensions" list in favor of a more human-centered, flexible model that entertained deep customer understanding and creative solutions while also adhering to the principles of science—all while preserving enough structure to be manageable. We felt strongly that too much structure and process would be more of a burden than a blessing and would diminish our results. And, since quality management was already tasked to another group in Mayo Clinic, we were free to pursue true customer-focused innovation.

It all led us to the Fusion Innovation Model.

What *Is* the Fusion Innovation Model?

The Fusion Innovation Model is, really, a mindset and a thought process.

As a thought process, it blends the disciplines of design thinking, scientific method, and project management together as a whole. As illustrated in Figure 3.12 at the end of the last chapter, the three guiding principles are "fused" to operate together rather than separately.

Really, it's a Zen-like absorption in the "truths" of the fused disciplines, a deep commitment to a single guiding light, as a single principle. It is not a doctrine or a manifesto or a checklist where we follow one discipline at a time, design thinking on Mondays and Tuesdays, scientific method on Wednesdays and Thursdays, project management on Fridays. We do *all three all the time*. It may seem idealistic, but it is not. We benchmark ourselves against this principle every day; it helps us achieve balance and move more efficiently through our innovations.

The Fusion Innovation Model fuses three distinct disciplines:

1. *Design thinking.* Blends a deep customer empathy and understanding with creative design and business constraints into attainable and marketable insights

2. *Scientific method.* Strives to turn controllable experiments and measurable evidence into unbiased and proven solutions
3. *Project management.* Moves a project forward in a manageable and demonstrable way, with a timeline and a set of structural guideposts and stages to ensure that it is accomplishing what is intended

These disciplines will be explained and illustrated by example throughout this chapter.

The Fusion Innovation Model is guided by the customer, not the process. The process fuses naturally to achieve customer objectives and organizational objectives alike. When you're doing right by the customer, especially the "greater" set of customers inside and outside your organization, you're more likely to get it right.

At the end of the day, the Fusion Innovation Model achieves what we think is the right balance of customer and customer experience, and process and process rigor. This organic balance helps us to overcome organizational barriers and antibodies that slow projects down and to bring more discovery and innovation to light more quickly. Ultimately, we believe it is the best way to transform the greater Mayo organization and the delivery of the 21st century model of care, and it is also the best way to introduce innovation into any complex environment.

We believe that the Fusion Innovation Model:

▶ *Achieves a greater synthesis.* The Fusion Innovation Model fuses our own experience and culture with what we observed outside Mayo at 3M, Procter & Gamble, IBM, and other complex organizations and what we heard from the experts at Doblin and IDEO and other innovation thought leaders.
▶ *Is simpler.* It is not a rigid "process" but rather, a flexible mindset.
▶ *Brings in technology the right way.* Technology is embraced, but it serves the innovation and strategy rather than being the end in itself.
▶ *Resolves conflicts.* The fused model is about balance from the beginning—neither "design" nor "science" nor "management" takes over. The true focus is on the customers, not the process.

▶ *Serves many masters.* Patient experience "wins," but so do the most scientific-minded and skeptical of our constituents—not just the patients but also the providers and payers.

▶ *Allows degrees of freedom.* Project teams can imagine, create, and experiment without following an exact formula. The process serves innovation; innovation doesn't serve the process.

▶ *Is flexible to the nature of the project.* One rigid process doesn't apply to all. Instead, there are many kinds and sizes of projects for many constituents. It's a guided framework for thought—not a rigorous checklist—and that makes it easier for our people (who are all different as well!) to work within it.

▶ *Avoids faster horses, organizational antibodies, and inertia.* This is the best feature of all: the Fusion Innovation Model is true to the customer and gets the most out of what we have to offer. It is fun, engaging, and creatively challenging for our people. It's also more interesting to manage.

▶ *Places trust in our teams and personnel.* Rather than strict adherence to code or protocol, we allow our teams the flexibility to approach a project as they see fit. We trust our teams to be thorough and smart about how they assess the customer experience before, during, and after an innovation, how they use experimentation and data to validate it, and how they identify progress and demonstrate results.

From here, we will proceed to describe the three fused disciplines of the Mayo Clinic Fusion Innovation Model— design thinking, scientific method, and project management. The discussion will be slightly weighted toward design thinking because it is perhaps the least tangible component of our model. Scientific method and project management are no less important, but they tend to be more understood and they are already deployed by most organizations.

What Is Design Thinking?

Part I of this book brings our story forward from the early days of innovation at Mayo to the early days of the Center for Innovation and our initiative to bring about a new, better, experience-driven model of care. As we began our journey, we knew we had to develop an operating philosophy—an approach—to seeing the world and defining *transformational* innovation within it.

Early on we engaged with IDEO, whose slogan "We create impact through design" resonated with us. We met with founder David Kelley and with Tim Brown, who is now the president and CEO and is also the author of *Change by Design*, an excellent read on the design thinking topic. Brown is also a member of our CFI External Advisory Council.

IDEO has evolved the concept of design from being a mostly tactical, analytical process for putting something together, making it work, and making it look good according to some predefined specification or set of requirements to being something that embraces a more strategic sense of understanding human and organizational needs and behaviors. For IDEO, these concepts all converge into something called *design thinking*.

The design thinking approach, in IDEO's words, "brings together what is desirable from a human point of view with what is technologically feasible and economically viable." A designer designs a product that works. A design *thinker* starts with gaining an understanding of customer needs, recognizing patterns, and developing a strong intuition about those needs. A designer *then* applies design tools and a healthy dose of testing and verification to validate the initial design concepts. Importantly, you don't have to be a designer to understand and apply design thinking. It is a discipline with a body of knowledge that can be taught and learned.

As we see it, design is tactical, and design *thinking* adds strategic elements that turn inventions into innovations. Those elements turn innovations into *transformative* innovations. For us, design thinking *starts* with the customers, and it incorporates not only an understanding of the customers but also a deep *empathy* with them. It adds what we call *contextual creativity*—that is, creativity applied with that true understanding of the customers and that functions within the boundaries of technology, business, and organizational needs.

The crowdsourced *Wikipedia* definition of *design thinking* works for us:

Design thinking is the ability to combine empathy for the context of a problem, creativity in the generation of insights and solutions, and rationality to analyze and fit solutions to the context.

What the Experts Say About Design Thinking

Tim Brown, president and CEO of IDEO, defines *design thinking* this way: "Design thinking is a human-centered approach to innovation that draws from the designer's toolkit to integrate the needs of people, the possibilities of technology, and the requirements for business success."

Roger Martin, dean of the Rotman School of Management, University of Toronto, adds: "Design thinking balances analytical thinking and intuitive thinking, enabling an organization to both exploit existing knowledge and create new knowledge. A design thinking organization is capable of effectively advancing knowledge and achieving lasting and regenerating competitive advantage." And a famous one-liner from Dr. Martin: "In this new economy, the winners will be the re-thinkers, not the re-trenchers."

Well said. It is time for us in health care to stop digging deeper holes.

At the risk of belaboring the concept, the Fusion Innovation Model does not stop at design thinking. Rather, it integrates design thinking with scientific method and project management to provide the discipline to move things forward in a demonstrably correct manner. Design thinking is the secret sauce that makes innovation really matter, by understanding and serving customer and business needs, exploring the possibilities, and making the unknown *known*. The scientific method rigorously tests concepts, and project management moves the known forward and makes it *possible*.

Time Out for Examples

As a means to illustrate, we'll take a small detour to describe a few actual examples of what we do. We'll use these examples to frame our discussion of the principles of the Fusion Innovation Model.

First is our Asthma Connected Care App, a project in the implementation phase, already a winner of an Edison award for innovation. The issue was how to help teenagers with asthma manage their condition more effectively and have direct contact with their medical teams. The second is the Smart Mirror, a project in a working prototype stage. Both are part of the Connected Care platform, and both also have significant hooks into the Health and Well-Being platform, as they are really designed to augment health and well-being on an ongoing basis, before and after health care events. The third project is our Jack and Jill Rooms, and it is part of our Mayo Practice Redesign platform. As one of our earlier successes, Jack and Jill Rooms redesigned the traditional patient exam room to improve patient interactions with physicians and staff members and to incorporate family members and others more comfortably into the process.

Staying Tethered: The Asthma Connected Care App

The Asthma Connected Care App (Figure 4.1) moved through the design and testing stages during 2011 and early 2012. The "small frame" goal was to create a way for adolescent—aged 13 to 19—patients with chronic and "persistent" asthma—requiring treatments two or more times a week—to keep up with their health regimen. By staying connected to care providers, care and well-being would improve, and they would avoid a sudden worsening of their condition and a likely trip to the hospital or emergency room.

The "big-picture" goal was to demonstrate the effectiveness of continuous, connected care for a broader assortment of chronic diseases by managing care locally with a connected app, tethering the patients to their care teams "asynchronously" through data exchanges and text messages and "synchronously" (in real time) as necessary. We felt that with

FIGURE 4.1.   ASTHMA CONNECTED CARE APP

the Connected Care app, adolescents would feel empowered, providers would have much more data with which to make decisions, and previously unseen trends would emerge. In the end, our intuitions were confirmed, and we learned a lot about effective remote disease management, including how to connect to those patients.

The Asthma Connected Care App shows how we are transforming care delivery, moving the center of gravity away from the traditional, physician-based exam room to the daily life and flow of the patients, in their home, place of employment, school, and community.

Seeing Yourself as Others See You: The Smart Mirror

The Smart Mirror is a prototype mirror designed for seniors (Figure 4.2). The Smart Mirror is used like a bathroom mirror, and it is connected to a small mat that the patient-user stands upon while looking in the mirror, as would happen during a routine morning "get ready for the day" sequence. The mirror has an electronic display, and it is tethered not only to the floor mat but also to the cell phone network for outbound communications. The mirror displays reminders to the user to take scheduled medications, and it collects data when the user

FIGURE 4.2. SMART MIRROR

acknowledges taking those medications. The mat collects data on the patient's weight.

The information is passed on to a caregiver in the responsible health organization. It is also set up to be passed on to chosen outsiders, such as the user's loved ones as a check on the patient's activity and appearance. Caregivers can check on weight as an evidence of diet or congestive heart failure problems and on the proper dosages of medicine. Like the Asthma App, this concept has many more possible applications not only in elder care but also in the broader patient space, as well as for chronic conditions beyond aging, skin disorders as an example. With a broader set of data collection tools, including nanotechnology and embedded patient sensors, the possibilities are endless. Also like the Asthma App, the emphasis is on health and well-being, not traditional health care events. The working prototype is under development in the CFI Healthy Aging and Independent Living (HAIL) Lab.

Both models incorporate enabling technology to make a more desirable model feasible for the customer. Additionally—and importantly—viable business models are emerging as health care finally catches up with other industries in offering technology-enabled delivery well integrated into process flows.

Rethinking the Outpatient Exam Space: Jack and Jill Rooms

The Asthma App and, to a degree, the Smart Mirror are designed to reduce dependence on clinical visits. But when visits do occur, we naturally seek excellence in that experience too. So we created a project to examine patient-doctor interactions—to make the exam and discussion of results process more comfortable and productive not only for the patient but also for the physicians and staff members, as well as any of the patient's family members who might be present. The project was conceived in recognition of the fact that outside of cosmetic changes in furniture and décor, outpatient exam rooms really haven't changed much since 1900. As we'll see, the name of the project *arose from* our findings; it wasn't even on the radar in the beginning.

A team of CFI designers studied patient-physician interactions and the involvement of families, and they quickly found a number of problems. Computers were set up so that the physicians could view them easily, but not the patients. There was little room for family members, and the space was dominated by the exam table, dressing area, sinks, and exam tools—even though most appointments following the initial evaluation tended toward conversations about the patient's history and symptoms. In fact, our research showed that 80 percent of the time used in an office visit was for conversation versus only 20 percent for examination.

Observation and experimentation led to a series of full-scale prototype exam rooms, first conceived and constructed using foamcore, cardboard, and similar materials in the CFI lab, then put into practice as a prototype. The setup that resonated most with the group was the creation of separate consultation and examination rooms connected by a doorway. The consultation room was outfitted with a round table, four chairs, and a computer monitor on a swivel. Real patient interactions were observed in the new configuration, and researchers noted that patients were more comfortable and relaxed, they asked more questions, and they were more interactive in creating their home health care plan.

But there was one more issue: what about the additional floor space these dual rooms would require? An innovation such as this must fit within business constraints to succeed. The design team came up with a solution that shared a central exam room with two consultation rooms—in the manner of the central "Jack and Jill" shared bathroom from the 1970s TV show *The Brady Bunch*. Solid soundproof doors, lighting changes in the rooms, and a system to signal occupancy rounded out the new design. The design not only resonated with patients and their families but also with physicians, who could use one room to type up notes while the patient changed in another. Staff could clean and set up the exam room for another patient while a consultation was occurring in the neighboring room. The improved patient flow more than made up for the extra space required. The Jack and Jill exam room was shown in Figure 3.3 in Chapter 3.

These descriptions are meant to introduce, not fully describe, these programs—obviously there is more to these stories.

Acquiring a Deep Understanding of Customers

In business, and in innovation, almost everyone talks about the customers.

These days, if you're part of an innovation group or organization and you are *not* talking about the customers, you're way outside the loop. You didn't get the memo that good innovation doesn't start with ideas, shiny technologies, or even existing products. It starts with the customers. To turn an idea or invention into an innovation, it must ultimately create value for customers and be accepted by them. Other ideas need not apply.

Many people talk about the customers, measure customer activity, collect customer inputs, pore over customer satisfaction survey results, and put customers into one of four neat market segments. But do they really *understand* the customers? Do they understand not only what the customers want and need but also what the pain points and dissatisfiers are? Do they understand the deep, *innate* wants and needs, the ones the customers can't always or don't always express or even think of? Do they look holistically at the *experience*?

Avoiding Faster Horses

To innovate, we must create more than a faster horse.

If we simply take customer inputs at face value, or if we evolve our products without considering the bigger picture of what customers want, we can find ourselves in the weeds pretty quickly. Consider the personal computer industry over the years. Did customers really just want faster processors and more storage and faster printers and better print quality—more "speeds and feeds," as the industry put it? Perhaps there *was* a need. These features made computing work better—within its current experience.

But if you had focused just on speeds and feeds, you would have missed the boat. People really wanted to connect to each other and to enterprises—the Internet. As we found out even later, they really wanted the simpler tablet format to do this. So while the industry kept producing faster horses, it took too long to satisfy the greater customer need and desire. Nowadays the PC industry struggles to stay relevant.

Did real customers in the general public *say* they wanted the Internet? Did they *say* they wanted tablets? Hardly. These innovations emerged from an analysis of *latent* customer needs. They arose from intense observation, intuition, and some experimentation with the customer experience—from highly synthesized visions, a clear-eyed view of what was possible, and a willingness to try things.

Indeed, Henry Ford himself saw beyond the stated need to go faster, to find a faster horse. He observed that it was difficult to get more than one person on a horse. It was difficult to get protection from the elements. A horse required care around the clock. A horse could be difficult to control. Combine these insights with emerging technologies (and many more to come), and you arrive at the automobile.

But no customers at the time would have *said* that they wanted an automobile. They didn't know it was possible.

They couldn't synthesize the need and available technologies into a big-picture vision. Innovators figured it out through observation, intuition, and a deep understanding of the customer experience.

Meeting Explicit Needs—and Going Beyond

It's obvious that health care is complex, and most customers don't know very much about it. To get customers—patients or people seeking information about staying well—to articulate what they really want in the health care space is a tall order, in no small measure because they don't know what's possible. Most can't know.

Most people have had some experience with health care. They can describe a few pain points, like long waits in doctors' offices reading outdated magazines. They can tell you—or show you—physical pain in the clinical setting, and we've done a lot in the medical community to mitigate that. But about the whole experience? About the greater health experience beyond the clinical visit? Probably not. Compounding this is the low expectation customers have of health care delivery, an expectation that is lower than they would have in other aspects of their lives. Therefore, their ability to tell us what they need is often limited. Yet that does not mean they do not want, need, or deserve much more. Many have simply accepted the status quo. It is up to us to find a way to understand these unstated needs.

Getting a true customer understanding starts with looking at the entire experience, then framing the large and small opportunities within it. It starts with gaining a deep understanding of what the customer really wants or needs, beyond what might be discovered through traditional means like focus groups, satisfaction surveys, or interviews—which are today's primary methods in the health care space.

We must identify *explicit*, *tacit*, and *latent* needs.

The model in Figure 4.3 evolved from a 1950s' analysis of knowledge and learning. That analysis held that some learnings are explicit and can be expressed in words, while others, like riding a bicycle, are *tacit*; that is, we know how to do these tasks, subconsciously, but we can't put into words how to do

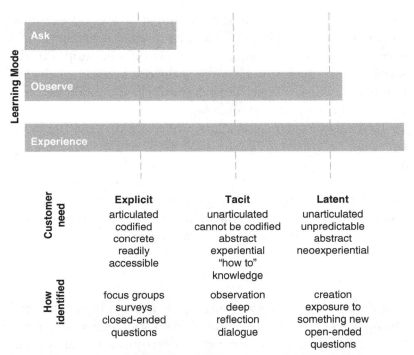

FIGURE 4.3. A KNOWLEDGE HIERARCHY OF CUSTOMER
NEEDS: EXPLICIT, TACIT, AND LATENT

them, and they're hard to convey to someone else. We can only observe them.

We have flipped this model around and added a layer so as to take into consideration the reality of innovation in a complex environment, integrating the *latent* needs of both the customers and the providers. We feel that transformative innovation can be achieved only when these latent needs are met and exceeded.

First, we substitute needs for knowledge in the model. Some needs are *explicit*, and the customers can articulate them. Other needs grow out of their behaviors and experiences, but the customers cannot articulate them easily. These are *tacit* needs.

Customers can articulate *explicit* needs, like shorter waiting times or clear, easy-to-read treatment programs, simply if you ask them. The other, more subliminal, or *tacit*, needs are difficult to articulate. However, you can often determine the needs simply by watching customer behavior. The need for, and advent of, Microsoft Windows is a good example. Customers wouldn't have articulated in a focus group or on a survey their need for multiple windows on a desktop. But the software designers would have seen the need clearly when they watched customers open one program, close it, open another, and repeat the cycle over and over.

To the explicit/tacit construct, we have added another layer: *latent* needs. Latent needs are so subliminal that not only can a customer or provider not articulate them but you're also not likely to observe them in practice. You simply have to infer and synthesize them from layers of customer-supplied and observed data, with an overlay of deep thought, visioning, and experimentation in a context of what's possible.

The Power of Latent Thinking

Automobiles, tablets, and many of the great transformational innovations of our times resulted from someone with a great vision, and the capacity for pattern recognition and synthesis, assembling customer inputs and observations with an understanding of the possibilities—to arrive at a strong and market-viable *latent* need. Recognizing the true big-picture latent need was the first step; the second was showing potential solutions together (or parts of them) to the customers to make them realize those solutions are what they *really* wanted. These steps, together, will take you to transformative innovation if done right.

The Asthma App: Always There for Me

At CFI we seek the latent needs in every customer experience. In our Asthma App, customers didn't just want a stand-alone app to manage dosage and provide treatment reminders. Eventually the novelty would wear off, and they would stop using it. We knew that from previous outside research.

Further, as an industry, we have thrown a dizzying array of health and health care apps at customers. If you search the Apple iTunes app store for "health," you'll find more than 40,000 apps that work on weight loss or fitness or that address more general health questions and problems. There appears to be a high demand for them, with an estimated almost 700 million downloads for apps in this category in 2013. But in a report by the IMS Institute for Healthcare Informatics, the researchers noted that the majority of the apps are spewing forth data that consumers cannot use to improve their health and well-being.

What our customers really wanted was the ability to avoid disruptive, time-consuming office visits—especially true for the 13- to 19-year-old age group we targeted. They also wanted to be able to contact care providers whenever a symptom changed or whenever they planned to do something or travel somewhere outside their normal routine so they could adjust their treatment. They wanted a live person to give feedback to them for any changes in symptoms. That contact didn't have to be in real time—asynchronous was okay—but having that person there really helped them feel confident, and it motivated them to stick to their care routines as well. They wanted to use technology that they understood, which in this case was a smartphone. We hypothesized this, and we put the app together to confirm our hypothesis.

The Smart Mirror: A Lifeline to Loved Ones

For our Smart Mirror, the latent need was for not just the caregivers but also for the *loved ones* to be able to monitor the elder without disturbance during their normal routine or without the caregivers feeling like they were imposing on somebody who likely was an authority figure in their past. Again, we had to synthesize this latent need from our intuition of the complete customer experience; it wouldn't have emerged from talking to the elders (or their caregivers) or from watching them in action. In this case, caregiver input helped us along, but we would do some assembly to get to the true latent need and final vision.

The Jack and Jill Room: Dressed for (Clinical) Success

One of the key tacit needs for the Jack and Jill rooms turned out to be very simple, and it was literally in front of our noses as we experimented with clinical room designs in our lab.

Almost amusing in its simplicity, here's the story. During one of our experiments, a Mayo Clinic patient stopped her physician in his tracks and got him thinking: "When I'm dressed, I feel healthier than I do in a paper gown," she said. Firmly and confidently, she equated the state of being clothed with the state of being healthy. "How can I talk about my health while sitting in a paper gown?" she continued and repeated: "When I get dressed, I feel healthier."

Indeed, in the Jack and Jill rooms, patients spend most of their time discussing their health while fully clothed, not in the paper gowns. The setting feels more like a living room. We hypothesized that patients wanted more comfortable surroundings and wanted it to be easier and more discreet for family members, but this was a surprise that really teased out a more tacit customer need to be clothed and comfortable. This need carried through this project and became a learning for other projects.

If we didn't strive to understand tacit and latent needs, we would invent a lot of faster horses. We would fine-tune the heck out of the patient office visit, making it as fast as possible with fresh magazines in the waiting room and designer gowns—and miss the big picture. We'd miss the true need or desire—that our patients would rather connect from somewhere with a care provider (not necessarily a physician) synchronously or asynchronously. But if instead we realize that if we meet this latent need to interact this way, our patients will be more positive about their health, and they will stay in contact more during health or when they need to manage a chronic disease. The outcome will be better health—and it will cost less.

In these cases, we would have missed tacit and latent needs if we had used traditional innovation methods. We had to take the extra steps to synthesize, create, and model these experiences—to "imagine" the experiences, before and after, to give the customers the "aha" and give our own organization the "aha." We listen to customers just as everyone else does. We *see* them in action when possible and when it makes sense. But we go a step further—to *feel* the total experience, to imagine, and to put new ideas out there to feel their response.

> Explicit, tacit, and latent.
> Listen, see, and feel.
> Discover and imagine.

Don't Outsource This

This is important. You can't just pay others to do this and forget about it. You can't pay market research firms or other outsiders to really understand your customers. Why? Because the resulting picture will probably be limited to explicit needs.

The best innovations start by making the observations and doing the synthesis yourself. All members of the team, including management and organization constituents, should be involved, not just the marketers. We went the extra step to hire professional designers into the CFI team. This was the first time designers were embedded directly into an academic medical center. We did this because we didn't believe that the experience assessment and resulting designs could come from outside. We didn't want to miss tacit and latent needs. This should not be taken as saying that there is no role for outside companies; we certainly took advantage of the considerable expertise of IDEO and Doblin to get started, and we often still collaborate with them on projects. Rather, it is meant to point out that we listened to good advice, but we didn't want others to do all our imagining.

The Power of Systemic Thinking

You've heard the well-worn expression "Think outside the box." As you've probably gathered by now, at Mayo Clinic we think outside the operating room, even outside the clinic and the bricks and mortar of our institution. Not that we don't think about what happens inside those four walls; it's just that we think of the broader context as well.

For a company that produces physical products—boxes—the exercise is to think outside that box as well. If you innovate inside and outside that box—into the delivery, supply chain, service and support, and other processes that turn your product into an experience, you'll not only be more successful but you'll also be far more likely to transform, disrupt, and eventually lead your markets.

Continued

Once again we return to our consultant, friend, and CFI External Advisory Council member Larry Keeley for a classic demonstration of this theme, the "Ten Types of Innovation" model depicted in his book of that name (full name: *Ten Types of Innovation: The Discipline of Building Breakthroughs*, republished by Wiley in 2013).

In Figure 4.4, we show the 10 types of innovation Keeley refers to, grouped into three categories: Configuration, Offering, and Experience. Note that the "product" in the sense we normally think of it is part of the Offerings. His premise is that you can innovate—and thus *differentiate*—in any of 9 other areas within your business to make your "whole" product better and thus gain market leadership in that area. Keeley wonders out loud why so many companies simply focus on the product. Further, through years of analyzing actual company behaviors, he has found that if you innovate successfully in 5 or 6 of these 10 types, you're well on your way to disrupting your industry.

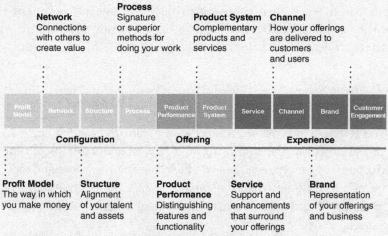

FIGURE 4.4. TEN TYPES OF INNOVATION
(COURTESY LARRY KEELEY, DOBLIN)

It's not hard to come up with examples of companies that have innovated in many if not all of these types and done it well. Amazon, Starbucks, Apple, Southwest Airlines, and others have all innovated well beyond the product itself to create new processes, channels, brands, and business models quite effectively.

We serve this up as a lesson for your business and also as a framework for how we think about ours. We think three dimensionally about the possibilities, not only across the 10 types of innovation offered by Keeley but also across the continuum of health care (Figure 4.5).

FIGURE 4.5. THE HEALTH CARE CONTINUUM

The point: when doing design research for the customer experience, "open up" your creative thinking to cover the entire experience and process and the product delivered by your enterprise. The solutions will be far more interesting, and they will have more impact; and you'll find new and greener pastures to deliver.

A Finger on the Pulse: What's New Out There?

We realize that a deep customer understanding, acquired only from our own observations and thought, might not go far enough. To develop a 21st century model of care, we must "frame in" what's going on in the outside world and, particularly, what's *changing* in the outside world.

As part of our design thinking process—most specifically, the "scanning and framing" process described shortly—we carefully study and categorize hundreds of trends in the outside world, representing social, technological, economic, environmental, political, and information advances. One way these learnings are shared is by assembling them into *trend cards*, available to all CFI and Mayo personnel. The cards each present an "orthodoxy challenged," that is, a concept in place that one might appraise as hard to change or

Continued

to do in a different way. The trend card summarizes the data and findings and sometime solutions (Figure 4.6).

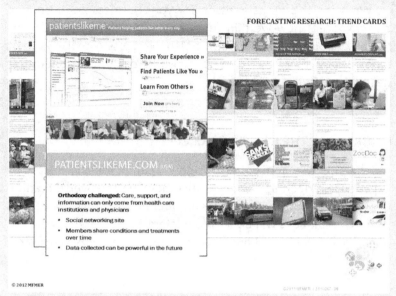

FIGURE 4.6.   TREND CARD: PATIENTSLIKEME.COM

In this example, the orthodoxy that "care, support, and information can come only from health care institutions and physicians is challenged by a relatively new medical social media website called PatientsLikeMe.com. On this website, patients with like diseases and symptoms can share experiences, conditions, and treatments, and they can create considerable data about their experiences too. Designers familiar with this emerging tool can incorporate it, and others similar to it, into their needs assessments and designs.

These trend cards serve as handy references and as a way to "drip irrigate" our staffers and the greater Mayo organization with current and emerging trends. By no means are these the only source of outside information. As we engage in any project in any field, we research and incorporate quantifiable and nonquantifiable trends, as we did with the Asthma Care App in assessing smartphone use, numbers of users, "stickiness" or willingness to continue using an app, and so forth.

Evidence, Please: The Scientific Method

So far, we've described the customer-centric but also business-constrained approach of design thinking. For many organizations, design thinking furnishes the core model for innovation.

With the complexity and the constraints of rigor and research naturally found in a health care environment, we must go further. Our innovations must fulfill the requirements of evidence and experiment, and they must meet the scrutiny of physician-scientists at once demanding of proven methods and skeptical of change. As a consequence, we must test, we must collect and present the evidence, and most of all, we need to maintain an exacting and unbiased approach.

This is where the scientific method comes in and is fused with other model components. The scientific method is based on measurable evidence, and it tests one variable at a time while keeping other parameters unchanged. It is, at its core, an unbiased approach to testing and proving a concept. The scientific method has four basic elements: making an observation, creating a hypothesis consistent with the observation, predicting something based on the hypothesis, and using experimentation to attempt to disprove the hypothesis. When the hypothesis can no longer be disproved, it becomes a conclusion that can be acted upon and communicated.

Multiple iterations may be used to test everything necessary, including new findings, ideas, and hypotheses from previous tests. The scientific method is not necessarily linear or circular. It yearns for solid, practical, evidence-based conclusions. Further, the learnings from one project or experiment are easily transferrable to another.

The scientific method entails a blend of testing, experimenting, observing, synthesizing, and documenting. We don't advance any given framework for our teams to do this; we instead simply require a scientific approach and let them figure out how best to do it—the details vary by project anyhow. When presenting a project, we expect our teams to come to us (and to the physician community) with documented scientific evidence in hand. Suffice it to say that our project presentations are loaded with graphs and charts measuring the outcomes.

Keep It Moving Forward, Please: Project Management

In every project we enter, we start with the end in mind. It's simple: get to prototype as fast as possible.

Of course, we'd like to get to implementation too, but we feel that implementation is too far down the road—a bridge to cross when we come to it. Why? Because if we do everything correctly up to that point, implementation should be fairly straightforward. Too, we don't want to bog down the early stages of any project with the notion of implementing a set of ideas we haven't even tested; for one thing, that would lead to predetermined conclusions, never a good thing.

At the same time, we recognize that the urge to innovate and the "golden moments" in seeing the success and "aha" of a project depend on getting something to work in the early stages. As most designers of personal technology products will tell you, the excitement really builds when you have a prototype in your hand to play with. The same principle applies to larger, and often more abstract, projects that you'd find in health care or other complex environments.

A Four-Step Approach

Our project management approach shies away from a template to follow in detail, though as we'll introduce below, we do have one. Like the other principles in the Fusion Innovation Model, we try to keep this flow free and flexible in form as well. Different projects will require different levels of rigor in project management; we leave that up to the teams to decide. More important, we understand that the project flow is seldom sequential or linear; most projects will have some circular flow to test new ideas or outcomes from earlier tests. We want to allow that, in order to get to the best, not

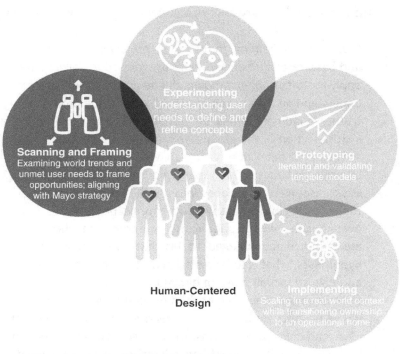

Experimenting
Understanding user
needs to define and
refine concepts

Scanning and Framing
Examining world trends and
unmet user needs to frame
opportunities; aligning
with Mayo strategy

Prototyping
Iterating and validating
tangible models

**Human-Centered
Design**

Implementing
Scaling in a real-world context
while transitioning ownership
to an operational home

FIGURE 4.7.   CFI INNOVATION FLOW

necessarily the fastest, solution. As we said earlier, we like to focus on what happens *during* the stages, not just the starts and finishes of each stage.

Figure 4.7 shows our conceptual *innovation flow*, which includes *scanning and framing, experimenting, prototyping*, and *implementing*. We should note that throughout this flow, we apply the principles of the Fusion Innovation Model consistently and continuously: design thinking, scientific method, and yes, traditional project management. And to repeat, these circles do not necessarily occur in sequence; there is usually a combination of linear and circular flow as the project team sees fit. For example, while scanning and framing, you can dip several times into the experimentation phase, as we did in the Jack and Jill Room project, to discover and round out tacit and latent needs.

Summarized, here are the four steps in the innovation flow:

▶ *Scanning and Framing.* In this step a project is conceived, and basic research begins. Teams are formed to collect data, apply customer understanding, define what further customer understanding may be required, and kick off the project. We feather in industry trends and develop personas representing a cross section of the groups we serve where it makes sense. In our detailed project map, we break this phase up into self-explanatory *initiate* and *plan* steps. The project is sized, resourced, and placed into the CFI Portfolio Roadmap to maximize connections with other projects, eliminate overlap, and leverage prior learnings. Internal stakeholders are identified and engaged. In this phase, we describe the hypotheses, what is to be tested and how it is to be tested, and give an overall sense of direction to the project.

▶ *Experimenting.* The all-important experimenting phase is where we discover the reality of customer needs, and we test ideas and deliverables against those needs. The experimenting phase begins with research, best described as knowing what is known or what can be observed. Experimentation follows, and it is a process of getting at what is not already known and must be discovered.

Design teams are free to construct the experiments. Some experiments are in our labs; others are conducted within the practices or even outside of Mayo. The goal is to identify tacit and latent needs, through observation and data collection, and to start to wire together some of the possible solutions in low-fidelity ways like foamcore models. It is in the experimentation phase where "failure" occurs most often, or rather, where something doesn't quite work but produces a learning that can be combined with other learnings to generate a new experiment. Experimentation leads us to create a prototype, a more formal and complete test of the concept in a live environment. Repeated and protracted experiments may arise from this phase; the timeline is simply "per project plan." Research reports and prototype plans are outcomes of the experimentation phase.

▶ *Prototyping.* As we move into prototyping, we synthesize the discovery findings from experimentation, and we develop potential solutions or alternative future states. In prototyping, we validate and generate the proof of concept for the solutions.

The prototype is a more complete, realistic, and on-location rollout of a concept designed to validate patient, physician, and staff benefits and to affirm the return on investment and financial metrics. Prototypes can be made in our labs or on location in community clinics or hospitals or, increasingly, in the customer's home. They include working examples of technology, and they are fully staffed according to the model being tested. Finishing touches and some fine-tuning are typically applied to the deliverable.

▶ *Implementing.* Prototyping may go on for some time until the concept is solid; during this phase we begin to *demonstrate* it to various constituencies within Mayo. A *project story* is created and distributed through our communications engine (discussed in next chapter), and a plan is put together to acquire the resources, train the receiving practices, and roll out the project. In many cases, the operational owner is anticipated and engaged early in the project, making the implementation handoff far easier. As an organization, CFI is accountable for generating value and results—hence we never let up on the implementation lever!

So You Think You Want More Structure . . .

Our Fusion Innovation Model may appear a bit loose and informal based on what we've presented so far. For those of you more used to a structured and detailed operational approach to innovation, specifically to project management, we'll provide some relief in this section.

Indeed, we have a more structured operating template, shared in Figure 4.8. In fact, we even have an "operations manager" responsible for this template and for documenting and checkpointing our projects through it. We're flexible—yes. But we don't ignore structure completely.

Continued

Working Methodology Elements and Responsibilities

CFI Goals	Focus on the human experience to identify needs and design services, products, and business models to meet them		Innovate care delivery that's accessible, affordable, and value driven Collaborate openly— internally and externally		Generate economic value by demonstrating financial return from sustainable delivery models, services, and products	
Phase	**Phase 0**		**Phase 1**		**Phase 2**	
	INITIATE	Accountable	**RESEARCH AND EXPERIMENT**	Accountable	**DEVELOP AND TRANSFER**	Accountable
	Identifying an opportunity's strategic alignment, scope, and fit. (Problem as stated)		Understanding world trends and user unmet needs to frame the opportunity. (Problem as Understood)		Prototyping, iterating and validating tangible models refined through co-creation with end users and operational homes	
Objective	Assess worthiness of project, and define/ assign initial PM/ Designer for plan phase.	Platform Lead	Approve research and prototype plan output and identification of operational home	Platform Lead	Approval of prototype validation, and ready for initiating transfer to operational home	Platform Lead
	Transfer of scope as stated to identified team		Approve additional resource needs (IT, Design, Other)	Platform Lead IT Lead	Approval of input and readiness of acceptance of handoff	Operational Home
			Determine Business Development Opportunity of prototypes proposed	Bus. Dev.		
Outputs	Scope document, and initial resources defined	Platform Lead or Project Sponsor	Charter Document and Control Book	PM	Validation Report and Diffusion/Transition Plan with Operational Home and institutional partners.	PM
			Research Plan including critique checkpoints, insights/ recommendations report	Designer and Design Strategist	Design Insight/and Final Presentation	Designer and Design Strategist
			Business planning/ Impact Analysis (what is success)	Innov. Coord.	Transfer Checklist and final report	PM
Activities	Platform leads engage with platform manager, design strategist, and business development for informed decision as applicable . Team included in initial stakeholder meetings as appropriate.		Design should immediately pursue user (patient) research as applicable. This along with secondary research will inform the opportunity area. Inform and engage potential support groups of the project content (e.g. S&P, eHealth etc.)		As identified in prototype recommendations. Prototypes should be created and engaged with institution operational homes and support structures for 3rd party validation of work (e.g. Practice, MSS, S&P, eHealth) Transfer of responsibility and tail of support for limited implementation to operational home to ensure smooth transition	
Timeline	T-0 Kick-off of project		1-3 mo.		3-9 months	
Controls	Leadership approval		Monthly status report to platform leads		Monthly status report to platform leads	
			Yellow or Red critieria defined		Yellow or Red critieria defined	
			Yellow or red brought to strategy meeting		Yellow or red brought to strategy meeting	
Metric	T-0 to resource engagement		Time to 1st user interview/observation		Time to 1st prototype complete NOI # of lives touched	

Decision Checkpoint appears vertically between Phase 0 and Phase 1, between Phase 1 and Phase 2, and after Phase 2.

FIGURE 4.8. CFI METHODOLOGY ELEMENTS AND RESPONSIBILITIES MATRIX

The Tools of the Trade

At this point we'd like to share some tools—or skills—that we feel are often overlooked in many innovation organizations. Teams often assume incorrectly that they do these things right. These skills are a focal point for us; we feel that they differentiate our approach to innovation and make it more robust, more tangible, and more likely to deliver results.

Using the Powers of Observation

There is no doubt that we are a visual culture. We would far rather see something in person. We'd rather watch a patient interaction with a physician than conduct a bunch of surveys about it. Why? Because in watching a real interaction, we feel we'll get the true picture, and we can observe tacit needs and behaviors that never would be captured otherwise. So, we place a lot of emphasis on observation; we closely "shadow" the actions and activities we test.

Where appropriate, we like to record audio and video clips from these observations. We carefully document and discuss the clips openly to "synthesize and interpret" what we saw. We have special project rooms generally papered with Post-it Notes (Figure 4.9). We make the best attempts to find the big

FIGURE 4.9. CFI PROJECT ROOM AND POST-IT NOTES

and small or detailed takeaways—most of all, the *behaviors that surprise*. Open eyes, open mind, and open thinking.

Brainstorming

Everybody does brainstorming, but not everybody gets a lot out of it. Brainstorming sessions can be dull, and results can be attenuated by organizational barriers and protocol.

We view brainstorming as a discipline, and we do it a lot. Our brainstorming sessions bring in diverse players, including members of the practice team. We encourage sessions to be visual and to "welcome wild ideas," to generate a lot of them, and to link them together where possible. We do not, however, let brainstorming teams make decisions. Those are up to the project teams and their synthesis of experiment and prototype results.

Prototyping

We rely a lot on prototyping, and we believe we do prototyping well. Our prototypes are complete and realistic, yet fast to arise and fast to give us proof of concept. We're not afraid to do a prototype a little "rough" to get it out there and see how it works. We get real patients, real physicians, real staff, real facilities, and real systems involved in prototypes as quickly as possible, and we don't shy away from adjusting or tweaking the prototypes once they're set up. Our prototypes not only prove concept but they also become vehicles around which to collaborate and for demonstrating our programs.

Innovation the Mayo Clinic Way: The Fusion Innovation Model

In this chapter we've presented an overview of the methods and guiding philosophy we use to imagine, initiate, and execute innovations into our practices. It's worth summarizing key concepts before moving on.

In creating the Fusion Innovation Model, we've recognized that both design thinking and the scientific method are powerful tools but also have some limitations. The data-driven scientific method takes time and often requires large investments to be able to come to conclusions. Design thinking brings in a focus on our customers, our intuition, and our creativity, but its output can be hard to quantify. In large complex environments such as health care, change is often looked at as a threat, and mistakes can be very costly, so a highly objective approach is needed to bring change.

In creating the Fusion Innovation Model, we combined these disparate schools of thought. The process adapts to what we're working on, but basically we integrate periods of intense experimentation, observation, and data collection with more intuitive and collaborative creativity sessions to complete our design thinking in a scientific manner. We may have several rounds of experimentation before we enter a prototype phase. We collect and analyze data from each of these experiments to frame the prototype, then use the prototype as proof of concept. We infuse a strong element of project management for coordinating and sequencing the tests and establishing the results. The resulting methodology combines the strengths of all three disciplines to achieve true innovation—all in a Think Big, Start Small, Move Fast framework.

All told, in the end, we're really driven by the customer. More specific takeaways:

▶ The CFI *Fusion Innovation Model* fuses the disciplines of *design thinking, scientific method,* and *project management* into a singular guiding approach to innovation.

▶ *Design thinking* combines a deep understanding of and empathy with customers together with contextual creativity and a rational approach to synthesizing customer experiences and solutions.

▶ *Deep customer understanding* entails understanding not only *explicit* but also *tacit* and *latent* customer needs.

▶ Design thinking and deep customer research should be accomplished at least partly in house. However, using consultants to learn how to do it and to collaborate with is, of course, okay.

▶ Design thinking is the secret sauce that makes innovation *strategic* and makes it really matter, while scientific method and project management make it *possible.*

▶ *Contextual creativity* is about nourishing creativity, removing risk, and looking beyond your product into all areas where you can deliver customer value.

▶ The *scientific method* removes bias by using measurable evidence to disprove a hypothesis or concept.

▶ Our *project management* approach combines intuition, experimentation, observation, collaboration, and deep prototyping to move a project forward, and it leaves a lot up to the design teams. We allow project teams to incorporate design thinking, scientific method, and project management principles as they see best to deliver a project.

From here, we move into the tools, skills, and processes we use to manage CFI and its presence in the greater Mayo organization. Chapters 5 and 6 cover what we call *transfusion*—the inbound and outbound communication and development and sharing of our innovative thinking. Chapter 5 explains our communications and knowledge management activities, and Chapter 6 explores our Innovation Accelerator. Both represent key skill sets and investments that set us apart from many other innovation organizations. The methods we use to manage and lead CFI inside a larger, complex enterprise are also revealing—and are covered in Chapter 7.

CHAPTER FIVE

Beyond Fusion to Transfusion

Communications and Knowledge Management

The single biggest problem in communication is the illusion that it has taken place.

—GEORGE BERNARD SHAW

We've seen this movie before, and you probably have too. It stars the typical, cliché, stereotype innovation center. Men and women in black clothes, designer eyeglasses, lots of Post-it Notes. What they do is a mystery to the rest of us. They're separated from the rest of the business by walls and keycard entries, and they're even in separate buildings.

They're ivory towers. Ivory towers that stand apart from, even look down upon, the rest of the business. Nobody knows what they do, and few of their outcomes or "successes" ever make it to the workplace, let alone to a customer. Sure, they may hit an occasional home run, they may come up with a new revolutionary technology or product. But have they made the rest of the organization innovative? Have they taken their cues from "the rest of us" on the floor? Not so much.

At the Mayo Clinic Center for Innovation, we're not fond of this model. We believe that innovation should be—to borrow a phrase—"of the people, by the people, and for the people" of the organization and the greater health care industry. We recognize that organizational engagement, for many reasons, is vital to what we do. We do everything possible to avoid ivory tower innovation.

We also realize that transformative innovation doesn't work in isolation. The working teams—in our case, the practices—must get it, co-create it, embrace it, and ultimately adopt it. And in order to embrace and adopt it, they must be *part* of it.

To accomplish that, innovation must be "transfused" between the innovation center and the larger organization. *Transfusion*, as we use the word, is a consistent and actively managed flow of intellectual capital around innovation—the ideas, successes, tools, techniques, trends, insights, and educational materials. Also the philosophy, ethos, and culture around what we do. It is inside out, outside in, and inside in. At its baseline, it is "Communication" with a capital "C."

But the story of transfusion doesn't stop with communication. CFI also recognizes the need for it to accelerate and facilitate the innovation process throughout Mayo Clinic, and to furnish a means to nurture and realize ideas that originate in the practices we work with. As a consequence, we've developed a platform called the Innovation Accelerator. The Innovation Accelerator actively reaches out into the greater community to find and fund projects to incubate (under the CoDE program—Connect, Design, Enable program), to provide tools and idea platforms for innovators in CFI and all across Mayo Clinic, to bring in outside speakers and experts, and last but not least, to hold a world-class annual symposium known as TRANSFORM to address the topic of innovation and transformation in the health care industry.

This chapter and Chapter 6 are about the all-important transfusion of innovation into the greater Mayo Clinic and the outside community. It is about how we consistently share and reshare our vision and process with the world. It is about how we enable innovation by staying connected and transfusing ideas among ourselves and our community. It is about how we *infuse* ideas, methods, techniques, information, and external best practices *into* CFI, and *diffuse* results, progress updates, knowledge, and leadership throughout Mayo and the external health care world. These two chapters cover how we work together, how we collaborate, and finally, how we build and strengthen the brand of innovation we practice at CFI and Mayo Clinic.

We feel—strongly—that our transfusion efforts and investments are a key differentiator and one of the important ways that CFI stands out among innovation organizations in complex environments. Through it we become more productive, build our identity, and stay relevant.

This chapter covers the strategies and tactics of the Communications and Knowledge Management aspects of transfusion. Chapter 6 covers the Innovation Accelerator.

What Are Communications and Knowledge Management?

The phrase *communications and knowledge management* by itself isn't hard to understand in the context of the CFI and the greater Mayo organization.

Communications refers to the strategies and tactics of getting the word out—*diffusing* the information—into the greater Mayo organization and beyond, about what we do, why we do it, and how we're successful. Our communication resources consist of print and Internet channels, including social networking media, and a public affairs engine all directed to and produced for internal and external audiences, all with a common theme and look and feel.

Knowledge management refers to the tracking of CFI's activities, contacts, inputs, and outputs into a knowledge base. It includes a communications archive, a project archive, and a contact management database. The purpose is to avoid duplicating efforts, to leverage learnings and tools, and generally to keep our ducks flying in formation.

The Communications and Knowledge Management function is embedded in the CFI yet it is connected with Mayo Clinic's public relations and marketing office. A manager coordinates the media components, aided by a diverse communications team of internal resources from the public relations and media support offices and external staff contracted for specific tasks.

The Message Is Out of the Bottle: CFI Communication Strategy and Tactics

Our diffusion strategy—what we communicate and why we communicate it—is not just to bring our efforts to light but also to truly make them part of the thinking in the greater Mayo organization and in the health care industry. They are designed to create interest and to keep CFI's activities and philosophy front and center in Mayo. They are designed to motivate both our greater organization and our own employees. They are intentionally multichannel and sophisticated in tone and form, they are substantial but not over the top in their graphic design or quantity, and they are informative but not advertorial.

Our Communications Goals
Our communications aim at four specific goals:

> ► *Information.* Our first priority is to provide essential information. We realize that communications, by themselves, don't drive change. However, they are a key part of building our relationships with the rest of the organization, for getting support, and for making what we do relevant. Communications pave the way to get the necessary collaboration and buy-in to move innovations forward; they are the first step in a chain reaction necessary for adoption.

> ► *Motivation.* Our communications do not only motivate the greater organization and health care world by providing information about "what's making a difference," but they also serve to motivate our own team. When our team members see their work presented to the outside world as a "product" or as a fascinating work-in-progress, it motivates them to Think Big, Start Small, Move Fast. Never underestimate the power of strong outbound communications to serve as "internal inspiration."

▷ *Professionalism.* Our communications take on a strong professional look and feel, which helps to elevate our credibility outside our organization. We think it also drives a greater degree of professionalism inside our team. Our communications elevate our professional ethos and depict us as anything but an off-the-beaten-path, ivory tower skunk works.

▷ *Brand.* Our communications help support Mayo Clinic's brand by publicizing the work we do. CFI brings trust, consistency, and credibility to innovation. And innovation is now a core strategic requirement of Mayo Clinic so the CFI is in a position to help the greater Mayo Clinic brand image.

Recall from Chapter 2 how former Mayo Clinic physician leader and current Vidant Health System CEO David Herman, M.D., framed a greater need for the health care industry to "separate the signal from the noise" to achieve innovation. Our goal and strategy is exactly that—to create a clear signal that can be heard about transformative innovation in health care delivery.

Our Audiences

The CFI has two main audiences: our internal audience, which is essentially all Mayo employees, and our external audience, which is our patients and the greater health care industry and beyond—really, anyone who looks at Mayo Clinic as a source of inspiration and accomplishments in the health care space. Our communications are crafted and channeled specifically to these audiences.

Our internal communications serve two goals. First, in the beginning and through the present, CFI was charged by Mayo Clinic leadership to create a culture and competency of innovation across the organization. Our communications serve to achieve that goal and to show the *value* that CFI brings to the greater organization—especially during this time of great angst in the health care industry. Second, and more practically, because CFI was "unknown" to most Mayo employees, we needed to deploy internal marketing to help create an understanding of the many ways staff can engage with CFI and the tools and lessons of innovation available to them.

The CFI's Communication Recipe

You might say we "eat our own cooking" by clearly communicating our communications goals each year as part of a detailed communications plan. In 2014, our stated communications goals were these:

1. Share our stories of how we are transforming health and health care and making a difference in patients' lives
2. Highlight CFI's alignment with Mayo Clinic's strategic priorities and mission
3. Show the value of the Center for Innovation to all audiences
4. Promote our collaborations
5. Explain our role in innovation, both internally and externally
6. Create partnerships with the Center for Innovation, both internally and externally
7. Grow our contacts and followers to aid in future communications and events
8. Increase awareness of the Center for Innovation as a national and international center for health care delivery transformative innovation
9. Attract new talent to the Center for Innovation, and Mayo Clinic overall

Externally, our *final audiences* include other health care organizations, including providers, payers, and suppliers of health care products, and moderators of public opinion on health care. Our *intermediate audiences* include general and trade press and media outlets—anyone with a stake or interest in what's going on and what's new in the health care industry. Additional audiences include but are not limited to potential partners, benefactors, potential employees, and other enterprises seeking to improve their customer experience.

Focus on the Message

Goals and audiences are nice, but do they really tell us what we're trying to communicate? It takes some thought—and some focus—to get centered on what the message is (really, what the message*s are*) before we step up to the communications plate.

If we're trying to create awareness and acceptance of CFI among Mayo Clinic employees, and to tell our practices how and why to engage with us, we must have a solid story. We want the greater Mayo organization, and its constituent physicians and care teams, to not only believe in us but to *work with* us. As a consequence, we must not only create a buzz about what we do, but we must also be very real and practical in our approach. How does what you do affect real patients, as well as physicians and staff? How do you work with us? What information can you get from us? And so forth.

When we create content, it is usually around one of the following five questions:

- How do we approach innovation?
- What is design thinking, and how does it work?
- What are our major platforms?
- What projects are currently in progress, what is their status, and what insights are they generating?
- How are we affecting the transformation of care delivery?

These are very real questions, the answers to which serve to tell our story, pique interest, and define a value to individuals and the organization as a whole.

The CFI Mark of Innovation

While not getting too carried away with it, we seek to build a strong, recognizable innovation identity as part of the overall Mayo Clinic brand. We seek all the attributes a strong identity conveys: positive image, consistency, and trustworthiness.

The communications effort itself is part of our mark, as is the Innovation Accelerator we will talk about in the next chapter, which nurtures innovation throughout the organization. Our identity begins with a distinct look and feel in our physical spaces and in all of our communication media. We use certain colors, symbols, typefaces, and other design elements that are easily identifiable with CFI. The look and feel is evident here as one first enters the CFI (Figure 5.1).

FIGURE 5.1. CFI MAIN ENTRANCE

In the monochrome image supplied, you cannot see the chartreuse color, but this is the anchoring color we use in our logos and designs (Figure 5.2). The graphics template for CFI was designed in house by our media support services and CFI team, but it has a vibe and presence that could be created by an outside group.

You'll see evidence of our style and identity throughout our communications. IDEO president and CEO and member of our External Advisory Council Tim Brown likens it to the simple, clear, consistent brand construct you might find in a successful retailer—Target, for instance. It works.

But no brand—or brand promise—works for long if it exists only in the organization's image, rather than in its products or services or customer experiences. We have a strong commitment to supporting our identity with what we *do*—design thinking, scientific method, project management, *transformative innovation*—and that extends even to the communications themselves. We've seen many enterprises go off into the weeds with fancy communications in which the basic message isn't clear, or worse, isn't true. Instead, we strive to make sure all of our communications support and build on the Mayo brand promise.

FIGURE 5.2.   CFI STYLE EXAMPLE

Outlets: Traditional and Social Media

At CFI we deploy a balanced and blended approach to communicating across the ever-widening assortment of communications channels—in traditional print media and public relations activities and Internet media including social networking websites.

Our strategy for traditional media includes using a variety of print media, mostly brochures and newsletters, that we put together to distribute to both internal and external constituents. We also maintain two separate websites under the Mayo Clinic umbrella: an intranet portal for Mayo employees and an Internet portal for external visitors. We write and distribute regular press releases about CFI news, events, and stories. In addition, we assemble a press kit that we send to key health care reporters and public opinion leaders, thus cultivating relationships with these important outside advocates.

Our social media strategy is aligned with a large Mayo-wide initiative called the Center for Social Media, which was launched in 2010 with a mission of "leading the social media revolution in health care, contributing to the health and well-being of people everywhere." The Mayo-wide initiative brings together like-minded organizations interested in the rapid dissemination of health-related information and the promotion of health-related social media tools.

At CFI we use social media to meet three objectives: one, to achieve rapid delivery of CFI news and updates; two, to get traditional media to cover CFI news as quickly as possible; and three, to propel us forward on the learning curve and apply what we learn to transform health care delivery. We recognize that social media has not only the potential to transform communications but also to transform health care.

Print Media

We develop and maintain an assortment of print media "collateral," mostly in the form of brochures and handouts that tell the story of CFI, individual platforms and projects, and innovation methods (Figures 5.3 and 5.4). Most are glossy handouts, like product brochures, and some are spiral-bound booklets. We use a variety of physical layouts according to our intended audience. Target audiences are mostly external constituents, including visitors, media interests, and even our benefactors, but our print media are also a handy and effective way to communicate with our internal constituents. Our print media consistently use our graphic design style elements.

FIGURE 5.3. BROCHURE RACK AT CFI ENTRANCE

FIGURE 5.4.   CFI BROCHURE EXAMPLES

Newsletters

Newsletters are prevalent at Mayo Clinic, and we make active use of them, both the corporate newsletters and our own, to get our message out. We write articles and blogs, and we encourage team members to contribute regularly to Mayo newsletters, including *This Week at Mayo Clinic*, *In the Loop*, and *The Scope*. All of our corporate media placements have allowed us to create a buzz and place our work in front of the Mayo practice and other Mayo constituents.

Corporate Newsletters

This Week at Mayo Clinic (TWAMC) is the main enterprise news center, created and distributed electronically and monthly to all employees. We at CFI try to place articles as often as possible to tell our story and especially to describe CFI programs that touch the entire organization. Examples include CoDE projects incubated in the practices and our annual TRANSFORM symposium (both are described in the next chapter) as well as CFI projects and successes. We also share stories about the way we work and the important lessons and techniques of innovation— all toward providing visibility for CFI and for strengthening the Mayo-wide innovation culture. Stories in TWAMC exhibit pictures of our lab spaces, which have encouraged visits from greater Mayo team members and even inspired workspace design in other parts of the organization.

At the institutional level, the every-other-day *In the Loop* subscription-based blog captures "news and views from around the Mayo system" in a slightly more quirky, bits-and-pieces format tuned more as a social media platform. The blog is meant to provide "stories that get at the kind of folks who work here," with a short, snappy, often humorous and even self-deprecating tone—all designed to "make us feel good about being part of this wonderful thing we call Mayo Clinic." Naturally, this newsletter gives CFI an active and continuous forum to communicate ideas and align thinking toward innovation, and it has been an outlet for CFI team members to communicate creatively and even humorously about what they do.

Created in 2012, the thrice-weekly *The Scope* news brief is targeted to Mayo physicians, specifically to address concerns and needs of physicians across the enterprise. Practice-related content includes new medical practices and alerts and also practice changes and other actionable items. (Background articles, strategic plans, awards, honors, and other nonactionable items are usually part of the TWAMC publications.) For CFI, *The Scope* is an important way to communicate CFI programs and changes that have come or are coming to practices.

Not surprisingly, especially in our newsletter-rich environment, we developed two regular entries of our own: *Innovation Insights* and *i on CFI*.

Innovation Insights

Innovation Insights is CFI's own free but subscription-based monthly newsletter for internal audiences (Figure 5.5). *Innovation Insights* includes four articles in each issue featuring different CFI platforms and projects. Articles are intended to create awareness about how we work and the kinds of projects we do.

i on CFI

Back in 2010 we started a brief update letter for our upper management, with the obvious goals of keeping them informed on CFI progress and activities. We send electronically a double-sided one-page newsletter to about 200 Mayo Clinic leaders each month (Figure 5.6).

FIGURE 5.5. *INNOVATION INSIGHTS* **ELECTRONIC NEWSLETTER**

FIGURE 5.6. *I ON CFI* LEADERSHIP UPDATE

This succinct bulleted-list update was received so well that the Mayo Clinic CEO, Dr. John Noseworthy, began asking other departments to create similar one-page update documents for senior leadership each month. It became a clear-cut example of "separating the signal from the noise."

Presentation Materials

Every year, and for an extraordinarily diverse set of audiences, we take our show on the road. Our road shows, which in 2013 happened in places as diverse as Singapore, the United Kingdom, Denmark, and Saudi Arabia, help to establish our place in the greater world of innovation and health care transformation. Our presentations help align and energize, and they are important showcases for our work.

We give dozens of major presentations each year to both internal and external audiences. We present our projects, our platforms, our philosophies, our guiding influences, our results, and our methods. We strive for a consistent professional look and experience, which we achieve by using a common template and graphic design for all parts of our presentations, including the videos. Figure 5.7 shows a sample cover slide for a recent CFI Overview presentation.

FIGURE 5.7. PRESENTATION EXAMPLE: CENTER FOR INNOVATION OVERVIEW

Posters

In the rapidly expanding world of high tech and social media, one wouldn't expect large graphic displays to take a high priority. But we feel that carefully crafted pictures can tell thousands of words to our teams and visitors, and they can extend our identity. Furthermore, as "wall art," they are inspiring to our internal teams.

If you visit CFI facilities, you're bound to notice several large *project posters* depicting the strategies and tactics of key programs. The example in Figure 5.8 depicts our Active Gaming for the Elderly project conceived and designed in our Healthy Aging and Independent Living (HAIL) Lab.

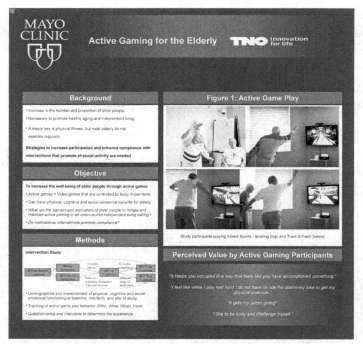

FIGURE 5.8. PROJECT POSTER EXAMPLE: ACTIVE GAMING FOR THE ELDERLY

CFI on the Internet

Our Internet strategy is very simple: "Own the CFI story on the Internet."

Externally we have two websites—one about the Center for Innovation itself and one for our annual TRANSFORM symposium. Both of these are embedded in the greater Mayo Clinic website found at http://www.mayo.edu. The CFI home page is found at http://www.mayo.edu/center-for-innovation (Figure 5.9), while the TRANSFORM home page, which includes specific information about upcoming TRANSFORM symposiums as well as highlights from previous events, can be found at http://www.mayo.edu/transform. Both sites are easily found in any search engine request.

Getting the Story Right

Among other benefits of our Internet and social media initiatives, we use our presence on those websites as a pointing

FIGURE 5.9. CENTER FOR INNOVATION EXTERNAL WEBSITE HOME PAGE

tool to send visitors to our own CFI websites, including the CFI blog, which will be covered shortly. Most of our traditional print media materials point to our websites as well. As a consequence, we grew traffic to the CFI and TRANSFORM websites by 200 percent from 2011 to 2013.

Importantly, a key part of our strategy is not only to create visibility but also to get the story out to the viewing public. Rather than asking outsiders to write a story about us or our projects, we write it ourselves first and publish it on the Internet, and we are then able to "take control of the story." Naturally, our web articles are also "consumed" by our internal audiences as well, which enables them to keep up with what is going on in CFI, and how it is being communicated to the world.

Content

Not surprisingly, you'll find a number of stories on our websites that are told using several media formats. Notes and articles on specific CFI project summaries and success stories contain links to more articles and supporting materials that are presented in text, video, and multimedia formats. These articles enable us to explain design thinking and our overall approach to transforming health care delivery. There are links to photographs of our workspaces and articles about our history and to our recent news releases and events. The CFI website is continuously updated.

The CFI Community and Social Media Platform

Embedded in the CFI website under the Connect tab is a multimedia platform known as the CFI Community. The CFI Community is designed to achieve a rapid, CFI-moderated, two-way conversation with internal and external constituents. The larger goal is not just to get the word out. It is also to enable innovation by learning from others, sharing ideas, and working together. It serves to build the CFI identity and to give our employees an opportunity to showcase their successes and build their own personal identities. The Community home link is http://www.mayo.edu/center-for-innovation/connect/center-for-innovation-community.

Within the community, you'll find the CFI blog and active interactions on social media outlets, including Twitter, Facebook, Pinterest, and YouTube:

- ▶ *Twitter.* Our hashtag is #MCCFI (Mayo Clinic Center for Innovation).
- ▶ *Facebook.* CFI operates a Facebook presence at "Mayo Clinic Center for Innovation" to share stories, to post events and videos, and to receive feedback from the friended community.
- ▶ *TransForum.* The TransForum social media platform disperses community information and solicits community response mostly around the annual TRANSFORM symposium (described in the next chapter); it remains active throughout the year.
- ▶ *Pinterest.* Pinterest allows anyone internal or external to CFI to post a photo—for example, a moment at a TRANSFORM symposium or a visual of a project being worked on.
- ▶ *YouTube.* A specially created YouTube playlist features over a hundred videos from previous TRANSFORM symposiums.

We also maintain an active conversation within Mayo Clinic using the Yammer social networking tool.

The CFI Blog

As part of our social media strategy, we use our blog to disseminate news stories quickly and to give our team members a way to make their work public and build their own personal presence through freelance contributions. We use the blog posts along with other team member contributions and other materials to feed posts to Mayo's social media, including Mayo's Twitter, Facebook, and YouTube pages.

The blog is one of the best and most current ways to keep up with happenings at CFI. It can be found at http://blog.centerforinnovation.mayo.edu/. Figure 5.10 shows a sample blog post from our CFI medical director about how the CFI is trying to shape the future of health care delivery.

Future of Health Care

Site Home / *The Center for Innovation Shaping the Future of Health Care*

Like 27   Tweet 28   +1 41   Share

Douglas L. Wood, M.D. (@dougwood) published a blog post · January 15th, 2014

The Center for Innovation Shaping the Future of Health Care

The delivery of health care in the United States hasn't changed much in over 100 years. The model created many years ago and still used today makes people travel to see a doctor on the doctor's schedule, when appointments can be fit in, rather than having a doctor try to find the best way to care for a person's need. The future of health care needs to shift to what people need, not what the current system needs. And it should shift to one of paying doctors for the health and well-being of people and patients, instead of the current emphasis on illness care and fee for service that is more costly.

The Center for Innovation at Mayo Clinic has been focused on researching, experimenting, piloting and building out new models of care delivery centered on human needs. We've been working with patients, care teams and Mayo Clinic physicians, and we've explored beyond that — in surrounding communities and people's homes. Patients tell us every day what they expect and what their experience with doctors and hospitals feels like to them. They share their fears and expectations with our team as we do our research, and they help us understand their experience and needs.

We have learned several important lessons that I find largely missing in the national conversation and should be the compass by which health care evolves. First, people fear the high cost of care more than anything else, even when they have insurance. They are confused and overwhelmed with appointment processes, the insurance processes and ever-changing information and broken promises. Most consumers are living on a thin line of financial security, and are frightened and stressed out over all these changes and the new financial expectations put on them.

FIGURE 5.10.   SAMPLE BLOG POST: SHAPING THE FUTURE OF HEALTH CARE

Public Affairs

At CFI we have long recognized the benefits and opportunities of getting placement in major journals, magazines, and blogs in our field of interest. We regularly submit press releases, articles, and commentary to the media for publication.

Additionally, we cultivate relationships with key health community reporters and bloggers. From our experience, it makes sense, once you have a story to tell, to start telling it in a similar manner to a carefully selected list.

Knowing What We Know: Knowledge Management

At the Mayo Clinic Center for Innovation, we are constantly creating new materials and documents around our activities. We're in constant contact with the outside world, and we receive numerous touches from outsiders in the form of visits and inquiries from colleagues in health care and other industries, the media, and so forth. As such, it is important to keep track of what we know, what we've said and documented, and whom we've talked to.

As a consequence, adjacent to the communications role, we've created a Knowledge Management function, a knowledge base—a "database plus"—to archive our contacts, inputs, and outputs. As we introduced at the beginning of the chapter, the goals are to avoid duplicating efforts, to leverage the most out of our learnings and tools, and to help us manage ourselves and our dialogue with others outside of CFI.

There are three components of our Knowledge Management function: a communications archive, a project archive, and a contact management database.

Communications Archive

"Institutional memory"—remembering and knowing what a large organization has already done and whom it has communicated what to—is a challenge for any large organization, particularly one driving change along many fronts within a complex enterprise and industry. We felt early on that it was important to track our activity and progress, and how we "messaged" that progress to the greater organization. Our communications archive is a handy way for us to keep on track, measure performance, communicate our "numbers" and successes, and keep our message clear to the outside.

At CFI we maintain a dedicated archive, run by a dedicated archivist who has a degree in library science. She acts as our "Radar O'Reilly" (from the TV series *M*A*S*H*)—aware of all that's going on. She is the go-to person when we need to remember or find something. As in the TV show, we'd probably flail—or even fail—without her.

Project Archive

CFI originally evolved from the SPARC Lab, a tiny team of a designer and an analyst. When the CFI was formed in 2008, the team grew quickly. At that time the young "lean and mean" team had very few processes in place, but one thing they *did* do consistently was to write elegantly about their project work. Why? Because they thought that someday someone who had no knowledge of their projects might need to learn from that work. With the growth surge brought on by the CFI's expansion, the ways of reporting and capturing naturally became more disparate. We didn't want to put too many restrictions in place, which might dampen creativity, so we began organizing the project information in two formats—as is and in a reproducible constructed way—in a common shared folder on our website. Today, team members can go there and find common deliverables for projects, and supporting documents can be linked to project stories.

Sharing what we know and the insights we have learned from our project work is a priority. That is the one common request we always get: "Tell me more about projects you've worked on and how they've impacted the practices." As part of the "voice of CFI," we created the project archive so that we can actively address this and similar requests, both from internal and external constituents. Since then, we've used the project archive as the primary resource to construct much of our story as we need it, including project stories shared on our external website (http://www.mayo.edu/center-for-innovation/projects).

Along the way, we developed a "Project Summary for Communications" project story template for our teams to use to communicate the essence of a project in concise form:

- ▶ Title of the project and platform
- ▶ Overview of the project (30 to 50 words—an "elevator pitch")
- ▶ Background (150 words)
- ▶ Project description
- ▶ Outcome (30 to 50 words)
- ▶ Think Big (overarching goal, 25 to 30 words)
- ▶ Start Small (initial steps, prototypes, and pilot programs, 25 to 30 words)
- ▶ Move Fast (how and where was it implemented, 25 to 30 words)
- ▶ Project resources (links to PDFs, one-pagers, web videos, or pictures from the project)
- ▶ Project contacts (names of designers, physicians, stakeholders, and others who worked on it)
- ▶ Project analysis (results and implications, short but no word count limit)
- ▶ Status report (if still in progress)
- ▶ Lessons learned (success lessons, barriers, failures, and insights)
- ▶ Closure report (if implemented or halted—where, what, and why)

This template and consistent approach help us standardize our approach to communicating a project, which makes it easier for others in the CFI and outside to stay on board with what we do.

Contacts Database: Our Innovation Customer Relationship Management Tool

It's amazing how many individuals we connect with during the course of a year at CFI. We interact with and host visits for hundreds of individuals and groups from health care and other industry organizations and the media. Our TRANSFORM symposium alone was attended by 850 individuals in 2013. We also connect with, and host visits for, dozens of individuals *within* the Mayo organization annually.

If we didn't track these contacts, we'd lose a lot of valuable information, insights, and potential partners going forward. So we keep a simple customer relationship database of whom we interact with—basic contact information, the nature of the contact, and so forth. The data can be searched and used to generate targeted communications and mailing lists tailored to areas of interest.

Innovation the Mayo Clinic Way: How to Make Communications and Knowledge Management Work for You

It's worth taking a moment here to summarize transfusion, and our strategy, strengths, and experience in the Communications and Knowledge Management portion of the transfusion:

- ► *Transfusion* represents the active intake (*infusion*) and dissemination (*diffusion*) of not only news and accomplishments but also the principles and practice of design thinking and Mayo innovation as a whole.
- ► Transfusion includes the Communications and Knowledge Management and the Innovation Accelerator, described in Chapter 6. Transfusion is a key strategy—and success story—of CFI.
- ► The Communications function goes far beyond the typical public relations efforts. It is *strategic* communication. As the name suggests, it combines a discipline of active communication across a wide variety of media to a diverse audience with the retention and memory of key concepts and contacts for CFI and the greater innovation community.
- ► Communication goals include disseminating information, motivating the employees of CFI and the greater Mayo Clinic, building a professional look and feel, and enriching and supporting a strong CFI identity and Mayo Clinic brand.
- ► The CFI identity includes a clear and consistent message, message style, and graphic style for both internal Mayo Clinic personnel and external constituents.

▶ Media include not only traditional print media but also websites and social networking media. There is also a traditional public affairs office active in sharing news with the health community.

▶ We use both traditional newsletter formats and a concise *i on CFI* monthly one-page summary of CFI activities for upper management.

▶ Online, our objective is to "own the CFI story on the web." We make broad and consistent use of our blog and social media tools to supplement our message, to "get the story right" in all channels, and to drive traffic to our other media.

▶ Our Knowledge Management efforts consist largely of maintaining a communications archive, a project archive, and a contact CRM database.

From here we step forward into the second major component of our transfusion: the Innovation Accelerator. Chapter 6 describes our most assertive platform for infusing and diffusing innovation from the CFI into the larger Mayo organization and the world health care community.

CHAPTER SIX

Accelerating the Transfusion

The Innovation Accelerator Platform

The nature of innovation . . . has changed. . . .
It's no longer individuals toiling in a laboratory,
coming up with some great invention. . . . It's
multidisciplinary, it's global, . . . it's collaborative.

—SAM PALMISANO, former CEO, IBM

Chapter 5 introduced the story of how the Center for Innovation facilitates an active *transfusion* of intellectual capital around innovation—a transfusion that deploys a wide array of communications media and knowledge management tools. Chapter 5 then went on to describe our Communications and Knowledge Management core, a broad and active two-channel conversation between CFI and its partners—both internal Mayo Clinic partners and partners outside in the greater health care innovation community. No doubt, the Communications and Knowledge Management core is a fundamental piece of CFI's strategy—and a fundamental difference between us and the traditional innovation organization.

While we consider communications and knowledge management vital to the transfusion of ideas between CFI and the greater community, from the beginning we wanted to take that mission a lot further. Early on we recognized the benefits of "thinking big" to drive the vitality of innovation from the *outside in to* the CFI, and from *inside* the CFI *out to* Mayo Clinic and the greater health care community.

These thoughts led to a substantial investment in another core activity to really drive innovation forward. Initially, this activity was championed by coauthor Dr. Gianrico Farrugia under the Culture and Competency of Innovation platform. In 2013, we expanded our activities both in size and strategic importance. We renamed the platform the Innovation Accelerator, and we gave it a dedicated manager and multidisciplinary team.

The Innovation Accelerator platform sets out to speed up and enrich the transfusion, to expand the Communications and Knowledge Management core even beyond the CFI walls. This platform actively brings in education and resources from the outside, houses idea management tools, and supports a unique internal incubator designed to facilitate ideas and projects originating across Mayo Clinic's operating units. More simply stated, the strategic objective of the Innovation Accelerator is to "build and catalyze a competency of innovation across Mayo Clinic."

There are seven active practices ("planks") within the Innovation Accelerator platform as listed below:

- ► *Connect, Design, Enable (CoDE) Innovation Awards.* Seed funding for growing great ideas
- ► *TRANSFORM.* A three-day symposium focused on transforming health and health care delivery
- ► *Thinking Differently: A Quarterly Series of Unexpected Conversations.* A series of renowned and refreshing speaker-experts on innovation from various fields
- ► *Eureka.* An Internet-based tool to engage employees in idea generation around specific challenges
- ► *CFI Innovation Toolkit.* A set of online case studies, tools, and resources

▶ *Innovation Catalyst Certification.* An immersive, hands-on experience to learn and apply innovation and design thinking taught in collaboration with Arizona State University
▶ *CFI Consulting Services.* A service to share innovation best practices with and for external clients

The CoDE for Incubating Innovation

Remember the Pediatric Phlebotomy Chair from the Introduction?

You may be surprised to learn that it wasn't really a CFI project—as such.

The Pediatric Phlebotomy Chair was developed in a Mayo Clinic practice—the Department of Pediatrics—as a CoDE project. It got seed funding—and some help—from CFI, but CFI didn't originate or develop it. So, what is "CoDE"? It is an abbreviation for "Connect, Design, Enable," and it is a descriptor of our innovation incubator model, which has become one of our richest success stories.

CoDE was born out of an early recognition that CFI has no monopoly on developing new ideas around the health care experience. Much of what's new and improved will come, in any organization, from the people with "boots on the ground" who deliver the services or products day in and day out. All of the staff members in our practices have great ideas, and we wanted to create something to help bring them forward. We recognized that many good ideas in large organizations die a death from a thousand cuts (multiple layers of review, "constructive criticism," funding lapses, and more). We wanted to protect those ideas.

At CFI we felt that it wasn't enough just to offer knowledge, tools, and encouragement. Better than just being "involved," we wanted the practices to be "hands on" in developing their ideas. We also strongly believe that innovative organizations find ways to provide employees with "thinking time"—a critical component to enable creative thinking—and that they should empower employees to work on projects they are passionate about outside of their normal work time. Google and 3M among others are well known for doing this.

As such, we felt the need early on to establish and manage an internal innovation incubator. To make it work, we needed a clear process to identify, select, and fund CoDE projects, and we wanted the greater Mayo organization to be very familiar with the program. So we branded it CoDE, and it has been a major CFI-led initiative throughout Mayo ever since. CoDE is the first award program at Mayo Clinic to offer funding across the enterprise to all employees.

CoDE has been in place for five years now, and it has generated dozens of first-class innovations—like the Pediatric Phlebotomy Chair—for Mayo Clinic (Figure 6.1).

How CoDE Works

For CoDE projects, the CFI acts almost as an internal angel investor. CFI gives annual grants each year, up to $50,000 for selected CoDE projects. Currently, about 10 projects each year are selected. A CoDE project must be completed in a year to ensure fast time to market and to avoid "feature creep" that might prolong a project's development and reduce its

FIGURE 6.1.   CODE: CONNECT, DESIGN, ENABLE

relevance. The program is open to all employees across Mayo Clinic—physicians and nonphysicians alike. CFI design, project management, and technology resources can be brought into the project, and most CoDE projects have both practice and CFI advisors on the team. Outside resources and services can be purchased, which many times are needed to meet the one-year implementation expectation.

Each year brings a new CoDE cycle. In the 2013 cycle, 88 ideas were brought forward, some of which were collected from the Eureka idea management tool described below. These projects were narrowed down by a review committee composed of CFI and broader Mayo practice team members into 25 project finalists. Final selections were made using nine criteria, including how innovative the project was, how the project would fit into Mayo's strategic objectives, and the overall value of the project.

CoDE award winners are announced with a launch party and great fanfare across the Mayo organization. A complete brochure is put together for all Mayo constituents broadcasting selections for each year and—importantly—sharing ongoing results from previous CoDE projects.

In CFI, the CoDE office is staffed by a full-time project manager and designer. Other CFI and Mayo resources, like IT or other practice personnel, can be tapped when it makes sense.

CoDE Project Examples

Most CoDE innovations are "adjacent," and they solve specific problems rather than being transformative by themselves. However, ultimately they fit into the greater "here, there, and everywhere" vision. Naturally, like the Pediatric Phlebotomy Chair, the end result primarily benefits the practice from which the idea originates, but the concepts and tools can and are often used elsewhere. CoDE projects can also extend CFI-advocated technologies such as remote patient monitoring.

In the five cycles of CoDE completed since 2009, some 47 awards have been made to 32 physician proponents and 15 awards have been made to allied health staff—62 in all. Note the awards to "allied health staff"—the CoDE program is open to all employees at Mayo, not just the physicians. It is actually unique in that regard, and it highlights that nobody owns innovation.

Here are examples of CoDE awards:

▶ *Optimizing Spine Surgery Throughput.* A redesign of the patient experience before and after spine surgery, improving the experience and operating room (OR) utilization

▶ *Telepresence for Remote Concussion Evaluation in Sports.* To monitor concussion and mild-traumatic brain injury

▶ *Exposure-Based Therapy Anxiety App.* App providing patients with exposure-based therapy and connections to health professionals for treating anxiety disorders

▶ *Mayo Clinic App.* Broad-based app for informing and messaging patients about their Mayo visits, helping them navigate where they need to go and how they need to prepare; app works like an "e-concierge" and is a resource for other Mayo information; app described further in Chapter 8

▶ *No One Dies Alone.* An adaptation of a model developed by a nurse in Oregon; offers a network of volunteers to be at the bedside for patients with no loved ones during the final 48 hours of life

▶ *Oxistimulator.* Tool for monitoring patient blood oxygen levels during light anesthesia and for automatically stimulating them if levels drop

▶ *Patient Imaging for Wheelchair Users.* Smartphone app and sensor to get pressure images; monitors high-risk points for pressure ulcers in everyday settings

▶ *Stroke Telemedicine.* Video link for remote or rural patient access for patient assessment and treatment dialogue

▶ *Teleconsultation for Surgical Pathology.* Computerized larger-scale imaging on a digital glass slide so as to replace conventional microscope slides with larger imaging slides; allows collaborative viewing and discussion for reaching clinical consensus

▶ *Pediatric Inflammatory Bowel Disease (IBD) Self-Assessment Tool.* An Internet-based game to educate pediatric patients on IBD; provides advice on treatment and adverse medication reactions, provides information on the benefits of good nutrition, and general disease care

It's not hard to see the diversity among these projects. In all, through four cycles, CoDE has delivered the following:

- ► 14 care delivery models
- ► 12 invention disclosures
- ► 6 filed patents
- ► 5 licensed products
- ► 2 service offerings
- ► 2 clinical trials
- ► 1 education delivery model
- ► 1 clinical consensus tool

Why CoDE Is Important

In a busy and complex organization like Mayo Clinic, with multiple approval steps for any initiative, it can be difficult to get the time, not to mention the resources, to spend on innovative thinking and projects. Not surprisingly, when days are carved up into time slots with patients and appointments, "free" time is hard to come by.

That's a big part of the reason we created CoDE.

CoDE provides a somewhat formalized and funded "lift" for new ideas coming from the people who directly interact with our key customers—our patients. It reinforces creativity and innovative practice throughout the organization, and—importantly—it builds teamwork and credibility with the practices. It also brings new ideas into production without consuming resources to generate new ideas. Further, the ideas generated have real-world roots. And perhaps most important, the CoDE program is open to all employees at Mayo. Its openness sends the message that innovative ideas can, should, and often do, come from anywhere.

We're approaching five years of experience with the CoDE program, and as you can see from the figures above, plus the intangible evidence below, CoDE has been highly successful. Comments from Mayo CoDE awardees are widespread, and they all echo common themes: CoDE is very important to the development of real practice ideas.

We hear comments like these from practice team members:

> "CoDE funding gives resources not usually available to innovate, and it engages your practice area in a rather unfettered way into other sources of funding."
> "CoDE not only brings a resource and an expertise but it also allows us to focus . . . and act passionately about those issues."
> "With CoDE, barriers are taken down."

Other CoDE learnings include these:

▶ A passionate and dedicated team is more important than monetary awards.
▶ Projects are more successful if CFI is actively engaged in running workshops, facilitating design thinking and user-centric research, removing barriers, and promoting networking and collaboration.
▶ It is important to establish institutional alignment early to accelerate project timelines, remove resource barriers, and support implementation into the practice.

At day's end, CoDE is really about developing teamwork and collaboration with practices, and it is about exhibiting CFI strengths and value.

TRANSFORM: The Biggest Industry Conversation of the Year

From its inception, CFI sought to make a "contribution to the world" in health care by starting, continuing, and growing a serious conversation about transformative change. In that light, we started an annual conference and worldwide forum—a "Woodstock" if you will—for innovation in the health care experience. We call it TRANSFORM.

The annual three-day TRANSFORM symposium (Figure 6.2) is held every September in the Rochester Civic Center in downtown Rochester, a few blocks from our main outpatient building, the Gonda Building. The goal of

FIGURE 6.2.   TRANSFORM 2014

TRANSFORM is to "nurture and facilitate an ongoing dialogue among a thoughtful and diverse group of committed individuals to bring meaningful, transformational change—impactful action—to health care." The TRANSFORM stage brings remarkable speakers and engaging venues to catalyze innovation and inspire action. It is part of CFI's efforts to build a community around innovation in health care and the transformation needed to fix it.

The program is moderated by the amazing John Hockenberry (more about him in a moment). The visually stimulating multimedia conference features CEOs and other leaders from health care and adjacent industries, health care providers and payers, journalists, and patients sharing their experiences. Speakers and panels dive into deep and sometimes controversial topics; every segment of the show is designed to leave an impression and does exactly that. TRANSFORM generates extensive media coverage, and many of the more engaging sessions can be viewed on YouTube—just run a search on Mayo Clinic YouTube channel, and use the term "TRANSFORM playlist" to see for yourself.

The Story of TRANSFORM

We started the conference six years ago in recognition that a go-it-alone strategy would not work. We wanted to collaborate with a greater audience and spearhead an industry-wide effort with industry-wide talent. Our first meeting (before it was called TRANSFORM) had 161 attendees—88 of whom were internal to Mayo Clinic. The Center for Innovation was actually launched at this meeting by then-Mayo Clinic CEO Dr. Glenn Forbes.

Over the years, TRANSFORM has grown rapidly, to 435 attendees in 2009, 728 in 2011, and 849 in 2013. In 2013, audience members came from 14 countries and 32 states. There were over 300 organizations represented. Some 119 of these were other health care providers, 37 were academics, and 37 more were design firms. There were 17 pharmaceutical and medical device companies, 16 health care technology providers, and 13 retail organizations in attendance. These statistics (and many others) are all captured in Figure 6.3.

For the first time in 2013, we had over 2,000 people watching *live* online. We also had a very special recognition in 2013, when Minnesota's National Public Radio (NPR) station reached out to ask if they could share our TRANSFORM talks on their midday news. We responded with an enthusiastic yes, and a number of the talks have been aired on NPR. A broader public radio strategy is under way.

We make a point to use the three-day meeting as a jump off for broader conversations. The TRANSFORM conversation continues through CFI's social media connections. Among other statistics for 2013, we generated 1,314 Facebook Likes for the TRANSFORM home page and over 18 million Twitter impressions. The TransForum CFI online community, described in Chapter 5, boasted over 2,000 posts.

We are careful to *not* make either CFI or Mayo the star of the show. Neither the content nor the presenters are Mayo or CFI centered; and only a handful of CFI projects are touched on during the three-day show. The TRANSFORM stage is carefully crafted to offer a state-of-the-art, expansive yet connected experience (Figure 6.4). In 2013, external attendees comprised 70 percent of the audience, nearly doubling the number in any previous year.

The three days of the 2013 symposium were moderated by John Hockenberry, journalist and former correspondent for *NBC News*, *ABC News*, and National Public Radio. It doesn't get any better than John Hockenberry. With an extensive understanding and experience covering health care, he led the dialogue, gave powerful opening and closing comments, synthesized what speakers said, and asked excellent questions

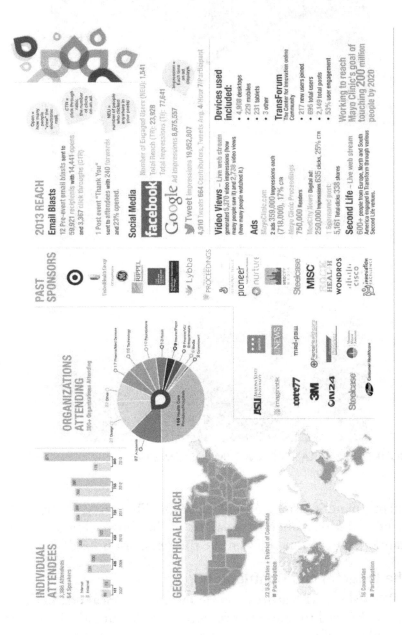

FIGURE 6.3. TRANSFORM 2013 SUMMARY

159

FIGURE 6.4.   TRANSFORM SYMPOSIUM STAGE

during panel sessions and after talks. The witty, clear, and insightful Hockenberry was a star of the show, while he constantly kept the limelight on the speakers, not himself.

The Program and Contributors

TRANSFORM features a large number of speakers, but it's hardly limited to one-way presentations. About half the show is made up of conversations on stage—with panels consisting of three or four experts from different backgrounds and sectors of the industry. Along with panel discussions, attendees see multimedia presentations with musicians, video clips, and heartwarming testimony from patients whose lives were impacted by transformation. There are lighter moments too, as when two local 5th graders presented a project identifying the challenges and opportunities in nanotechnology for health care. TRANSFORM is both serious and fun, and it is loaded with impact and insight.

Here is a sampling of speakers and panelists from TRANSFORM 2013:

- Maria Bartiromo, anchor and journalist, CNBC
- Tim Brown, President and CEO, IDEO; CFI External Advisory Council member
- Nancy Snyderman, M.D., Chief Medical Editor, *NBC News*
- Sally Okun, R.N., Vice President for Advocacy, Policy, and Patient Safety, PatientsLikeMe.com
- David Erickson, Ph.D., Director, Center for Community Development Investments, Federal Reserve Bank of San Francisco
- Michael Green, M.D., Professor of Medicine and Humanities, Penn State College of Medicine
- Roy Beveridge, M.D., Senior Vice President and Chief Medical Officer, Humana
- Paul Jacobs, Ph.D., Chairman and CEO, Qualcomm
- Jacky Jennings, Ph.D., M.P.H., Associate Professor, General Pediatrics and Internal Medicine, Johns Hopkins University
- Sam Ho, M.D., Chief Medical Officer, UnitedHealthcare
- Larry Keeley, President and Cofounder, Doblin, and Director of Deloitte Consulting LLP; CFI External Advisory Council member
- Eric Manheimer, M.D., Fellow of the American College of Physicians, Chief Medical Officer, Bellevue Hospital, New York
- Kevin Ronneberg, M.D., Associate Medical Director, Target Corporation
- Dallas Smith with Susan Mazer, musicians and producers for the C.A.R.E. patient television channel

TRANSFORM content is too broad and diverse to describe in detail here. However, examples of panel discussions from TRANSFORM 2013 (many of which can be found on YouTube) include these:

- ▶ *Science Sunday.* Pathways to living better and longer (which included the aforementioned 5th graders).
- ▶ *Reframe.* Looking through different lenses to understand the big picture of health care today.
- ▶ *Collide.* How health care is changing business and how business is changing health care.
- ▶ *Scale.* How the uncertainty of change is reduced when we learn of new models that have successfully scaled.
- ▶ *Unravel.* Why patients' needs must be at the center of untangling the complexity of health care.
- ▶ *Rebuild.* Pain points for consumers, and how a "retail" model can help change the patient experience.

Making TRANSFORM Happen

Holding a symposium on the scale of TRANSFORM is a major commitment and investment, but we feel it's worthwhile as a transfusion mechanism and as a way to maintain a leadership brand in our industry. The commitment and investment include a full-time project lead who draws from internal Mayo resources and external event professionals, which results in a team of about 15 people. The costs and some of the planning efforts are offset by a small group of partner sponsors, which have included names like Steelcase, Target, Cisco, Intel, and 3M.

As an investment in transfusion and branding, we've been highly satisfied with TRANSFORM results.

A Series of Unexpected Conversations: Thinking Differently Speaker Series

As part of our mission to continuously "drip irrigate" our enterprise with new thought, and as part of a strategy to extend TRANSFORM, we host a series of notable speakers and personalities at Mayo for CFI teams and the broader Mayo audience. We call it: Thinking Differently: A Series of Unexpected Conversations.

The broader goals are to learn from outside experts and to introduce new perspectives to our work. We bring in one speaker each quarter, and as we'll see, these speakers come from diverse backgrounds. Topics are specific or general; formats are usually a combination of presentations and conversations. One could think of these sessions as "two-hour TRANSFORMs," as makeup sessions for those who can't attend TRANSFORM and as continuations and enhancements of TRANSFORM-like dialogues.

Speakers are typically world-renowned experts from various disciplines and fields. They visit Mayo and have an immersive experience in an area they are particularly interested in. They then share their insights and inspirations on their topics of expertise, thus informing and expanding our work in health care. Presentations are recorded for all Mayo employees to access.

Since its inception in 2012, the series has brought several speakers to Mayo including these:

- ▶ Mark Smith, M.D., President and CEO, California HealthCare Foundation (CHCF)
- ▶ General Hugh Shelton, 14th Chairman of the Joint Chiefs of Staff
- ▶ David Kelley, founder, IDEO
- ▶ Dave Grey, founder, XPLANE, an innovative visualization and graphic design firm
- ▶ Dr. Michael Crow, President, Arizona State University—our partner in the "Innovation Catalyst" certification described shortly
- ▶ Sara Miller Caldicott, grand-niece of Thomas Edison
- ▶ Dr. Tachi Yamada, Executive Vice President, Takeda Pharmaceuticals and former President of the Bill and Melinda Gates Foundation's Global Health Program
- ▶ Jim Hackett, CEO, Steelcase

I Found It! The Eureka Idea Collaboration Tool

Health care is not a nine-to-five job. Mayo Clinic and its hospitals are open 24/7 and spread over several states.

Many entities have highly specialized jobs; for example, one division is responsible for putting together the instruments needed for each operation, tailored to that operation. Collecting as many ideas as possible from such a broad and also highly specialized base is a significant issue, one no doubt shared by many readers of this book.

We therefore wanted to create a simple, open, 24/7, electronic idea submission system that would allow easy collaboration, evaluation, and management. We learned from outside companies like IBM who had already created such systems. IBM had built its successful "jam sessions" programs created internally to connect employees and to solve vexing problems. We examined existing idea management software tools so we could move quickly and not get stuck in building a homegrown tool. We selected our platform from a company called Imaginatik (http://www.imaginatik.com). Imaginatik's Innovation Central idea management platform is a crowd-sourced ideation and solution tool designed to "harness the collective wisdom of employees, customers, and partners."

We launched Innovation Central internally and called it Eureka. This software tool allows specific Mayo departments or groups to "ideate" solutions online and interactively as a way to address their own challenges and problems. The CFI helps the group frame the *challenge*, and then the department-based team moves through the *challenge life cycle* of collection, assessment, selection, and execution of the best solutions. Importantly, we allow that life cycle only a 5- to 10-day period to get a fast and energetic response.

Eureka speeds up problem solving by allowing everyone to contribute solutions and to build on one another's ideas to organizational challenges and changes. A Eureka "event" typically has a sponsor and a review team. Participation is enhanced through pre-event marketing, group meetings, and so forth.

The event team as a whole can vote on ideas and comment, and they build off one another's ideas. The platform has a powerful assessment tool to evaluate the content across a number of different criteria and subject matter experts, allowing the best ideas to bubble up to the top based on collective team wisdom. Team members take ownership of the best ideas and move the ideas through to project completion.

CFI helps to filter, identify, and synthesize themes, and it can moderate and facilitate the process. Eureka-generated ideas have identified new opportunity areas, and they have been used to initiate CoDE projects. To date, eight departments within Mayo have made use of Eureka to host their own jam sessions.

More Tools in the Toolbox: The CFI Innovation Toolkit

Want help with a specific challenge? Want to learn a new technique? Want to read a case example on the application of design thinking? Need an alternative approach? The CFI Innovation Toolkit makes that easy, and it is an important way we diffuse design thinking knowledge into the organization.

The CFI Innovation Toolkit is an online repository of techniques, knowledge, and insights related to design thinking (Figure 6.5). Tools and specific skills, like brainstorming, prototyping, and wireframing, are available for quick reference or deep learning. The toolkit is a repository of best practices, case studies, and examples, presented with easy Internet access and in some cases, short videos. Tools are generated by CFI or adapted and edited from the outside. Toolkit materials are available to CFI team members and the greater Mayo organization.

FIGURE 6.5. CFI INNOVATION TOOLKIT

Get Certified: The Innovation Catalyst Certification

As one travels through life, professional credentials are always a good thing. Meeting the education requirements to gain a credential gives you time out from the daily routine, an opportunity to really absorb something new, a sense of accomplishment when finished, and connections to a team of fellow accomplices. At Mayo Clinic certification of competency in a particular skill is essential; after all, you want your intensive care nurses to be formally trained in their vocation! It was natural that Mayo Clinic employees started asking about innovation certification.

In 2013 we moved forward with a program to certify Mayo staff in innovation by developing a curriculum in innovation and design thinking with Arizona State University and its Master of Healthcare Innovation degree program. The curriculum combines an immersive and interactive weekend of on-site learning with a six-week online course and an application of the learning to a specific project. The program was launched in early 2014 with 35 Mayo Clinic participants.

Those who complete the course become Certified Innovation Catalysts, and they receive a confirming certificate.

Beyond Our Borders: CFI Consulting Services

As you've followed along in our book, you've probably realized that we have developed considerable technique and experience of value in helping other innovation teams, particularly in complex organizations and industries. At first reluctant due to our laser focus on generating results for our own innovation efforts, we're now offering consulting services to others in the industry and/or with similar environments. Simply put, we want to take our message and our practice outside of Mayo to help others set up innovation centers and achieve results.

We've found that others want to learn our story and incorporate some of our experience and best practices. We want to leverage our brand and competencies around principles of innovation and design thinking and other parts of our practice. Naturally, we also build the transformative innovation story by connecting and networking with partners in health care, and we can also learn and experience best practices of other organizations.

Initially and somewhat informally, we've already had a number of engagements with organizations as far away as Japan, the United Kingdom, and Singapore. We are codifying our activities under a dedicated consulting group. Stay tuned to Mayo Clinic and the Center for Innovation for more on this one.

Expanding the Innovation Community: Emerging Components of the Innovation Accelerator

We've just explored the seven major "planks" in the Innovation Accelerator platform. But we also recognize that there are more than seven ways to accelerate innovation in a large enterprise. Two other CFI programs, both of which bring forward innovative ideas and help to move them along faster, deserve mention: (1) our fellowship and internship program and (2) our foray into the world of open innovation. They aren't officially part of the Innovation Accelerator yet, but they operate with much the same principle and purpose.

CFI Fellowships and Internships

Like many organizations, over the years we've recognized the win-win proposition of engaging with interns and research fellows: we at CFI expand our core skills and get help moving projects forward; the interns and fellows get valuable experience toward building their careers. In a few cases, the "test drive" may result in our finding someone spectacular for our team as a permanent addition.

CFI has engaged with an assortment of colleges and universities to offer internships and fellowships for undergraduate, graduate, and Ph.D. students from design, business, and engineering schools. "Design coops" and MHA/MBA students from leading design and business schools join a CFI project team for a three- to five-month hands-on learning experience. Our William Drentell Research Fellowship in Health Care Innovation offers candidates already employed as health care professionals or who are faculty in a complementary field a half- or full-year immersive experience. Recently, a Ph.D. engineering candidate from Purdue University was embedded in CFI to conduct her thesis work on the development of a remote patient-monitoring system. And a group of MBA students from the University of Minnesota helped build a new CFI "garage" function that incubates ideas with strong potential for commercialization.

Another internship program brings in journalism students from the local Rochester campus of the University of Minnesota (UMR) to write up our projects for our blog and project archive. The sidebar on OpenIDEO that follows was actually written by a UMR student as a guest post on our blog.

Open Innovation

Open innovation is a popular buzzword in today's innovation lingo. We get it, and in a space so driven by patient experience, we feel the need to listen to the experiences—and ideas—of our patients, not to mention the ideas of others in the greater health care community.

Naturally as a consequence, we're open to ideas. But in order to maintain our focus on our immediate goals and objectives, we don't spend too much time collecting and sorting through the thousands of ideas and observations that might emerge from a true open forum. Instead, we like to use open innovation to address specific problems.

Our most recent experience with open innovation was with OpenIDEO, a dedicated open innovation platform offered by the design consulting firm IDEO. OpenIDEO is "an online platform for creative thinkers," designed to include a broad range of people in a design process by presenting challenges. It is a bit like the Eureka platform mentioned earlier, but it "opens" the challenge up to problem solvers across the global community. At this point, to conclude this section, to illustrate OpenIDEO, and to give an example of how our journalism interns help us, here is a sampling of a recent post, written by Katie Nelson, a UMR intern, on an OpenIDEO challenge presented as the following question: "How might we all maintain well-being and thrive as we age?"

The Healthy Aging Challenge: A Guest Post Written by Katie Nelson

OpenIDEO is a global platform that partners with organizations who wish to address a specific problem. Together, they propose a challenge that becomes open for all creative thinkers to weigh in on. How it works: once a challenge question is posted, individuals are able to share their ideas and experiences. Favorite concepts are then chosen by the sponsoring organization, and the ideas are continually narrowed down until the winning concepts are chosen at the end of the challenge. With hopes of learning about some potential solutions for a challenge that Mayo Clinic is no stranger to, they opted to sponsor a challenge back in June: The Healthy Aging Challenge (Figure 6.6).

FIGURE 6.6. THE HEALTHY AGING CHALLENGE

Continued

Mayo Clinic challenged people to come up with ideas to answer the following question: "How might we all maintain well-being and thrive as we age?" This topic was chosen because as the years go on, the number of people reaching the age of 65 and older will continue to skyrocket. So, it is crucial to think about the factors that affect people as they age.

Hundreds of people participated in the challenge, and the three winning concepts were announced in August. Designers Annie Nguyen and Sylvia Stein authored the winning ideas which they presented at the TRANSFORM symposium in September 2013.

Annie's first winning concept was the idea of utilizing a Caregiver's Wellness Toolkit. The transition into a caregiving role often occurs quickly and unexpectedly, putting a strain on "even the most resilient of people." The purpose of the caregiver's toolkit, then, is to provide resources and information on how to be a great caregiver so individuals do not feel quite as overwhelmed. How-to videos and physical "goodies" like candles and meal certificates would ideally be inside these toolkits, to make leaving the hospital a little less chaotic.

Innovation the Mayo Clinic Way: Stepping on the Innovation Accelerator

Here is a short summary of how we actively infuse and diffuse the innovation experience through the use of the Innovation Accelerator platform:

▶ The Innovation Accelerator is an active, multichannel, multiresource program designed to diffuse innovation ideas, skills, and best practices from CFI to the greater Mayo Clinic organization, as well as the greater health care community. The strategy is to build innovation competence and to strengthen the collaboration with constituents external to CFI. The Innovation Accelerator also serves to bring best practices to the CFI.

- The Innovation Accelerator helps CFI "lead the conversation" on health care transformation and to be the most "innovative innovator" in the space.
- There are seven active practices, or "planks," within the Innovation Accelerator platform: an innovation incubator (CoDE), an international symposium (TRANSFORM), a speaker series (Thinking Differently), an idea management platform (Eureka), the Innovation Toolkit, a certification program, and an external innovation consulting practice.
- CoDE is a robust program that provides seed funding for great ideas incubating and implementing care models, services, and products in the Mayo practices and beyond.
- The annual TRANSFORM symposium leads the conversation on transformative health care innovation and builds connections between CFI and the greater health care community.
- The Eureka idea management platform helps departments solve problems, gather ideas, and collaborate with Mayo constituents.
- The Innovation Toolkit provides innovation and design thinking resources for the greater Mayo community.
- The Innovation Catalyst Certification program formalizes an innovation and design thinking credential.
- Beyond the Innovation Accelerator, CFI also connects with the outside through sponsoring internships, fellowships, and open innovation "challenges."

From here we shift focus in Chapter 7 to the bigger picture of managing the Center for Innovation and how we've "transformed" our leadership model and culture for the future.

CHAPTER SEVEN

Leadership in Transformation

The Story of CFI 2.0

Innovation is fostered . . . by journeys into other disciplines . . . from active, collegial networks and fluid, open boundaries. Innovation arises from ongoing circles of exchange, where information is not just accumulated or stored, but created.

—MARGARET J. WHEATLEY

Originally, during our frequent meetings to plan this book, we wanted this chapter to be about how we manage the Center for Innovation. It was originally intended to give you the full picture of how we manage an innovation organization, from top to bottom, from motivation and hiring to results measurement and rewards. It was to be about the nuts and bolts of moving a large innovation team forward within a larger complex organization.

As we began writing, we found ourselves to be less excited about how we got to where we are today and way more excited about where we are going. So we'd like to scrap that construct and do something different.

We've shared how CFI came about. We've shared the industry state (the "problem") and the vision (the framework of the "solution") throughout the book and especially in Chapter 3. All of that has provided a solid backdrop for our work. We've also shared some of our successes against that backdrop, and we will share a few more in the next chapter.

We've had the usual challenges faced by other managers of embedded innovation teams. We've had to manage people. We've had to manage the natural tensions between design and science, between creativity and risk. We've had to manage large budgets, measure results, and justify our existence. We suspect that's not much different from the experiences of everyone in our reading audience.

We've already described our path to our present state. In this chapter we'd like to talk more about leadership than management per se. We'd like to talk about the transformation of our leadership style.

That transformation of our organizational model, dubbed "CFI 2.0," was borne out of a combination of our own experiences and of the insights provided by our experts and closest trusted advisors—our External Advisory Council team. With their insights we've transitioned to a new and evolved leadership model—which we're pretty excited about and feel could be central to designing the leadership model for *your* organization too.

So that's what we'll do. We'll talk about how we're "innovating innovation"; how we're transformed to a new, more collaborative, more fluid leadership style. We'll talk about how we evolved from a more traditional functional management structure to a more self-directed "village" approach to leading the organization—really, to expanding collaboration and letting the organization lead itself. It's an exercise in a more fluid, autonomous, self-directed approach to moving the team forward—and we think it will extend our Think Big, Start Small, Move Fast identity and style.

If It Ain't Broke, Should We Fix It?

All in all, we think we've done a pretty decent job getting to where we are. We've built a great team. We've built a vision and platforms and projects within that vision. We know how to get results. We know how to share those results—and the ethos of what we do—through the transfusion mechanisms described in the last two chapters. We've established credibility inside Mayo Clinic. We've established credibility at a *strategic* level by recently elevating innovation to a core strategic require-ment of the organization. We've established credibility at an *operational* level by creating a distributed model and weaving innovation into our fabric. And we've established credibility in the outside health care world.

Really, we don't have much to complain about.

Since its formal inception in 2008, CFI has grown pretty big pretty fast. We've done a lot of things well, although, as expected, not always perfectly from the first steps. Every organization has change, some self-directed, some induced or inflicted from the outside. Every successful organization learns and adjusts as it goes, and we've done a lot of that. In our book that's a *good* thing. We don't want to be resistant to change or to get bogged down in the tentacles of tradition.

Despite these successes we decided to transform our inno-vation model into CFI 2.0. For us, change is good. Not just for the sake of change, but for the sake of moving forward. We have always been uncomfortable with the status quo.

Before describing the changes effected by CFI 2.0, it makes sense to review some of our major successes that we wanted to build upon.

Establishing the Vision

We have a vision. In fact, Mayo Clinic has one vision that can be summed up as "Health and health care, here, there, and everywhere." As described in Chapter 3, we view health and health care in a longitudinal way—"in sickness and in health," as the saying goes. We view the provision of health care as something that happens not just as a discrete visit when sick but also as a continuous connection or "tethering" in wellness. That tethering can also streamline care in sickness through electronic connectivity tools that bring patients in contact with providers—and specialist providers in contact with pri-mary care providers—remotely, anywhere, anytime.

In other words—health and health care—when I need to come to you, when you can come to me, when I never knew I needed you.

The vision is really our centerpiece and our core. From that vision we built CFI's four major platforms: Mayo Practice, Connected Care, Health and Well-Being, and the Innovation Accelerator. The vision has worked well, both internally and externally, as a centerpiece for communication, guiding our innovation teams, and nurturing our innovation activities.

Building the Team

We adopted the principles and methods of design thinking early on to build our CFI team. Those principles created considerable interest among our current—and our potential—employees. Who would have thought a big health care machine like Mayo Clinic would hire professional product designers? Anthropologists? Architects? Fashion designers? We did, and we deliberately hired people with diverse experiences from diverse walks of life to work with us full time, to be embedded in our practice, to integrate with the Mayo mystique, and to influence it from completely different perspectives.

The results have been amazing—a true win-win. They've learned from us, and we've learned from them. The interdisciplinary teams we've embedded have worked well. Everyone approaches our health care challenges with passion and a combined spirit that, we believe, leads to far greater productivity than would be the case if we hired designers only on a consulting basis.

In addition to a solid team, we feel we've built a solid culture—a culture that embraces the customer, a culture that is creative, a culture that embraces change, a culture that gets things done. "Real artists ship" is the timeless quote from Steve Jobs. We feel that we have real artists who can and will create a new health care experience and that we deliver.

Establishing the Metrics

As any viable and accountable organization should, CFI has a set of core metrics. Like the metrics used by any organization, these have evolved over time, and as you might expect from our scientific approach, we are driven by metrics. Here are our three core metrics:

1. *Time to first completed prototype.* You've heard and embraced Think Big, Start Small, Move Fast. As you can see from this metric, and its placement as the first one, dexterous speed is very important to us. Choosing the metric of time to first completed prototype was also deliberate. The prototype is often the first time when our Mayo collaborators have an "aha" moment—they see the possibilities. Getting to that point is critical. In our organization the next big thing always demands everybody's attention. We know, therefore, that if we're going to keep people's attention on the task at hand, we have to get to the first completed prototype as quickly as possible. But there's also an important subtext here. We need to move fast to deliver the change needed and expected by our constituents, and—importantly—we know we can trust our teams to do it right even within the context of "speed is the number one goal." Without the right kind of leadership and culture, teams would fail with such a mandate—the pressure to "move fast" would overcome the imperative to do it right.

2. *Number of patients' and persons' lives touched and impacted.* This big-picture metric is important, for it is a barometer of whether we really make a difference, whether we really are delivering transformative change. If we focus merely on a few specialties and/or small sustaining innovations, will we transform health care? Probably not. So this metric is key—as is the stated Mayo Clinic goal of yearly touching 200 million lives by 2020. We estimate that CFI touched 720,000 lives (patients and consumers) in 2013. While this is still quite a bit short of the stated 200 million organizational goal, it is highly energizing to our teams, our constituents, and our leadership. That said, we also measure how deep we touch a patient's life. The Pediatric Phlebotomy Chair did not impact many thousands of lives, but it had a big impact on those it did touch. As we outlined in the Introduction, it too met our definition of a transformative innovation. So we measure both numbers and impact.

3. *Return on our investment (ROI).* Despite the fact that we're a not-for-profit entity, we must justify and pay for our existence as does any other organization. As we already stated, Mayo Clinic needs to invest hundreds of millions each year in research and education. Every project is evaluated for its revenue stream and cost impact on the practices and on Mayo Clinic as a whole. Projects are grouped by their primary purpose (new patient engagement, new revenue, cost reduction), and one of our measures of our effectiveness is revenue generated or expenses reduced—that is, the projected financial impact on Mayo's practice.

The example in Figure 7.1 of how we show our metrics comes from a presentation we gave to the Mayo Clinic Clinical Practice Committee. Although the graphic presented is intended to "sample" our metrics, that is, how we view them and how we present them, you can begin to get an idea of the size and scope of some of our projects. Incidentally, in Chapter 8 we'll cover a few projects—Mars, Optimized Care Teams, and eConsults—that support a major financial goal to reduce outpatient practice expenses by 30 percent.

Catalyzing the Process

From the beginning, we were big believers in the disciplines of design thinking, scientific method, and project management. Over time we developed those disciplines and infused them into the CFI team using a more or less traditional management approach. We sponsored and conducted training, assembled resource materials, deployed metrics, and created vehicles such as the CFI Project Control Book and the CFI Portfolio Roadmap to manage and balance our portfolio and keep it moving forward.

Over time, and quite naturally, designers became the stewards of design thinking, project managers became the stewards of project management, and we all became stewards of the scientific method. Our designers reported to a design lead, our project managers reported to a project management lead, and so forth. However, quite frankly, this structure catalyzed silos, not integration; it caused problems; it limited the value that

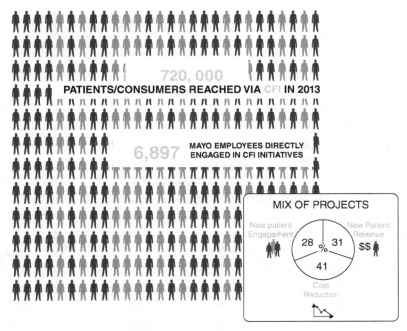

FIGURE 7.1.   CFI METRICS SAMPLER

individuals from one group could see in what individuals from another group brought to the innovation process.

As described in Chapter 4, we sought a better way, a better and more balanced approach to innovation. We sought a model in which every member of the team, management included, treated the innovation method as a singular, fused model, which you now know to be called the Fusion Innovation Model. All projects and programs would be managed forward by all people on the teams with a balance, an innate and natural emphasis on all three disciplines. Essentially, we fused the people just as we fused the disciplines.

The idea of the fusion model was not only to make sure all three disciplines were incorporated into a project effort but also to reduce friction within the teams. If everyone on the team lives and breathes all three disciplines, little time will be wasted addressing a dearth of scientific method or an overemphasis on design thinking or a failure to keep constituents updated. Projects could move forward in balance, without the friction created by team member "agendas," by the natural tensions between creativity and deadlines, between data and intuition, and between customer and process. Popular stereotypes go away—for example, designers not being able to keep deadlines or project managers rushing the user research to get to the next stopgate or checkpoint.

In creating this model, we really manage a team of "specialist-generalists"—people contributing a distinct specialty expertise such as design or IT skills but who also function very well in other roles. When team members remain siloed into a single discipline or specialty, it requires the work of other team members—and often the resolution of tensions and conflict—to move things forward. We feel, from our experience, that any innovation team is well served—and easier to manage—if team members are conditioned and rewarded for a fused and holistic approach to their jobs. From the early days of CFI, we've emphasized the development of team members as generalists in addition to being the specialists they were when they joined the team. We prefer that individual members think of themselves first as innovators and second as designers or project managers or scientists.

We should also note the idea introduced in Chapter 3 that informality and trust are very important ingredients of our management style. We're not talking about dress code here—Mayo expects a certain level of attire, and as an embedded organization, we're quite compliant with that. But we have also adopted the open-floor and open-door attitude of many of our technology peers. There is little in the way of organizational hierarchy; everyone is on a first-name basis, and informal conversation is encouraged throughout the team. Even in a manager's office (there are only two of these), the glass doors are seldom shut except for conference calls. One door has a sign: "If you have a good idea, no need to knock."

Prior to the recent CFI 2.0 transformation, our designers sat in a design team with a design team lead nearby, and our project managers sat with their lead—the floor was organized by discipline. Now, there is little in the way of physical separation or hierarchy—no walls or other barriers to separate those teams. Everybody's desk is set up the same way; a team lead is just one of the team. In many organizations, trust is built by formality and hierarchy. Ours is just the opposite—we maximize interaction, and we trust everyone to perform without the traditional mechanisms of physical hierarchy.

Managing the Portfolio

People often ask us: How do you evaluate the "return potential" of a specific innovation project? As we've shared, we currently organize around Big Idea platforms—Mayo Practice, Connected Care, Health and Well-Being, and the Innovation Accelerator. Each platform has a portfolio of projects that meet a range of criteria in terms of their complexity, value and financial impact (for example, new revenue or expense reduction), or societal impact (for example, access for an underserved population). We think a lot about innovation with impact and innovation that addresses Mayo Clinic's most significant challenges in areas such as access, value, efficiency, service, affordability, and integration. In the beginning, we needed to demonstrate significant financial *return on innovation* so we selected projects with more of a bottom-line impact. In contrast, we now have a more balanced portfolio approach so we now continue to consider financial return but also *societal* impact.

We also tend to favor projects that have leverage into other projects; for example, many of the prototypes for electronic care delivery or for redesigned care teams have a reach into other platforms. Those projects tend to create a lot of value and give support to the total "here, there, and everywhere" vision. We know it can be limiting to think of the platforms as individual silos; so today when we prioritize projects, we look at the entire vision, not just an individual project and its *return on innovation* in a single platform.

We should also add that the Center for Innovation is funded from three sources—Mayo Clinic operations, philanthropy, and revenue and/or equity from new products and services. The CFI has been in a building mode over the past five years, and it required a more significant investment in the early years. Now that we are established, the CFI is committed to generating a return that many times over exceeds its operational expenses.

Gaining Strength Through Collaboration

Many innovation organizations approach their existence as an organizational silo, unable or unwilling to interact with the outside or even with potential stakeholders, contributors, or test beds within their own enterprise. Not so with CFI.

Not just to survive but also to build bonds, leverage resources, and flourish, CFI continuously connects internally, with committees, departments, divisions, and business units, and externally, with companies, universities, and academic centers. Internally, our value to other departments lies in what we can bring: our processes and methodology in how we approach our work, the design studio staffed with innovation experts and design researchers, the Outpatient Lab to prototype and test our projects, and the discipline of design thinking. Externally, we have established relationships with world-class leaders in their fields—Delos, MIT, Cisco, Destination Imagination, Verizon, Intel, Aetna, Mercy Health System, Blue Cross and Blue Shield of Minnesota, Arizona State University, GE, IDEO, IBM, University of Minnesota, Doblin, Best Buy, 3M, Yale University . . . the list goes on. We are inviting more people into the conversations around transforming health delivery. Although it requires time and a deep commitment to manage these collaborations, our approach enriches both the process and the result.

Changing the World

From the beginning, we've sought to "change the world" of health care, both within and outside Mayo Clinic. That will never happen if we keep our innovations to ourselves or if we simply install them as changes into the practices we work with to develop prototypes and prove the concepts.

As a consequence, all through the evolution of CFI, we have emphasized and invested in communication. Really, as Chapters 5 and 6 describe, it goes further than traditional communication into a broader, deeper transfusion of intellectual content around the health care experience—from innovation methods to the latest industry conversations heard, to the TRANSFORM symposiums we lead, to the projects that are initiated in the practices but gain traction through CoDE.

This transfusion not only improves our competence and credibility but also maximizes the impact of each innovation. People not only learn about the vision but also see how it works and see how it fits together. The transfusion builds our capabilities and our successes and furthers Mayo Clinic as a whole as a health care leader.

The value of the transfusion, and the importance given to it by us as transformative leaders, is hard to overstate.

Approaching CFI 2.0

As a natural consequence of rapid growth and a need to organize and channel this growth, as stated above, we initially adopted a more typical siloed approach and structure to managing the individuals on the teams. While we managed our projects around our vision, our people were still managed in silos built around expertise and activity—design teams were led by a design manager, project management teams were led by a project management lead, and then there were a few embedded skills and resources like IT and communications that reported to functional managers wholly outside of CFI.

Because of the flat and informal organizational structure, and with the physical interaction and comingling described above, it worked pretty well. Design, project management, and other teams within CFI reported to a single layer of CFI leadership—our administrative director, our medical director, and our associate medical director—a.k.a. your coauthors. The frictions and inertia of hierarchy didn't run too deep—things got communicated; things got done.

But we remained concerned about the siloed, functional approach. When executing on a holistic vision of providing health and health care "here, there, and everywhere," could one really manage separate silos and groups addressing this singular, grand vision? Would team members building electronic interfaces for Health and Well-Being consider, or leverage from, similar interfaces being developed for Connected Care?

The answer, knowing our informality, the absence of physical barriers, and an innovation "space" conducive to interaction on the floor, and at the watercooler, was probably yes. Team members and team leads *would* talk to each other; they would share, out of a natural curiosity to keep up with what was going on and consistent with the general camaraderie and gestalt of the greater CFI team.

But we felt, especially going forward, that there would be challenges. The team was growing. More team members (60), more projects (100), more constituents, more technologies, more of everything. We were experiencing a gradual evolution from managing a small, entrepreneurial startup to a large enterprise-scale team. We felt a greater complexity and interplay between our platforms and projects. The scope and impact of our projects were expanding as well; there was a greater quest for a major transformation, a societal impact, extending well beyond improving individual patient experiences.

As a consequence, we saw an opportunity to take our organization another step forward, to take the process of management of CFI from "good" to "better." We wanted to gain from the exchange of ideas from highly networked, collaborative, and sharing teams that did not have individual objectives or agendas. We wanted everyone to march forward together in equal step toward our vision, without large amounts of management direction and redirection. We wanted everyone to lead themselves toward the goal. We also wanted to balance the natural tension that occurs between structure and autonomy.

We wanted to emulate the models of many high-tech companies, where innovation teams can see the customer, get the vision, and execute on it with a minimum of direction and a maximal view of the "end in mind." We wanted our teams to be able to "touch it and play with it" and see how the customers and the marketplace react; that in itself would provide plenty of motivation.

Our hunch was that we needed to keep the flat organization, and we needed to make the teams as "self-leading" as possible. We knew we were at a good starting point, with talented physicians, designers, and project managers with a wide range of experience and an intense interest in the end vision. We just weren't sure we had the organization or process of management in place to "get there" the best way.

You might say we were looking to transition from a "process of management" to a "process of leadership." A *process of management* implies more structure, rules, and day-to-day handholding of subordinates and subordinate processes. A *process of leadership* implies more self-direction, more self-motivation and resourcefulness. Peter Sander, in his book *What Would Steve Jobs Do?* (McGraw-Hill, 2011), defines *leadership* as "getting people to want to—and to be able to—do something important." It's that sense of self-actualization and self-reliance, toward something important, that we wanted to make central to CFI.

So we had our own jam session. We met as managers, team members, and constituents, and best of all, we brought in some of the experts from the External Advisory Council to give us their take on how to move forward into CFI 2.0—our leadership model of the future.

Change by Design: A Jam Session with our External Advisory Council

You may recall from Chapter 3 our discussion of the External Advisory Council (EAC), our group of external "innovation whisperers" from whom we've received valuable insight from the beginning. Normally we meet with the nine-member EAC twice a year.

We developed a list of four questions for the EAC members to try to get to CFI 2.0—our leadership model of the future:

1. What are ways to minimize silo thinking and silo behaviors?
2. What is the optimal size of a team?
3. How much leadership structure should be in place at the platform and/or core level?
4. What other advice do you have for us to work more effectively?

We presented this list and received a fabulous set of observations and prescriptions.

Their observations were so insightful that we decided to share them in summary form as useful advice for your own innovation enterprise. Most of these observations center on change, organization, communication, collaboration, and leadership.

Observations and Prescriptions from EAC Members to Get to CFI 2.0

Change

▶ Mix it up every so often to keep people on their toes; change is good. But do not do anything that does not feel right.

▶ Recognize that a major reorganization or restructure is very stressful.

Organization

▶ Conflicts are constant. Solve them by seeding team members in interdisciplinary villages—nobody's next-door neighbors do the same thing that they do. Different people with different interests and different ways of working. Each person has a home in an *interdisciplinary village*. They understand each other and respect each other. When they move to a different environment, with multiple disciplines, they have a respect for the craft that the other people are representing. They listen to each other then.

▶ Best number of platforms or teams is always the smallest number. As teams become larger, the wasted time becomes larger. Smaller is better.

▶ No one in an organization should be focused on just one area. Natural connectivity and cross-fertilization and collaboration happen when assigned to at least two areas. Consider a major and a minor area of responsibility.

▶ Do more than one thing—people need to see the bigger picture.

▶ People move around from one project to the next—that's the biggest force for collaboration.

▶ Always have a client on the team.

- The more junior people are, the less good they are at multitasking—good multitasking is a function of their experience and cumulative number of projects over time.
- Driving *program efficacy*:
  - *Platform team structure.* All platforms should be staffed with a small core team (accountable for tasks, timetables, and tangible deliverables), plus a larger steering team (accountable for mission, vision, goal setting, and metrics).
  - *Platform status reviews.* Frequently, perhaps weekly, each platform leader should produce a crisp, engaging, and clear description of status, emphasizing exceptions or obstacles to expected progress (this can often be social).
  - *Platform deep reviews.* Occasionally, approximately once a month, platform core teams should conduct a deep session, designed to solicit broad input on key challenges.
- Once-a-month workshops. Get to borrow someone from another team—socialize by sharing people, not just information.
- Ideal size of project team: maximum of six to eight people, no fewer than three—anything more than that, you have a meeting and not a team. People can hide in their commitments and obligations.
- Never isolate design.

Communication, Collaboration, Meetings

- Meetings are almost always ad hoc. Don't waste your time in meetings.
- Two meetings a month of the entire team. Show work (content delivery). Different people host the session—post or blog cool stuff they are seeing in the world and doing—very action oriented.
- Offer *know-how sessions.* Lunchtime, one-hour talks.
- Weekly program reviews with senior execs. Reviews go deep and are really quick with elevator pitches that are under five minutes.

Continued

► Regular program reviews. Get everyone to bring empathy and skills to the table. Be aware of each other's challenges. Learn to help each other. Show humility. Iterative—build on solutions: I need help with this key problem for a client.

► Cross-pollination. Share, drag, or move (whatever it takes) learnings across teams—socializing the content and information. Make each other aware of each other—rip and run with insights across teams.

► Socialize people and information across groups and initiatives. It's about leveraging knowledge, building bench strength skills, and most of all trust and respect across diverse disciplines. Explicitly think about connective principles—across disciplines within a project and across platforms and initiatives. Shared passions and democratic behaviors can be built on these shared beliefs that can be expressed in project or program tenets and principles.

► Shared investment. Everyone—all disciplines—should have individual and collective beliefs that all of the platforms matter and are equally passionate about the need for the platforms to succeed. They should each passionately invest of themselves and their projects, but also cross-support the others when instances of opportunity to help present themselves. For example, episodically participate in a workshop on another's project.

Leadership

► There should always be a team leader who is responsible to make sure that the team is working productively and will make its goals and/or deliverables. She or he will supervise or manage (but do not do much of that)—just giving the guidance that the team may need. He or she will see to it that the small team is operating at the highest level.

► Leadership belongs to everyone in the organization. Lead down and up and horizontally. People in the mailroom lead. Leadership is a very broad thing. Everyone knows everything going on at every moment—I do not hold information or only share it with a few. Never misuse power or authority. Maintain a very open and collaborative environment.

▶ Foster diversity in as many ways as possible—skills, knowledge, cultures, experiences, and above all the ways of thinking. (Roger Martin's "validity/reliability" gets used a lot in my group as a tolerance mechanism.) Teach the organization through formal understanding and repeated experiences to value the power of diversity. There is fact-based evidence that more vectors on a complex problem will create a much more dimensionally robust solution (Scott Page). It's messy, and there is a place for "fair fights" within the team in making "wise" choices, that is, topically focused debate, but the democracy of information and the will to behave democratically should be the dominantly ambient state of teams, initiatives, and platforms.

▶ Understand the relationship between culture and process. Our experience is that culture can change process, but attempting the inverse only gets a temporary state change. The character of collaborative trust-based relationships may be a cultural shift problem, particularly in organizations that have a tendency toward independent actors, independent departmental structures, professionally defined departmental structures, and/or are predominately hierarchical (explicitly or the more difficult, implicitly). The change to a different state, even amplification of what is desirable to retain, or likely some of both, will require persistence, patience, and time. The dilemma lives at the intersection of intellectual and emotional complexity and therefore will take longer than you think (and certainly would like) and involve tolerance and formal and situational teaching.

▶ In designing high-performance teams where collaboration is critical, behavior trumps expertise and power. One needs all, but bias toward behaviors in creating sustainable teams and expertise and power will resolve itself—this is the nature of self-selecting teams. Project leaders should be skilled in spotting, teaching, coaching, and correcting. If they are a part of or perpetuating the problem and only work better as individual contributors, they cannot be the leaders no

Continued

> matter how otherwise qualified they are in the topic. Team collaboration is fundamentally a social methodology enabled by trust and respect. Collaborative behavior, while it can be readily understood and externally agreed to by reasonable people (the intellectual), the internalization (the emotional) is much more complex, and only time, coaching, and most of all practice with reinforcing outcomes will shift it . . . that's the "human dilemma."

CFI 2.0: It Takes a Village

Not surprisingly, it took some time for the collective wisdom just presented to sink in and turn into actions on our part. You'll note, for instance, that not every idea or thought was in agreement, like meeting formats—we had to work through those ideas too.

We leaned in to our team to build CFI 2.0. We had an off-campus retreat at an arts center to exchange thoughts and ideas and begin to formulate a roadmap, articulating how our work integrates to one coherent vision, how we organize, how we plan and sequence our work, and how we allocate resources. We started by identifying a set of principles characterizing what we value as individuals and teammates to carry us forward with CFI 2.0:

1. Mutual respect
2. Trust, honesty
3. Open, authentic conversations
4. Accountability
5. Personal and professional growth; continuous learning
6. Seeing everyone as creative, helping each other build creative confidence
7. Generating results—for the CFI, for Mayo Clinic, and most important, for our patients

We partnered with our human resources colleagues and incorporated such leading-edge organizational trends and practices as highlighted in *HR* magazine, "Try Leading Collectively" (January 2013):

- ▶ There is a transformation under way toward more complex, interconnected, and dynamic structures.
- ▶ There is a trend toward shared responsibility and mutual accountability toward a strategic direction.
- ▶ There is greater use of "collective leadership" and mutual accountability-based approaches and structures.

What came through the process, loud and clear, was the idea of reorganizing by platform—and making each platform a dynamic "interdisciplinary village" reminiscent of smaller, early-phase startups where everybody tends to do everything—"All for one, one for all" might be the motto. We also fully embraced the idea of rotating CFI members across platforms—to gain the experiences and to expand the breadth and depth of each platform as they touched it.

We also reviewed our methodology to determine how to accelerate the pace, with a bias toward agility, speed, clarity, and implementation.

As a result, today we are organized by four platforms: Mayo Practice, Connected Care, Health and Well-Being, and the supportive Innovation Accelerator. Each platform is an interdisciplinary "village" with a manager and an interdisciplinary team of designers, project managers, innovation coordinators, IT professionals, and others.

In the end, our Mayo Clinic human resources team supported a precedent-setting new structure, moving from a functional orientation to a team-based model with platform managers supervising very diverse employees. The teams sit in comingled fashion with adjacent desks; designers sit next to coordinators, project managers, and embedded IT folks. There are no physical or organizational barriers between members of a platform team, and with rotation, each team member contributes and becomes an expert on the adjacent platforms.

Evolving Our Portfolio Structure

In Chapter 3, we introduced the hierarchy of platform, program, and project—which we clarified and defined in the new

CFI 2.0. Each platform (transformative) has a small number of programs (strategic), and within the program, a smaller subset of projects (tactical). Here, once again, is our definition of the levels in the hierarchy—really, the *portfolio* of activity within CFI:

- ▶ *Platform.* A collection of programs grouped together to facilitate effective management of that work to meet strategic business objectives
- ▶ *Program.* A group of related projects managed in a coordinated way to obtain benefits not available from managing them individually
- ▶ *Project.* A temporary endeavor undertaken to create a unique product, service, or result

Appendix B lists and illustrates our current portfolio of CFI projects and the platforms they fall under.

Making Other Communication and Leadership Changes

The new CFI 2.0 includes other changes:

- ▶ Weekly team meetings are now held and dedicated to sharing our work across platforms.
- ▶ For each platform, a physician lead has been named to partner with the platform manager.
- ▶ The former design lead in the previously structured "design" group has been recast as a design strategist, advising user research across the platforms and serving as a mentor for the designers.
- ▶ Designer and project manager career ladders with three levels have been crafted and implemented.

With this new structure, we feel we are gaining the rich interchange of ideas and the self-directed and self-motivated qualities of many leading innovation organizations. We have transitioned from a team that needs to be managed to a team that leads itself—an important transition in any organization. We have evolved from being managers to being enablers and communicators of the greater vision and design and all the components thereof.

Dashboard (Metrics)

We have a new Dashboard that we implemented as part of CFI 2.0, and it is shown in Figure 7.2.

Objective	Measure	2012	2013 Target	2013 Year End	2013 Status
People					
Workforce of the Future	Mayo employees engaged with the CFI intranet site (views)	43,011	47,312	59,813	Achieved
	Number of students / interns engaged	13	14	37	Achieved
	Number of Mayo colleagues involved and authoring innovation	6,091	6,700	6,897	Achieved
	Depts, units of Mayo sponsoring or touched by new initiatives	331	364	396	Achieved
	Number of staff invited to participate on task forces, advisory boards etc.	4	4	5	Achieved
	Practice-related design workshops facilitated	8	9	14	Achieved
Outcome					
Financial					
Practice	Projects in process supporting new patient engagement	20	28%		Aligned
	Projects in process supporting new patient revenue	22	31%		Aligned
	Projects in process supporting cost reductions	29	41%		Aligned
	Patient Access: Physician In-Clinic Appointments Saved - 2013 eConsults (7500), Video Visits (910) - 2012: eConsults (6470), Video Visits (418)	6,888	7,577	8,410	Achieved
Philanthropy	Development Funds Received	NA	NA	NA	Achieved
Commercial	Commercial Revenue Generated	NA	NA	NA	Achieved
	Companies launched	1	2	1	Not Achieved
	Disclosures filed	8	9	12	Achieved

FIGURE 7.2. CFI METRIC DASHBOARD AND PERFORMANCE SUMMARY

Continued

Objective	Measure	2012	2013 Target	2013 Year End	2013 Status
Other					
Brand Recognition	Number of patients and consumers touched in 2012 from this year's work	1,104,904	1,215,394	11,095,886	Achieved
	Number of in-person visitors touched by CFI tours\events\ conferences	4,397	4,837	4,925	Achieved
	Publications and videos distributed to global audiences	161	177	199	Achieved
	Number of patients and consumers touched by CFI efforts (including research subjects)	8,608	9,469	11,429	Achieved
Customer Satisfaction	Project Success Rate	94%	94%	95%	Achieved
	Recommend CFI for future engagements	90%	90%	95%	Achieved
	Customer Satisfaction (5 = Excellent)	4.5	4.5	4.6	Achieved

FIGURE 7.2. *(CONTINUED)*   **CFI METRIC DASHBOARD AND PERFORMANCE SUMMARY**

Innovation the Mayo Clinic Way: Evolving the Leadership Model

In this chapter, we've talked about leadership and how we're innovating innovation to get to CFI 2.0:

▶ The most effective innovation organizations will evolve from a management model to a leadership model—a model where the customer and the vision provide the basis for self-leadership, and day-to-day management direction and review are less necessary.

▶ The leadership model is more likely to be based on interdisciplinary villages built around platforms than to be based on a traditional structure isolating disciplines into separate silos.

- ► Interdisciplinary villages combine skills and disciplines into a team, avoiding physical and organizational barriers. All members work toward a common vision.
- ► Rotation between villages expands contributions and strengthens the linkages between the platforms, while also expanding the skill sets and experiences of team members.

In Chapter 8, we offer examples of how leadership and other principles we've covered are put into play in our three delivery platforms: Mayo Practice, Connected Care, and Health and Well-Being (the fourth platform, the Innovation Accelerator, was discussed in Chapter 6).

PART III

THE MAYO INNOVATION MODEL IN ACTION

CHAPTER EIGHT

Here, There, and Everywhere

A CFI Project Showcase

Innovation that works is a disciplined process.

**—LARRY KEELEY, Cofounder and President,
Doblin; Director, Deloitte Consulting LLP; and CFI External
Advisory Council member**

We will use Chapter 8 to share specific projects from three of our four platforms: Mayo Practice, Connected Care, and Health and Well-Being. (The fourth platform, the Innovation Accelerator, was described in Chapter 6.) In this chapter, we'll take you on a short flight through a series of CFI projects.

We start with a low-altitude flight through the Mars Outpatient Practice Redesign project as an example of scanning and framing, experimentation, and prototyping to transform the Mayo Clinic outpatient practice. No, "Mars" is not an acronym. Rather, it's a from-the-ground-up construct to answer the question, "What if we were to start from scratch and set up a new medical practice on Mars?"

As part of Mars, we'll take a more detailed tour through a subproject called *microConsults*. microConsults use electronic tools to incorporate specialty consultations into a single visit, avoiding a second appointment and trip to our facilities. You're at the Mayo Clinic for an orthopedic treatment, and the orthopedist recommends a neurologist consult? Done, then and there, on site, in real time, electronically. No referral appointment, no second visit. Estimated savings? Over 38 minutes per appointment for microConsults-enabled appointments—that's part of a 30 percent reduction in outpatient cost at Mayo Clinic, which is the overall financial goal of the Mars practice redesign—and more important, the benefit to the patient of a far smoother and more effective health care experience.

From there, we give shorter, higher-altitude summaries of other key parts of our four-platform vision. For example, as part of Connected Care, we look at eConsults, which leverages digital technologies to extend care beyond Mayo bricks-and-mortar facilities. We examine our Optimized Care Teams project, reinventing care team staffing, and the adjacent Wellness Navigators project from our Health and Well-Being platform. Finally, we wrap up with the Mayo Clinic Patient App project, which came through our CoDE incubator. Although they originated in separate CFI platforms, you'll see how these projects connect with each other and how they play into our greater vision for transforming the 21st century model of care.

A Flight Plan for Our Projects

Before taking off on our showcase tour, let's review how we map our projects into the 21st century model of care vision and how we get these projects off the ground.

Revisiting the 21st Century Model of Care Vision

First, here's a quick refresher on our 21st century model of care vision, which can be stated as "Always be there for me":

- ▶ "When I need to come to you"—Mayo Practice (Mars), "Here"
- ▶ "When you can come to me"—Connected Care (eConsults), "There"

▶ "When I didn't know I needed you"—Health and Well-Being (Optimized Care Teams, Wellness Navigators, Mayo Clinic Patient App), "Everywhere"

Project Presentation

Here is a quick recap to prep you for the flight.

Scanning and framing is the first major step of any project or program. Here, we scan the world around us, examine the situation, do our initial research, and frame the opportunity or problem to be solved in the broadest context.

Next, we develop and document our *research path*, which includes a sequence of experiments and prototypes designed to test our insights and the tools, processes, and technologies that we think will solve the problem and that may lead to a deeper customer understanding or a reframing of the problem in many cases. The scientific method really takes over at this stage, and the exact course of a project may change radically here, especially at the experimentation phase.

Then, to maximize the value of our learnings as well as to demonstrate them to constituents inside and outside Mayo Clinic, we *summarize* the findings of both our experimentation and prototyping efforts. Our findings can lead us to more prototypes and to implementation as well as serve as a vehicle to document concepts that can be used in adjacent projects or platforms.

Finally, once settled on the mechanics of a project, we develop an *implementation plan* to guide our practices to adopt it. Typically these program write-ups include descriptions of the new tools and processes and their impacts, a description of the staff needed for implementation, and a complete, typically self-paced training guide to walk the practices through it.

From here our showcase tour will give you important examples of where we've gone and how we got there. To start, we'll take you on a rather long flight to Mars and back to present an in-depth example; then we'll take several shorter flights to round out your tour of key CFI projects.

A Journey to Mars

Think about the last time you went to see a physician. Chances are, if you're relatively healthy, you had some measurements taken upon entering the office, and then you had a brief consult with the doctor, you received advice and maybe a prescription or two, and you moved on.

Such simple, one-stop visits happen all the time, every day, all across the country. But suppose your situation is more complex. You have multiple complex symptoms, or you have something the doctor would like to have checked out by another specialty. Can that happen during today's visit? You'll get a referral, and most likely you'll have to make another appointment, come in for another visit on another day, and go through another round of discussions, lab tests, and treatment planning.

And you still might not be done. Perhaps a third specialty needs to come into the picture. The visits start to add up: time spent in waiting rooms, time documenting medical records, and worst of all, from your point of view, time spent in repetition of the same information and the same questions. All in all, for you, these are seemingly endless trips to a clinic or hospital. Medicine, especially the treatment of complex diseases, is a complex thing. At Mayo Clinic we are famous for and proud of making things happen during the same visit day but, even here, many times this is not possible.

The Background

So we set out to address this complex patient experience. Our interest, of course, centered on the patient, but really, the same inefficiencies that were blanketing the patient experience were also wreaking havoc in our practices—in this case, our outpatient practice. Patients would make the trip to Rochester and schedule an appointment, only to find out that they needed another appointment, which we would try to get scheduled on the same day but which could be days out. More inconvenience, more effort, more documentation, more check-ins and checkouts—we just wanted to start over and create the "perfect" practice for these patients.

Very quickly, we started to call this project "Mars"—what if we were to scrap everything here on Earth and create the perfect multispecialty outpatient practice on Mars? What would we do? How would we design the practice from the ground up—the physical spaces, electronic tools, administrative support, the staffing—to get the job done with minimal inconvenience to our patients and most efficiently and cost-effectively?

We had a strong sense that something big could be done here. With the right research and combination of innovations, we could streamline the patient experience. We could react better to the patient condition known before and after the initial visit. We could avoid costly and disruptive stops and starts in the treatment process, reduce repeat visits from referrals and separate inputs from multiple specialties, and save our payers a bundle of money in the process.

Project Mars was born. We set a specific goal to improve the patient's experience as well as the provider's practice experience and to reduce practice costs for Mayo Clinic. We created a team and let it proceed.

Understanding User Needs

So with these strong hunches in mind, we set out to scan and frame our trip to Mars. What would the perfect practice, created from the ground up, look like? How would it work? How would it address the nagging issues out there? And how would our discoveries and prototypes in the Mars project, part of the Mayo Practice "When I need to come to you" platform, support the Connected Care and Health and Well-Being platforms?

We started this practice redesign project with big expectations of discovering efficiencies and applications of technology that would help across the health care spectrum. From the outset we "went big" with the discovery process to develop a complete list of insights through hours of external scanning, detailed observation, and listening.

A Patient Care Continuum

We developed a patient continuum to describe why most patients seek medical help (Figure 8.1).

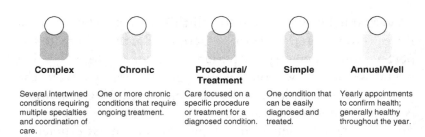

Complex	Chronic	Procedural/ Treatment	Simple	Annual/Well
Several intertwined conditions requiring multiple specialties and coordination of care.	One or more chronic conditions that require ongoing treatment.	Care focused on a specific procedure or treatment for a diagnosed condition.	One condition that can be easily diagnosed and treated.	Yearly appointments to confirm health; generally healthy throughout the year.

FIGURE 8.1. PATIENT CARE CONTINUUM

For Mars, our specific focus was on the more complex patients who would require the care of multiple specialties. The more complex patients using our outpatient practice generally fall into the two left-hand categories, so-called *complex* or *chronic patients.* Complex patients are the most challenging to schedule and move through the process due to the combinative nature of their diseases and the care required to address them. In some cases care is delivered when specialists can consult together; others can be handled in discrete consultations. But in all cases, the need to consult multiple specialties produces a logistics challenge.

Chronic care patients may or may not need to see multiple specialists, but they do require repeat visits, so easy and efficient scheduling is also important. For chronic patients, as well as others across the continuum, we began to have a notion that progress could be made by looking at the big-picture Mayo Practice—that is, Mayo Clinic as a central practice containing the specialties sitting behind Mayo, or the non-Mayo but partnered with us, primary care facilities local to the patient. A chronic care patient could get treatment locally with an electronic consultation with a specialist in a Mayo outpatient practice—if the logistics surrounding scheduling, medical records, and interactive technologies could be managed.

The upshot: we realized that Mars discoveries would be significant throughout the patient experience for all kinds of patients. A large-scale research effort was warranted.

Practice Research

We began a major practice research campaign to observe and discover what was really happening in our outpatient practices and to develop insights from that research. The campaign was conducted by CFI designers over a period of eight months in our practices. Specifically, the exploration included 200 hours of interviews and observations across the 50+ practices and specialties. We talked to patients, physicians, nurses, clinical assistants (C.A.s), and other staff members. We conducted 35 ethnographic patient interviews in three cities to understand patient needs, goals, and motivators. We also completed a thorough external assessment of best practices and trends, summarizing the state of the industry with "trend cards" (introduced in Chapter 4).

In all, it was a from-the-ground-up, start-from-scratch exercise in understanding what was really going on in our practices (the scan) and where we could best direct our innovation efforts toward solving the most important problems (the frame). Of course, the research didn't *stop* here—it just got us started! Experimentation and further research would get us closer to true customer—explicit, tacit, and latent—needs.

Practice Insights

From our deep observation, we identified a list of 238 insights in 12 categories to describe the current state, the key challenges and issues, and general observations about what occurred daily in the practices.

Here are the 12 categories. You may find these categories also apply to your organization's main challenges:

- ▶ Mayo Organization, Culture, and Beliefs
- ▶ Access
- ▶ Coordination of Care
- ▶ Predictability and Preparation
- ▶ Variance and Flexibility
- ▶ Care Team Dynamics
- ▶ Systems and Practice
- ▶ Communication

- ▶ Patient Types and Behaviors
- ▶ Patient Experience and Relationships
- ▶ Care Models
- ▶ Billing and Financial Issues

Framing the Problem

Even when the insights are grouped into 12 main categories, it took us a while to synthesize the body of research—that is, the 238 insights—into an actionable set of problems. Eventually, we did boil our outpatient practice redesign down into *seven* encompassing issues and problems to be solved:

- ▶ *Lack of standardization.* We maintained different processes for scheduling, treating, and managing patients, as well as different team compositions, even though the institution desired standardization.
- ▶ *Only one type of patient visit offered.* We essentially had only one offering for all patients: a face-to-face appointment, although we could vary it in length and provider type.
- ▶ *Patient complexity.* Scheduling needed to classify people as each having one condition, and additional needs were visible only after the patient arrived.
- ▶ *Lack of timely access.* Different departments and providers had better access than others; access time ranged from a few days to a couple of weeks, months, or even a year.
- ▶ *Patients not transitioning back to primary care.* Once patients became part of the subspecialty outpatient practice, they rarely transitioned back to primary care.
- ▶ *Lack of systemic recovery.* If the needs of the patients changed or if they were not originally scheduled correctly, care teams found it hard to readjust the patients' schedules.
- ▶ *Clerical burden.* Providers and care team members had to use, and move between, multiple, mostly fixed, IT systems, causing significant clerical burdens.

Creating a Research Path

Fast forwarding just a bit, we felt that we could define the basic problem areas as (1) identifying correctly the care needed, and thus the care process and schedule, of a patient before the visit and (2) more effectively reacting to true patient needs during and even after the visit. By applying new technologies, including *synchronous* (real-time) and *asynchronous* (not real-time) *interconnectivity, predictive modeling*, and even the promise of *genomics-based disease modeling*, we could design and create "an intelligent adaptable system to provide an unparalleled experience."

This led to identifying the main lines of experimentation that we felt would lead to the creation of an *intelligent adaptable system* and ultimately the redesign of the practice. Here are the seven Mars research paths, or "families," grouped in four larger categories—know the person; provide the right service, in the right place, at the right time; optimize services and experiences; and create awareness and flexibility:

1. **Know the person**
   - *Pre-visit question sets.* Establish an automated and standardized process for obtaining patient clinical and psychosocial information at the time of the initial appointment request and/or prior to a patient's appointment.
2. **Provide the right service, in the right place, at the right time**
   - *Customized education.* Provide education to patients in a format, location, and timeline that is more convenient and better prepares them for their visit and to create care team and provider efficiencies.
   - *Shared medical appointments (group visits).* Create appointments for small groups of patients in situations in which meeting together would support the medical and social needs of the patients and that would support the availability and needs of the care team.
   - *Remote follow-up.* Conduct follow-up or return visits with patients remotely in an asynchronous or synchronous manner.
3. **Optimize services and experiences**
   - *SmartSpace: reducing the clerical burden.* Automatically record conversations between providers and patients, and auto-fill clerical information (billing codes, notes, and orders) to allow providers to be more efficient and reduce clerical resources.

- *microConsults.* Enable one provider with a patient to connect with another provider to answer a focused question.
4. **Create awareness and flexibility**
   - *SmartSpace: increasing our situational awareness.* Use a Wi-Fi–enabled mobile application to provide near-real-time, geospatial views of the care team members, panels of patients, and workflows in a space throughout a day. This will allow us to respond more quickly to changing conditions, potentially including more day-of or week-of appointment scheduling, real-time triage, and systemwide "air-traffic control" with visibility and oversight to the system.

These research paths, or families, ultimately became sub-projects under the Mars umbrella, based on the results of further experimentation. Figure 8.2 summarizes the research progress toward identifying the seven initial experiment families. From here, we will drop down into one of these paths—microConsults—and give a tour of the specific experiments and research done on this emerging subproject.

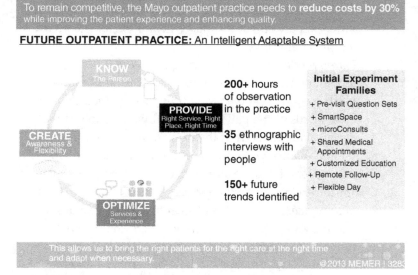

FIGURE 8.2. MARS: THE DISCOVERY BEGINS

Systematizing Practice Flexibility with microConsults

The microConsults project is designed to allow a practice to schedule an electronic consult from another specialty based on need discovered during a patient visit.

The scenario described at the beginning of the chapter serves as an example. A patient arrives for an orthopedic exam or treatment, and the scheduled physician decides that a neurological consult is in order. That consult could be scheduled and delivered in near real time using electronic means—a short, perhaps 15-minute video consult, with shared charts, texts, X-rays, and electronic medical record (EMR) data. This construct was the basis of our set of experiments.

The microConsults Concept

From our observations and initial data collection, we realized that it was common, especially for complex patients, to require a secondary consultation from another specialty. As we'll see later, that percentage varied by practice; through our research it averaged about 31 percent of patients with a range of 25 to about 50 percent.

Further, we realized that in many cases, again varying by specialty, patients were forced to leave the clinic and come back another day, to receive the secondary consult. That consult could happen the same day but rarely did through a formal scheduling process. If a secondary specialist saw a patient at all, it was usually through an informal contact and a "curbside" visit—usually a drop-by visit or a consultation from the primary to a secondary provider by phone, if, by chance, it happened to work out.

With microConsults, the vision was that a primary provider, upon deciding that a secondary provider opinion and/or treatment was in order, could systematically see the availability of a secondary provider and contact that specialist, in real time or near real time, to deliver a short, electronic three-way consult between the patient, the primary provider, and the secondary provider. The orthopedist could call in the neurologist; the neurologist, if available then or later that day, could review the patient case with the primary physician in a real-time, video chat. If successful, a treatment or treatment plan could be developed by both physicians together, usually in the presence of the patient too. The secondary physician could be called in without the time consumed and interruption of a full face-to-face visit.

While the business case is not always clear in the early stages, in this case it was very strong for Mayo Clinic with the move away from fee-for-service accounting to total-cost-of-care and bundled payments accounting.

Designing and Scoping the microConsults Experiment

With this idea in mind, we began a deeper exploration of the basic need and workflow concept. We began our exploration by holding co-creation workshops to understand the challenges and identify the opportunities. We hosted and facilitated four co-creation sessions over a three-week period, involving 19 provider participants across different medical departments and specialties.

In these workshops we identified different patient types who could benefit from increased integration including acute and nonacute complex patients, simple patients, and surgical patients or those who are considering surgery. In the workshops we also outlined a workflow that walked through a way to connect two providers and the patient. At this stage, we gave this workflow the name *microConsults* and developed a definition:

> *microConsults is an integrated care model where multiple providers meet with a patient simultaneously in a clinical space using technology that allows them to virtually connect and collaborate. A microConsult will be typically effective for a focused question that leads to diagnosis and adjustment to treatment. Many take 10 minutes or less. A microConsult can take place as a short scheduled consult or as a real-time unscheduled event.*

After scoping the type of interaction and appropriate patient types, we then wanted to understand the potential scalability of this idea in different departments. We completed a retrospective review with five practices to understand how many patients could have been appropriately served with a microConsult.

We evaluated 154 appointments, our sample being composed of new and established patients, and we determined that 31 percent of the appointments could have been handled as microConsults. This study helped us understand that there is a significant opportunity for microConsults across Mayo Clinic.

Two Iterations

The next step was to design the experiment. The team laid out two phases, or iterations, to move forward. The first iteration was designed as a live proof-of-concept exercise to confirm the value of the microConsult concept to the practices and to the patients; the second was to develop the operational model and confirm that it could actually work in practice without CFI involvement or interaction.

Iteration 1: Proof of Concept

Iteration 1—essentially a formal, electronic curbside consultation—was designed to confirm the value of microConsults to both patients and providers; to confirm the anticipated efficiencies in reducing repeat visits, scheduling overhead, and so forth; and to confirm the overall viability of microConsults to Mayo Clinic. The experiment began by creating a set of design questions that defined what we wanted to learn in the context of the challenges identified prior in our research (Figure 8.3).

Here are some examples:

▶ Does a microConsult effectively reduce referral appointments?
▶ Is a microConsult appropriate in some situations in which the redundancies of the rooming, history, and exam are not needed for each patient?
▶ Is there value and satisfaction in this interaction to both patient and the initiating and receiving providers?

We also decided that Iteration 1 should not include a test of different technologies. Instead, we would go with Apple FaceTime as the primary interface tool plus additional enhancements to practice scheduling systems. A complete set of User Requirements (too detailed to present here) was created.

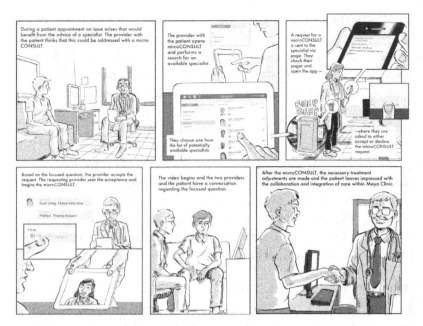

FIGURE 8.3.   MICROCONSULT PROCESS
(DRAWING BY NICHOLAS BREUTZMAN)

Partnering strategies and concepts were a big part of Iteration 1. Our initial studies led us to work with General Internal Medicine due to the relatively high concentration of potential microConsult-eligible cases in this practice. We decided to add in a test of a specific group of chronic patients—acute dialysis patients.

We recruited individuals from primary and secondary practices to participate in the experiment; overall, there were 12 initiating and 37 receiving specialist providers.

Iteration 1 Metrics

Our metrics included the following:

- ▶ *Appointment length.* The length of the microConsults
- ▶ *Referral status.* Whether the patients were being referred following the microConsults
- ▶ *Impact and acceptance of the technology.* Captured qualitatively through debriefing interviews with both providers

and the patients regarding their impressions of the technology from a performance and overall acceptance perspective
▶ *Value.* Captured qualitatively through debriefing interviews with both providers and patients regarding the value of the interactions
▶ *Patient and provider satisfaction.* Captured qualitatively, and in most instances through numerical rating, with both providers and patients, regarding the satisfaction and overall thoughts about the interactions

Iteration 1 Results

Initial microConsult measurements were encouraging. In the initial iteration, we completed 27 microConsults over a period of six weeks. The average length of the microConsult session was 9 minutes, 25 seconds.

Obviously, to shed more light on potential patient and practice efficiencies, we needed to quantify the savings in time spent with patients and in administering the visits. We compared the time utilization between the microConsult and what it would have been in a typical referred consult. The results were substantial: over the 27 microConsult appointments, we measured a savings of 1,035 appointment minutes (17.25 appointment hours), or just over 38 appointment minutes per appointment.

But that wasn't the whole story. What about the patient experience in terms of the time savings? In all we estimated a total savings of 118 *itinerary days*—that is, days spanning the initial and secondary consults as they would have happened, or about four days per patient. That's a lot of travel and hotel dollars saved for the patient, not to mention anxious time waiting between appointments, family member travel costs, and so forth.

We also measured satisfaction through surveying for overall satisfaction with the experience, on a 1-to-7 scale:

▶ The average ranking for initiating providers was 6.1.
▶ The average ranking for receiving providers was 5.7.
▶ The average ranking for patients was 6.2.

We also collected initiating provider, receiving provider, and patient comments:

▶ *Dialysis, initiating provider.* "We were able to schedule an upper endoscopy for the patient. This allowed patient care to move forward quickly, and it satisfied the patient who was significantly impacted by the condition."

▶ *General Internal Medicine, initiating provider.* "The microConsult expedited the process a great deal, and after confirming the diagnosis with Endocrinology, the patient changed his travel plans and opted for surgery the next day at Mayo Clinic."

▶ *Gastrointestinal, receiving provider.* "This is excellent. Far superior to a face-to-face consult with the patient because the dialysis nurse practitioner was present, and she could help interpret the relevant medical information. There is great potential for this process. We could potentially do six of these in an hour, saving everyone time and money."

▶ *Employee Community Health, patient.* "The most positive thing is that we are all immediately on the same page. My doctor knows what the specialist said and can ask questions I wouldn't have thought of. I don't have to try to remember for my next appointment. Everyone already knows the story."

Moving on to Iteration 2

Iteration 2, which is in progress at the time of this writing, is designed to fully automate the process, removing CFI from the loop, and to make it possible or easier for an initiating provider to schedule a "scheduled" or even a real-time micro-Consult directly and independently of CFI and administrative help. The team is presently recruiting additional partners. Metrics are expected to stay the same.

Upon completion of this iteration, the expectation is to "go live" with a version of microConsults and to eventually expand it to most practices, and to many initiating providers outside the outpatient practice.

From the example, you can see the Fusion Innovation Model at work. There was plenty of design thinking and co-creation—in this case, the patient *and* the practice customers. You could see the blending of scientific method (hypothesis, experiments, detailed measurements) and project management (phasing, reporting, communications) inherent in the effort. And there was constant iteration through the various stages of research and project development.

Being There and Everywhere with eConsults

From here, we want to summarize some of our other more illustrative projects. To respect your reading time, we offer these next "showcase" reviews at a "higher altitude," more of a big-picture summary.

As you probably noted, the Mars Outpatient Practice Redesign project covers a wide gamut of issues related to the physical destination practice. Among other things, we introduce asynchronous and synchronous connectivity to achieve greater practice flexibility and to deliver medicine beyond the walls of the clinic by bringing in specialty consultations through microConsults.

The principles and technologies of microConsults were not so new; for Mars, the *application* to achieve secondary consultations in near real time, without a follow-up appointment, was new and transformative, particularly for the patient experience. Really, microConsults borrowed principles and technologies already developed in our Connected Care platform, conceived to connect patients (and other providers) to Mayo physicians from "there and everywhere"—that is, without coming to a Mayo Clinic facility.

A Triple Win

Since 2009, CFI has been researching and developing "connected" models to deliver Mayo primary and specialty care without patients traveling to a Mayo facility. These models transform patients' lives by bringing Mayo Clinic specialty expertise conveniently to them. Furthermore, the e-models reduce the cost of care and help Mayo leverage its provider capacity in a manner that can help the most patients. The combination of patient experience and enterprise benefits makes these Connected Care initiatives especially important. In our lingo, we would describe it as a "triple win."

Among several projects within Connected Care is eConsults, an asynchronous electronic consultation model allowing remote secondary consultations to occur behind a Mayo or non-Mayo local primary provider.

Developing eConsults

The eConsult model offers an efficient way to access specialty consultations when a face-to-face visit with the patient is not required. The project is in an expanding implementation; we have defined 170 medical conditions appropriate for an eConsult, and we have completed 14,000 eConsults since the model was fully launched three years ago.

Problem to Be Solved

This innovation was developed out of the opportunity to electronically deliver cost-effective specialty care to patients with established primary care providers, in place of traditional face-to-face specialty consultations. This model would then allow remote patients to receive Mayo specialty care, providing an affordable and convenient option and open access for patients most in need of face-to-face care.

We looked at two delivery approaches: *synchronous* (real-time dialogue with the care provider) and *asynchronous* (non-real-time—answered quickly but not instantaneously). It had to be easy to use, particularly in that non-Mayo users in non-Mayo primary care facilities had to be able to access it and receive results seamlessly.

Understanding User Needs

We began our work by collaborating with our largest commercial payer, Blue Cross and Blue Shield of Minnesota (BCBS-MN). We worked together on the eConsult Model of Specialty Care, which would be more convenient for patients, would strengthen our relationships at the local community primary care level, and would reduce the cost of care. We selected a BCBS-MN–affiliated clinic, located in Duluth,

Minnesota, hundreds of miles from Mayo Clinic Rochester, to develop a pilot model.

We collaborated with providers in Duluth and with our Mayo Clinic primary care and specialty physicians to understand the clinical situations for which an electronic consult (eConsult) could replace a face-to-face consult. Just as a technical investment analyst might "backtest" an analytic model, we reviewed medical records to further define the scenarios of use, and we surveyed our physicians to understand their needs and willingness to use this type of model. Through this initial research, we estimated that about 30 percent of secondary referrals could be handled through an eConsult and that 85 percent of the physician specialists surveyed believed that an eConsult would be feasible.

We also worked to understand the patient experience and how best to deliver care at a distance, and we built a model that incorporated key features of the Mayo model of integrated and patient-centered care. We felt that the savings in patient time and travel by avoiding a second appointment and trip would be obvious, but we did make a point of getting patient feedback and testing eConsult response times to ensure minimal latency in getting a specialist response.

Experimenting and Prototyping

Our initial research proved so positive that we decided to launch a large experiment, really in scale, a full prototype, with the BCBS-affiliated Duluth clinic. The experiment initially covered 120 specialty consultations with the external practice group over a seven-month period. It then expanded to a larger scale prototype across Mayo over a two-year period with participation from 39 specialties and for 158 medical conditions.

We flowcharted the current process of face-to-face consults, including the patient touch points, operational aspects, and interactions with the electronic medical record. We then prototyped an eConsult delivery method and tested it to ensure the quality of the process. We piloted it with a few primary care providers at the BCBS-affiliated clinic in Duluth, and we started with one specialty practice (cardiology). Once proven to be effective, we gradually spread the eConsult model from the Duluth practice to our own primary care providers at Mayo Clinic and specialty practices (Figure 8.4).

To properly execute the experiment, we had to take on some important issues. First, since electronic consultations are generally not covered by existing payers, that is, insurance or government payers, we had to establish payment through BCBS. Naturally, we also had to develop easy-to-understand patient communication materials that the primary care providers could utilize when discussing this modality of care with their patients.

We worked with specialty practices to understand the conditions for which eConsults could be provided and the prerequisites for specialists to render the consultations. For example, if the eConsult is for endocrinology/osteoporosis, it would require a bone mineral density completed within the last six months, a serum calcium level, and a list of current medications.

We developed a tool to assess the satisfaction of both the primary care providers and specialists with this new model of care. We also undertook a similar exercise for patients to compare this eConsult to the face-to-face consultative model.

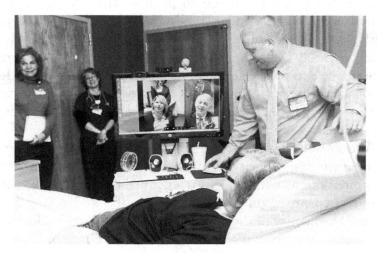

FIGURE 8.4.   ECONSULT IN PROGRESS

Experiment Findings

The large-scale experiment told us a lot:

- ▶ *Volumes.* By September 2011, we had completed 6,253 eConsult orders to Mayo Rochester. About 65 percent were adequately completed using the eConsult method; 35 percent required further face-to-face consultation.
- ▶ *Time for completion.* Typical eConsults took 15 to 20 minutes, about a third of the time of a face-to-face consult. About 27 percent were complete in the same day, 83 percent were completed in one business day, 93 percent in two business days.
- ▶ *Quality.* Through random sampling and registered nurse (RN) review, we learned that about 98 percent of the consults requested were appropriate for both the condition for which it was ordered and the clarity of the question in the requesting physician note.
- ▶ *Physician satisfaction.* Based on physician surveys taken during and after the experiment, 84 percent of referring primary physicians who had ordered an eConsult were either very or somewhat satisfied.
- ▶ *Patient satisfaction.* Detailed surveys and interviews were conducted with patients, and they reported high levels of satisfaction—over 90 percent very or somewhat satisfied. Not all physicians were early proponents of this type of care, and engaging with early adopters to demonstrate and lead the way was critical to its acceptance. Fear of not having the personal relationship or personal touch was a component of this model that needed to be overcome. It helped to ease this concern by having the specialists be involved in determining the appropriate conditions for eConsults.

We should also note another factor responsible for the model's success: the passion and commitment of a CFI physician, Dr. Rajeev Chaudhry, who led the project and an engaged interdisciplinary team of designers, project managers, physicians, nurses, financial and systems analysts, and staff members from operational areas across Mayo Clinic. The team won the revered Mayo Excellence in Teamwork Award for the eConsult project. This project was co-creation at its best.

Implications

It was pretty obvious early on that eConsults offered a new modality for providing specialty care. This is especially appropriate for situations in which knowledge transfer is needed between primary care providers and specialists. With key health care challenges including the increasing complexity of care (especially with new tests and medications), excessive costs, fragmentation, a projected shortfall of physician capacity, and emerging paradigms of patients as consumers, there is value in providing remote collaborative tools for primary care physicians and specialists to work together.

As of the end of year 2013, we had completed over 25,000 eConsults. In 2013, we performed almost 8,000 at Mayo Clinic Rochester, almost 2,000 at our other Mayo practice sites in Florida and Arizona, and about 1,800 in our Mayo Clinic Care Network and international affiliate practices. In 2014, volumes had increased 40 percent from 2013.

Connecting Faraway Places: Synchronous eConsults to Alaska

Cancer is the second leading cause of death among Alaska Natives over age 45, according to the Intercultural Cancer Council, a non-profit organization that promotes policies, programs, partnerships, and research to eliminate the unequal burden of cancer among racial and ethnic minorities and medically underserved populations in the United States and its associated territories. Not surprisingly, Alaska has a limited number of physician specialists such as oncologists or breast health experts, especially in remote regions of the state.

So we partnered internally with the Mayo Clinic Cancer Center and Breast Diagnostic Clinic and externally with the Alaska Native Medical Center (ANMC) to develop a program that would provide access to Mayo Clinic breast cancer expertise for patients in an underserved area. "Underserved area" refers not only to geography but also to demographics, so the "connected" nature of our model would go beyond saving enormous travel complexities. To all intents and purposes, it would make the care available—period.

We established a synchronous audio and video eConsult to connect ANMC with Mayo Rochester for use by patients and their primary physicians simultaneously. The model has worked well, delivering over 200 eConsults since 2010.

With eConsults, we at Mayo Clinic can truly be "there" and "everywhere."

The Nurse Is in Today: Optimized Care Teams

The Health and Well-Being platform is our third platform in the "here, there, and everywhere" vision. The essence of this platform is a broadening of the definition of *care* to include health maintenance and enhancement beyond the traditional physician visit. Major thrusts of this platform include the Community Health Transformation project, which we'll explore further in a moment, and the Healthy Aging and Independent Living (HAIL) projects targeted to seniors and the chronically ill and managed through our HAIL Lab.

For our showcase, we'll take you on a high-level tour of another project that intersects closely with the Mayo Practice and Connected Care platforms: Optimized Care Teams (OCTs).

Background: Care When and from Whom You Need It

Optimized Care Teams is really a subproject under a larger Community Health Transformation umbrella project. The central idea of the Community Health Transformation is to provide the right mix of care based on need, geography, and cost. In our thinking, three themes intersected to bring about this project.

First, we recognized that today's care model is linear and centered on a break-fix model—you need care, you call a doctor, you schedule an appointment, you visit the doctor, you get a treatment, and you're done (and possibly repeated over several iterations). This *conveyor belt model* (described in more detail shortly) generally fails to provide care or make care available during periods of wellness. It also centers on a physician visit, which is more expensive and less convenient to the patient than many of the alternatives.

Second, we recognized that this model works best in large cities, where there is a "critical mass" of hospitals, primary physicians, specialists, labs, and other services located near each other. What about the many remote areas or smaller towns and cities? Can these folks get the care they need without traveling back and forth to the Twin Cities or Rochester? Or do we have to build small and inefficient hospitals in remote places, fully staffed and equipped, to meet patient needs?

Third, the health care world is moving rapidly toward the pay-for-value and the accountable care organization (ACO) models we noted in Chapter 2. With pay-for-value, we can't afford to keep full-time physicians in place to serve locations with low population densities, but we could afford to keep professionals there who had lesser credentials and were connected electronically to Mayo Clinic in Rochester or one of Mayo's other locations.

We took these three issues and formed this hypothesis (the scientific component of our fusion method): "By developing a flexible, team-based model of care with a convergence of the right technology, access points, facility design, and team approach, we could deliver the *right care* at the *right time* in the *right place* by the *right person* in the *right way*—all at the *right cost*."

Thus, the Optimized Care Team model was born for further research and implementation as part of the larger Community Health Transformation project.

Defining the Care Model

We had a sense that the current model of care could be improved, but we wanted to approach it in a way that was inherently measured, scientific, and demonstrable to the current constituents.

We felt it extremely important to get to a visible, working prototype very quickly (Think Big, Start Small, Move Fast). As such, we worked fast to develop an alternative care model that could be tested in practice, exercising a care team concept and providing a real patient care experience. In this case, the experiment was used to do most of the research.

The first step was to identify the "current" care model and evolve it to a future model for testing in research and in practice. The current model is illustrated in Figure 8.5. This model is recognizable and doesn't need much description—it is face-to-face, it is generally but not always with a physician, it is reactive, and it happens only when someone is sick and needs a remedy.

The "future" care model would "wrap around" the patient in all phases of sickness and health, with all levels of medical disciplines in contact at the right time and in the right context. In this model, care would be delivered by a team, either in preventative or reactive mode (Figure 8.6). The "team" would include a blend of M.D.s, R.N.s, L.P.N.s, and R.N. care coordinators, nurse practitioners, medical residents, community health workers (C.H.W.s), and later on, "wellness navigators."

While the details are beyond the scope of this book, the operating model included a group care team calendar with team "huddles" to discuss patients, to triage care, and to assign care to the appropriate team member.

The Current Model: Conveyor Belt Care

The current model of care is built around face-to-face interactions between the patient and physician, nurse, or other clinical staff member, with a focus on the acute and a tendency toward the reactive.

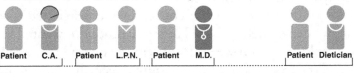

Patient   C.A.   Patient   L.P.N.   Patient   M.D.   Patient   Dietician

FIGURE 8.5.   CURRENT MODEL OF CARE: A CONVEYOR BELT

The Future Model: Wraparound Care

The future model is focused on patient-driven, longitudinal care and a population health and prevention mindset that requires the care team to adopt a more proactive approach and optimize the value of the visit experience.

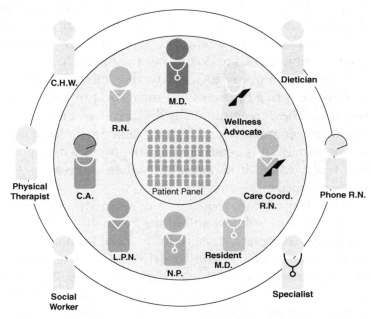

FIGURE 8.6.   THE FUTURE MODEL: WRAPAROUND CARE

In Sight, It Must Be Right

Kasson, Minnesota, is a small town in Dodge County of about 6,000 residents with a typical Midwestern downtown, a unique stone-based water tower built in 1895, and an annual Festival in the Park celebration. It also just happens to be 15 miles west of Rochester, and it also happens to have a clinic that is part of the Mayo Clinic Health System.

To get quickly to proof of concept, we constructed a series of on-site experiments at the Kasson Clinic. We wanted to see what would happen if we created a care team and managed the patient flow from all of Dodge County according to the needs of the patients and the skills and locations of the providers. We wanted to see how the flexible care model would work, and we wanted to measure who actually saw the patients, what care was given, and how the team and the patients felt about it. We learned from our experiments that there was significant potential for utilization of the broader health care team. Patients in many instances could be better served with nurse-only visits or nonvisit care or with a more integrated care team experience (Figure 8.7).

In these pilots, as Figure 8.7 illustrates, we found that, set up properly, the flexible, or optimized, care teams allowed our staff members "to operate at the top of their licensure," that is, to give care according to their skills and the patients' needs, all of which could be decided on in the huddle prior to the patient arrival. By making the best use of the R.N.s and N.P.s, only 6 percent of the incoming patients needed to see a doctor initially. There was also less paperwork, and since much of the

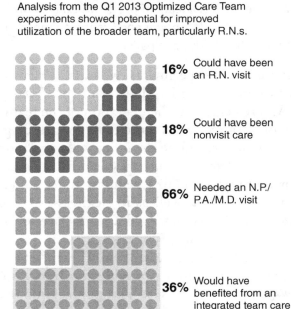

WHO NEEDS TO SEE THE PATIENT?

How can we best meet patients' needs?
Analysis from the Q1 2013 Optimized Care Team experiments showed potential for improved utilization of the broader team, particularly R.N.s.

16% Could have been an R.N. visit

18% Could have been nonvisit care

66% Needed an N.P./P.A./M.D. visit

36% Would have benefited from an integrated team care as part of the visit (e.g., pharmacist)

FIGURE 8.7. RESULTS: WHO NEEDS TO SEE THE PATIENT?

flow was worked out in advance, there was a smoother patient flow. That was because there were fewer "stop-and-starts" as patients had to pass on from one care provider to another.

As is the norm, we also collected qualitative feedback from care team members and patients, to make sure the data wasn't steering us in the wrong direction:

> "What may seem like a complicated patient may not be if you know the person well."—M.D.
>
> "I'm glad my doctor didn't need to see me. That means I'm not sick enough! I know they sent the right person to take care of me today."—Kasson patient
>
> "When the larger team is involved, it really gets the physician to think more broadly."—M.D.
>
> "I'm really enjoying hearing the doctor's conversations and learning more about how they think. It will really help me to pull out useful information during the rooming process."—L.P.N.
>
> "It feels like there is a team of people working in my best interest. It feels efficient and like there is good communication."—Kasson patient

From these initial experiments, we learned that there was more work to do to optimize the role of the *clinical assistant* (C.A.). C.A.s are central to the operation of the team and the scheduling of resources; with more tools and training at their disposal, we could streamline the process. As we "morph" the model into more of an ongoing care (versus acute care) model, we will pay more attention to scheduling nurse contacts with patients in "wellness" as well as in sickness—and so-called *nonvisit care*. Finally, we designed a workspace ideal for the OCT and the team huddle (Figure 8.8).

As we explored the spectrum of "well" care between acute sickness events, and how to provide the best, most cost-effective ways to achieve this, an idea popped into our heads: What if we set up some volunteers—community-minded folks connected with our clinical staff—to help our patients maintain and improve their health without medical intervention?

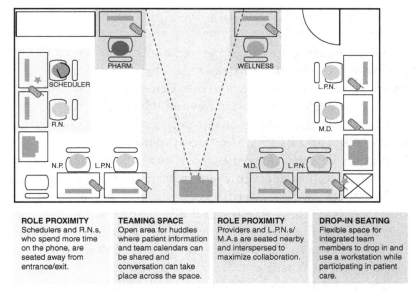

ROLE PROXIMITY	TEAMING SPACE	ROLE PROXIMITY	DROP-IN SEATING
Schedulers and R.N.s, who spend more time on the phone, are seated away from entrance/exit.	Open area for huddles where patient information and team calendars can be shared and conversation can take place across the space.	Providers and L.P.N.s/ M.A.s are seated nearby and interspersed to maximize collaboration.	Flexible space for integrated team members to drop in and use a workstation while participating in patient care.

FIGURE 8.8. OPTIMIZED CARE TEAM WORKSPACE

We felt that a "wellness navigator" could provide a contact point for these individuals and point them to good community resources, including our health resources where needed. The wellness navigator would provide someone to talk to, sort of a "health concierge" available for community use. We developed the Wellness Navigator project, and we fully piloted a new wellness navigator team member who could eventually be a core team member.

We (and our constituents) were very encouraged by these pilots, and we could see some real merit to this approach. There's a lot of potential synergy between the OCT model and our Mayo Practice and Connected Care platforms—all three connect well to deliver our greater vision.

Guiding the Implementation

Finally, we put together a 64-page booklet, called *Optimized Care Team: Implementation to Adoption Toolkit 1.0*, to assist any clinic anywhere in the system to implement the Optimized Care Team model.

Mayo Clinic Patient App

Finally, we finish up with a case example—the Mayo Clinic Patient App—that demonstrates the "here, there, and everywhere" vision—and happens to be a CoDE project originating in the practice and expanding beyond. Here's the story.

In order to meet the growing expectations of Mayo Clinic patients and to enhance the overall patient experience, the Center for Innovation gave a CoDE award to create a unique, simple, portable electronic environment for Mayo guests and visitors. Two areas at Mayo came together to apply for the award—Public Affairs and IT Workstation Support Services—to create an app, which would be an electronic tool that would act as a Mayo Clinic concierge to enhance patients' visits by helping them navigate around Mayo.

The app was made available in a soft launch in the Apple Store in May 2012 (Figure 8.9). In its initial launch, the Mayo

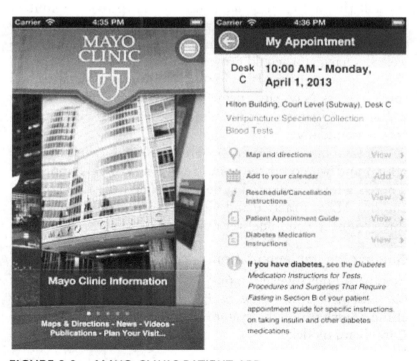

FIGURE 8.9.   MAYO CLINIC PATIENT APP

Clinic Patient App provided an easy-to-use tool to navigate a visit while at a Mayo Clinic campus. The Version 1 app included instructions for finding one's way around the clinic and hospitals, community information, and directions to local restaurants and entertainment. On the first day, the app was downloaded 1,000 times.

In typical CFI fashion, at the post-launch, the small CoDE team continuously tracked comments about the app on social media. On the day after the download, a patient made a comment on social media that caused the team to dig deeper and learn more from him. The comment was this: "You guys really missed the boat on this one." The team reached out, and it turned out that the patient was blind, and he called out some serious flaws that prevented the app from being usable by those with impairments. Some behind-the-scenes IT magic and a few weeks of effort was what it took to fix it up and offer a platform that would be accessible for everyone.

The team kept working in the manner so common for the CFI. How can we keep revising the product or service to help more patients? What additional user needs are out there that we can try to serve? Additional features were quickly added to the app, including the ability for the first time for Mayo Clinic patients to have 24/7 access to their personal medical records, their lab results, appointment schedules, and other services using their individual Patient Online Services account (easy to set up—a patient just needs his or her Mayo Clinic patient number). The team further expanded the functionality to include the latest news, publications, and health information such as videos from Mayo Clinic. All of these improvements made it a true "here, there, and everywhere" cross-platform tool. Just as important, the establishment of the Mayo Clinic Patient App and its successful patient- or person-centered navigation have set the stage as a standard for other Mayo apps to follow.

It even made a splash at Apple. Tim Cook, Apple's CEO, introduced the 2012 Apple Worldwide Developers Conference on stage by highlighting the Mayo Clinic Patient App. Since then, the app has expanded to the Motorola DROID and to virtually all other mobile platforms, and it has been downloaded almost 200,000 times. It is Mayo Clinic's most downloaded and used app!

Hopefully these snapshots have given you a good sense of how we approach our projects and our 21st century model of care vision. Instead of summarizing this chapter here, we'll take you straight to Chapter 9, our final chapter: a "user's guide" to implementing successful transformative innovation in complex enterprises—from our experience and our hearts.

CHAPTER NINE

Innovation the Mayo Clinic Way

~~A Prescription for~~ An Experience in Innovation

You cannot transform by amending the status quo.

—TIM BROWN, President, IDEO, and CFI External Advisory Council member

Ah, there it is. Or there it *was*. The "P" word, the word *prescription*. You know we are health care professionals, and perhaps with Clayton Christensen's seminal work *The Innovator's Prescription* in mind, you've expected us for eight chapters to "prescribe" how to innovate and to "prescribe" how to change the future of health care. From us to you, written on a small piece of paper and signed (or its electronic equivalent)—a formula for fixing something and moving forward.

We may be employed by one of the top medical practices in the world, and we may be from the top echelons of our professions. But we know that we do not have the exact solution—a "prescription"—for all that ails health care, let alone, an exact solution to bring you success in the oh-so-elusive frontiers of innovation.

For that reason and many others, we've held ourselves back from using the "P" word. It's overused in the medical field anyhow. This isn't a prescription, or a "treatment plan," a formula we hand down to you for success. Rather, it is a list of ideas, principles—learnings, lessons, failures that informed our progress, our evolution, ripe for you to incorporate into your own organizational framework to achieve success.

We hope we have given you a clear-eyed view of the opportunity to transform health care, and you've seen how we've gone about approaching the opportunity ourselves. Your opportunity may or may not be related to health care, but we suspect you face similar challenges in moving your own complex organization forward toward important goals—as obvious or unobvious as those goals might be today.

So rather than a prescription or treatment plan, what we offer is more of a checklist for developing a solid structural and cultural foundation to achieve important innovation in complex environments. It should help you figure out *what you need to do, what to do,* and it should help you figure out *where to invest.* It's more of a plan for innovation health and for innovation *team* health.

For you, it may start with something that is broken—or it may not. Our goal is to help you build organizational health and vitality so that, in your own innovations, success becomes more of a self-fulfilling prophecy in a way similar to good health becoming a natural outcome for people who follow good health habits. Good innovation habits bring good innovation health, just as good personal habits bring good personal health.

Here, for the record—and to conclude our book—are 10 principles, based wholly from our experience, for achieving successful, transformative innovation in complex environments and enterprises. These principles—above all else—are crafted to help you Think Big, Start Small, Move Fast.

1. Create a Distinct, Embedded Team; Build a Unique Identity

Over and over again we see individuals or small groups in complex enterprises gather some resources "under the radar" to go off to try to move something forward as a skunk works.

While this is successful at times, and while this may be a place to start, and while our early beginnings had some of this DNA, we firmly believe in quickly evolving to building a highly visible, embedded innovation "center" literally in the center of the enterprise.

Locating in the center of the enterprise helps your work gain traction by it being clearly visible, and it also helps expand the dialogue, the interaction, the collaboration, and the *involvement* of the rest of the organization. By nature, people possess an innovative, creative spirit. As IDEO founder and Stanford professor David Kelley summarizes, creativity is not the domain of a chosen few but is inside each of us. We need to help people unleash their creativity, and for those who have lost touch with it, to build up their creative confidence.

People want to move their ideas forward, and when they see a legitimate, funded, resourced entity at the center of their organization carrying this out, they can join in without fear or risk of wasting their time, or worse, stepping in something not sanctioned by the greater enterprise. They get ideas and inspiration *from* it; and they contribute ideas and testing opportunities *to* it. By embedding and centering the innovation group, you get the "gains from exchange" not otherwise available. The embedded innovation organization should become a showcase—both physically and intellectually—for the organization. It should be an exciting, uplifting place to visit. It should have an identity congruent with transformative innovation, and it should present well to constituents.

Realistically, you may not have the funding or organizational backing to start in this position; we get that. But you should start with the end in mind—in this case, a formal, embedded, established innovation center. Even hanging an innovation shingle on a wall in an open, collaborative space is an important first step, and in fact, how we got started. Build it, and they will come.

2. Seek Diversity

If you simply bring existing organizational players into your innovation team, guess what? You're likely to get pretty much the same perspective and style of work already inherent in your organization's DNA. This isn't all bad—you need some people who know how to play your enterprise's game.

But there is so much to be gained from the experiences, intellect, and perspectives of people who enter your organization from the outside. People with different educational backgrounds and skill sets and people who have worked in different organizations and different industries or even on their own bring a fresh, new way of framing and solving problems that usually turns out better results, and more quickly. Fresh insights can be priceless for those who want to Think Big, Start Small, Move Fast.

Especially in our industry, where there is a strong "button down" tradition of how things are done, this is important. If you want a new solution, you need fresh perspectives, and if you want fresh perspectives, you're best served to bring in smart people and smart insights from a variety of backgrounds. The best mix is a healthy combination of "new blood" and well-established, credible internal performers who know how to navigate the shoals of your enterprise.

We initially built our diversity by engaging with concept champions like IDEO and Doblin, visiting other innovation centers, especially those in other industries, by bringing in interns and other outsiders where we could do so on a modest budget, and by selective hiring.

3. Take an Integrated, Holistic Approach

We know it sounds sort of late-1960s "groovy," but we've found over time that it makes sense to approach transformation—and how we staff and organize to approach that transformation—with a holistic, big-picture approach.

What does that mean? First, as we approach the health care problem, it means that we look at the problem as a whole, "Health and health care, here, there, and everywhere." We don't align our focus and our troops to just one aspect of that problem, for example, acute episodic care delivered in the clinic. We look at health care and health care transformation as a *system*.

The risk, of course, is that we try to "boil the ocean"—that is, we overextend our resources and bandwidth so as not to do any one thing well, or even to completion. That risk is offset by the synergies and benefits we get from applying our learnings and tools to several corners of the problem at once, as we've seen by applying Connected Care technologies to both in-facility and remote care. We also avoid the boil-the-ocean thing by carefully structuring programs and projects within the "whole" in such a way to be certain that we start with smaller defined initiatives and make good progress on all fronts with high-return projects. We don't get lost in the weeds with something too big to handle or too off-center to be meaningful. We truly live by our motto Think Big, Start Small, Move Fast.

THINK BIG start small MOVE▶▶ FAST™

The integrated, holistic approach has also come to apply to our people. Most organizations tend to "silo" their employees as project managers, designers, IT specialists, and so forth. We recognize the need for expertise, but rather than creating internal friction by having different groups with different perspectives and metrics interact with each other from under their own secular roofs, we've created the Fusion Innovation Model, whereby the three disciplines of design thinking, scientific method, and project management come together as a whole. Furthermore, we've organized our group into "villages" around platforms, programs, and projects rather than organizing by our areas of specialty.

As a consequence, our team members have become "specialist-generalists" capable of applying holistic methods to a holistic problem. They have become like small business owners who have to do a little bit of everything to make it work. From our experience, this leads to better, more integrated solutions to problems, and it's an easier and more rewarding way to work as well.

4. Champion a Clear Vision

We don't believe any innovation organization can survive—let alone prosper—without a clear vision of where it is going and how that differs from today.

Mayo Clinic has invested a lot to arrive at the "Health and health care, here, there, and everywhere," the "Always be there for me" vision. We've conceived it, worded it, put graphics around it, and spread it through the organization at every possible opportunity. In the CFI we continue to fine-tune it and to personalize it with the likes of "When I need to come to you," "When you can come to me," and "When I didn't know I needed you" slogans.

The 21st century model of care is a complex thing, and nobody knows for sure exactly how it is going to look. Our vision evolves a little every time we start a project, complete a project, go through an environmental change (like the Affordable Care Act), or see something new outside of Mayo. It is organic and iterative. It is presented as a sequence—not just a picture of the future state but a picture of the evolutionary path to getting there (see Figure 3.4 for a refresher).

In sum, good visions are clear, they define something important, and they set an aspiration and destination to facilitate designing a path to get there. They are adaptive and organic, and they are communicated clearly to all parts of the organization. As a consequence, they are top of mind both for the innovation center and for enterprise constituents.

5. Communicate, Communicate, Communicate

It happens all the time. Great ideas, great innovations from great people, great teams with great leaders—but nothing happens! Thought leaders are left scratching their heads. What happened? What *didn't* happen? And why?

Chances are, their ideas, their efforts, even their very existence may remain invisible to the powers that be and to the rest of their enterprise.

We recognized the importance of *transfusing* what we do to our constituency. We recognized the need for clear, appealing, meaningful communications about what we do and what we think across all channels available inside (and outside) the enterprise. We invested in an identity, in pleasing, professional-grade graphic collateral, in multimedia presentations, and in clever, brief updates like *i on CFI* that regularly feed a clear message to busy people in important places in the enterprise. We treat communication as a must, assigning resources to make sure it happens and having a regular communications timetable, rather than communicating as afterthought when somebody asks a question.

In all, we use communication not only to get the word out but also to accomplish two other critically important purposes. First, high-quality communications add an aura of professionalism to our work. We are not an under-the-radar skunk works but rather a permanent team embedded within the enterprise, and we are to be taken seriously and watched closely. Second, our communications serve not only to inform and motivate our constituents but also our own team. How motivating is it when you see your project go to print in a fine, four-color glossy Mayo Clinic publication?

From what we've observed outside Mayo Clinic, innovation teams regularly overestimate what the organization knows about them and underestimate the return on investment for providing excellent communications.

6. Accelerate, Accelerate, Accelerate

In the beginning, we quickly recognized the need to *transfuse* our evolution, our vision, our works-in-progress, and our successes into the rest of the Mayo Clinic organization, and to the outside as it made sense to do so. As we developed our communication strategies and vehicles, we began to feel another purpose and important element to this transfusion: the dissemination of innovation *intellect* throughout the organization and to the world outside.

What do we mean by "intellect"? Here, we're talking about the know-how, the technique, and the inspirations that make innovation happen, that make it *work*. We also recognized that we hardly have a monopoly on innovative ideas and that we could serve the organization well not only by developing our own innovations but also by fostering and incubating the innovations of others.

As a consequence, the Innovation Accelerator has become the "other half" of our transfusion strategy. Within the accelerator, we collect and distribute ideas and tools about innovation. We incubate and fund projects originating outside of CFI but inside the enterprise through our CoDE program. We lead the health care experience transformation conversation through our TRANSFORM symposiums, which leave a major transfusion of ideas and inspiration in their annual wake. And we develop and implement curricula, teaching modules, and learning venues that provide opportunities for everyone in the organization to improve their innovation competence.

Effective innovation teams in complex enterprises don't just produce great innovations. They also lead the conversation about innovation and give the greater enterprise the motivation and "muscle memory"—consciously or subconsciously—to be part of the innovation process themselves.

7. Collaborate, Collaborate, Collaborate

From the beginning, we knew we couldn't do this ourselves.

Transformative health care innovation, in a large, generally conservative medical provider organization was going to be challenging under the best of circumstances, and it wouldn't be possible without reaching out to others for guidance, resources, teamwork, experimentation, and prototype "test-beds," and other forms of cooperation.

From day one we collaborated with industry experts like IDEO and Doblin, and we created important alliances with important Mayo Clinic decision-making entities. We also collaborated with others from the outside—for example, Blue Cross and Blue Shield of Minnesota, Cisco, Good Samaritan Society, Philips, and Target, all of whom were looking to extend beyond their walls as well to innovate toward transforming health care.

Most of all, we collaborated and co-created with Mayo Clinic employees to involve them in ideation, design, and especially testing. We knew from the beginning that collaboration breeds involvement, involvement breeds support, and support ultimately leads to adoption. If you break this chain at any step along the way, it's much harder to get to implementation—if you get there at all.

We spend a lot of time and energy seeking and nurturing our partnerships—both inside and outside Mayo Clinic. We seek the win-win scenario, the relationship that builds the CFI and Mayo image, gets things done, and helps the partner out as well. We believe that modern innovation without collaboration, especially in complex environments, is destined to failure.

8. Start Small and Iterate

We talked about the folly of boiling oceans in item 3 above. It's easy, when taking on such a "giant hairball" as health care, to try to do everything at once, to, in American baseball vernacular, swing for the fences, to try to hit it out of the park.

We use a different way, and it works. Especially with complex innovations, rather than describe, design, and detail the idea to perfection, it works better to create a small prototype so constituents (and we, for that matter) can *see* it in action. Rather like many technology products, once we see it, we get a better grasp of the "aha" and the influence on patient and provider experience, and we can build from there. It's easier to communicate, it's easier to align support, and it's easier to visualize what the next steps are.

So rather than create huge projects with massively wired and bulletproof underlying technology, we go for experiments and rich small-scale prototypes. They provide proof of concept, something to see, feel, and measure experience response, and something to build on. We start small and iterate to the larger vision, often weaving pieces of the vision together as we go. Back to baseball vernacular: we hit singles, load the bases, hit a few more singles, and we score a lot more runs than teams inclined to swing for the fences—who miss much of the time.

Naturally, "starting small and iterating," getting to that first completed prototype, is a big part of our Think Big, Start Small, Move Fast doctrine.

9. Know and Navigate Your Enterprise

In a large, established organization like ours, especially one that delivers complex products and services where a customer's life is at stake, you're bound to run into some bureaucracy. It's inevitable.

We can't choose to avoid bureaucracy. If you avoid it, you are avoiding the heart of your organization, and you will not effect change. Bureaucracy is inherent in our constituency and our customers. Bureaucracy—and its incumbent processes and process checks—is important. It may seem at times like "1 in 10 syndrome" is at work—for every person advancing an idea in the organization, there are 10 people employed to figure out what's wrong with it.

We accept all of that—it's there, and it's part of our reality. Our mission is to learn how to best navigate through it.

First and foremost, we deal with bureaucracy by trying not to be too bureaucratic ourselves. We try to act like a team, all supporting each other, all friends with each other, with a minimum of process checks and forms to fill out to move forward. We can be formal when we need to be formal, but more often we are informal and go out of our way to be easy to work with, both internally and with our constituents.

Beyond not being too bureaucratic ourselves, we seek to embrace the administration in several ways. As already pointed out here in our 10-step approach, we seek involvement and collaboration. By collaborating with our constituents from the beginning, we avoid rejection from organizational antibodies who seek to find the fault in something they didn't know about.

We seek to mitigate bureaucracy through the "generalist" approaches identified above, where team members inside and outside CFI are "general" enough to see the other side of the fence. It becomes one's duty to support a design effort, even if you're a project manager. It becomes one's duty to support practice staff members as parts of a team. When they see that you're supporting and collaborating with them, they will support and collaborate with you. It's a chain of empathy and unity that goes far to mitigate the "not invented here" syndrome and other tentacles of bureaucracy. We do not rail against bureaucracy. We understand it, and we know it has positive aspects. We feel we have developed a way to know when it is helpful and can lead to institutional change—and when it is less so and should be circumvented.

Next, part of the reason for our extensive investment in continuous communication is to help reduce the negative effects of bureaucracy. We believe in transparency. No hidden agendas, all things shared, all proactive—and *no surprises*. What you see is what you get with the Mayo Clinic CFI.

Finally, bureaucratic tentacles tend to become the longest and most numerous when you're taking risks, particularly risks that people don't understand or accept. We do like to take risks, and we feel that risk taking is important to move forward—and really, to avoid bureaucracy. But we insist on making those risks *prudent*, and we make them *transparent*. "Prudent" is one reason we involve the practices and insist on medical leadership in the CFI management structure. "Transparent," again, comes back to communication.

We'd be naive to claim that we've completely avoided the negatives of bureaucracy—or that we'd even *want* to. Bureaucracy serves its purpose. It is a check on our balance and a balance on our check, and it can often serve to give us ideas and feedback on things we never even thought of, and it may save lives. What we try to do—and feel we've succeeded with—is attain some freedom from the extreme negatives—the biggest tentacles—of bureaucracy that would likely envelop us if we didn't approach it right. In that we've been successful.

10. Don't Stop Until You Get There

This one hardly requires further explanation.

An innovation organization, if done right, should bring energy to the enterprise; so naturally, as leaders, you should bring energy to your innovation organization. How you channel that energy, especially in the beginning, means a lot, for sooner or later, you'll achieve successes—small at first, and bigger as you go.

Those successes start to supply some of the energy in their own right—innovative energy becomes a self-fulfilling prophecy. Your innovation organization is set in motion and gains momentum. It steers itself for the most part and supplies its own energy through its own desire to succeed and its own pattern of success. Your role evolves more to mapping out where it is going and evangelizing and rewarding the success.

When you get to this point, you know you've done the right thing.

Gianrico Farrugia, Barbara Spurrier, Nicholas LaRusso

CFI Partners from Across Mayo Clinic

The following is a list of 85 departments, divisions, and centers from across Mayo Clinic that have partnered with the Center for Innovation.

Allergic Diseases
Alzheimer's Disease
   Research Center
Anesthesiology
Bariatric Surgery
Biomedical Imaging
Breast Diagnostic Clinic
Cancer Center
Capital Contracting
Cardiovascular
Center for Individualized
   Medicine (IM) Clinic

Center for Science and Health
   Care Delivery
Center for Sleep Medicine
Child Adolescent Psychiatry and
   Psychology
Colorectal Surgery
Community Health
Community Pediatrics
Department of Medicine
Dermatology
Destination Medical Center
Development

Dietetics
Discharge Planning
  Standardization
Education
Emergency Department
Employee Health
Endocrinology
  (Pediatric and Adult)
Engineering
Facilities
Family Medicine
Gastroenterology and
  Hepatology
General Internal Medicine
Gynecology and Obstetrics
Gynecology Surgery
Health Care Policy and
  Research
Healthy Living Center
Hematology
Human Resources
Illustration and Design
Infectious Diseases
Information Technology
Language Services, Kasson
  Clinic
Mayo Clinic Care Network
Mayo Clinic Health Systems
Media Support Services
Medical Genetics
Medical Oncology
Medical Students
Nephrology
Neuro Spine
Neurology
Neuropsychologists
Nicotine Dependence Center

Nursing
Oncology
Ophthalmology
Orthopedic Spine Surgery
Orthopedic Surgery
Otorhinolaryngology
Palliative Care
Pathology
Pediatric and Adolescent
  Medicine
Pediatric Gastroenterology
Pediatric Inflammatory Bowel
  Disease (IBD) Clinic
Pediatric Postural Orthostatic
  Tachycardia Syndrome (POTS)
  Clinic
Physical Medicine and
  Rehabilitation
Preventative Services
Primary Care Internal Medicine
Psychiatry and Psychology
Psychiatry Research
Public Affairs
Pulmonary and Critical Care
  Medicine
Quality Management Services
Radiology
Referring Physician Services
Robert and Arlene Kogod Center
  of Aging
Simulation Center
Social Services
Surgery
Thoracic Surgery
Transplant
Urological Surgery
Volunteer Services

Center for Innovation 2014 Project Listing

Count	Platform	Projects	Description
1	Innovation Accelerator	Eureka	Online ideation and problem-solving platform for organizational and external collaboration. Speeds up the problem-solving process by allowing everyone to contribute ideas and solutions to key challenges.
2	Innovation Accelerator	Toolkit	Robust learning kit filled with education about design thinking and innovation. Instructional videos, project summaries, stories, and workshops are available to Mayo Clinic employees to learn how to apply innovation to their work.
3	Innovation Accelerator	TRANSFORM 2014	The TRANSFORM symposium is a three-day event, with a focus on innovation and design solutions that transform the delivery of health and health care. The symposium offers forums for networking and collaboration, hands-on workshops, and inspirational main-stage presentations.
4	Innovation Accelerator	Speaker Series	*Thinking Differently: The CFI Series of Unexpected Conversations* is a quarterly speaker series for all Mayo Clinic employees. It hosts global thought leaders and innovators from various industries.
5	Innovation Accelerator	Innovation Catalyst	An immersive, experiential program in innovation management and design thinking, offering certification as an Innovation Catalyst. The program is a collaborative effort jointly developed by the CFI and Arizona State University.

Continued

Count	Platform	Projects	Description
6	Innovation Accelerator	CoDE 1: Virtual Gym for Spinal Patients	Offers virtual participation for people with spinal cord injury and/or dysfunction focusing on health and wellness. A "virtual gym" provides wellness to those unable to access a health club or facility while guiding them with the most appropriate, evidence-based, and adapted wellness program for strengthening, stretching, and endurance training from their own home.
7	Innovation Accelerator	CoDE 2: Peds Pain App	The Pain Coach App is a tool to help improve the quality of care for pediatric patients with pain, reduce clinic expenses, increase access, and provide an effective, mobile treatment option for patients after they leave Mayo Clinic.
8	Innovation Accelerator	CoDE 3: Individualized Preoperative Rehabilitation Toolbox	An individualized preoperative rehabilitation (iPREHAB) program to improve patient resilience and surgical outcomes. Utilizes the time starting when patients make an initial appointment at Mayo Clinic until surgery to optimize the patient condition prior to a complex surgical intervention using the iPREHAB toolbox.
9	Innovation Accelerator	CoDE 4: Mobile, Cognitive Screening Exam	Thousands of patients seek evaluation at Mayo Clinic for impairment in cognitive function. A neuropsychological exam typically requires three to four hours of clinician time, and it is not always necessary for diagnostic referral questions. The new model offers a portable and computerized cognitive screening exam, administered within the primary care environment, to help triage patients who would benefit most from comprehensive consultations.
10	Innovation Accelerator	CoDE 5: TeleVision	Since ophthalmologists are not available at both Mayo Clinic Arizona locations, the use of a smartphone and lens adapter to take a comparable image and transmit it remotely can completely redesign delivery of care for acute eye issues.
11	Innovation Accelerator	CoDE 6: Telehome Care	The Telehome Care model is a knowledge-based integrated patient and disease-specific care management process delivered in an e-format. These e-care management teams will help evaluate and provide ongoing home-based care for patients with congestive heart failure and/or atrial fibrillation.
12	Innovation Accelerator	CoDE 7: Breast Cancer Decision Tool	The Patient Decision Support Tool for Breast Cancer Care is a tool for newly diagnosed breast cancer patients to use so they can be well informed about their treatment options. The tool will be fully implemented across the Mayo breast cancer practice and extended into medical decision making for other types of care.
13	Innovation Accelerator	CoDE 8: Centralized Checker Desk	This project is designed to provide an easier way for patients to check for earlier appointments. It will leverage existing systems by creating a centralized Checker Desk for patients to check for multiple appointments at one time. This could dramatically shorten patients' stays and fill no-show and cancellation slots.

Count	Platform	Projects	Description
14	Innovation Accelerator	CoDE 9: Remote Diabetes Technology	Many people with diabetes live with insulin pumps and continuous glucose monitors. These technologies require intensive patient involvement and are limited both by technical competence and changes in device settings that are generally made only at visits to the health care provider. This new model will help to empower patients and optimize their daily diabetes management plan.
15	Innovation Accelerator	CoDE 10: Cancer Survivorship Software	Design and implement software to allow Mayo clinicians to easily generate a survivorship care plan for patients who have completed their cancer treatment.
16	Connected Care	Video Visits	A service to enable nearly any provider at Mayo to offer a video consultation to any established Mayo Clinic patient when an on-site visit is not required. Will incorporate process, security, and technology to enable a Mayo Clinic quality experience.
17	Connected Care	Diabetes Project	Help patients optimize their living with type 2 diabetes, identifying gaps in clinical care, communications, and technology, as well as social and environmental limitations, and offer services and products that address the gaps.
18	Connected Care	Bariatric Behavior Modification App	This project utilizes the Asthma mHealth architecture through the incorporation of a mobile device. This application will provide a mobile platform, allowing the care team of specialists (endocrinologist, registered dietitian, psychologist, and so on) to better assist and assess the patients' presurgical behavior modifications.
19	Health and Well-Being	Healthy Aging and Independent Living (HAIL) Lab	The HAIL Lab is a place for designing, prototyping, and piloting new services and technologies to help seniors remain at home, safe and connected. The lab has room for focus groups and observations, an assistive technology lending library, and a mock-up apartment for in-lab studies, as well as rooms for other experiments.
20	Health and Well-Being	Patient-Centered Discharge Summary Tool	Regaining health and independence are key goals when patients leave the hospital. We are working with an array of stakeholders to rapidly reenvision Mayo's processes and materials to provide patient-centered tools and support to enable people and their families to have the most successful transitions and connections with ongoing care possible.
21	Health and Well-Being	Healthy Living Lab	The CFI is collaborating with an external partner to design, build, and operate a Healthy Living Lab in Rochester to study and validate health and wellness products and services in a simulated home environment.
22	Health and Well-Being	In-Home Monitoring: Recliner	Patients with congestive heart failure (CHF) generally have low adherence levels with weight monitoring. For high-risk CHF patients who spend a vast majority of their day in a recliner, we can place sensors under the legs of the chair and connect them to a device that sends data to determine if there are dangerous trends. Outputs will inform impact on patient health and functional/experiential needs.

Continued

Count	Platform	Projects	Description
23	Health and Well-Being	Transition Aid	This is a qualitative research project with the intention of identifying reasons for readmissions that correlate to some degree with Krumholz's "Post Hospital Syndrome" paper. By observing the patient journey at the hospital and in the home, we hope to find opportunities to intervene in situations that would have otherwise led to a hospital readmission for the patient.
24	Health and Well-Being	Student Health and Well-Being	The CFI and Arizona State University (ASU) believe there is significant opportunity to help students enhance their health and well-being. The CFI and ASU wish to explore and understand the needs of students and formulate approaches that enhance the daily lives of the ASU student body and contribute to the Mayo objective of connecting with 200 million people by 2020.
25	Mayo Practice	Population Health Model	The CFI is partnering with Mayo's Office of Population Health Management to create, pilot, and implement a population health model that: – Recenters the system on the patient's needs—clinical and nonmedical – Delivers coordinated, integrated care at the right time, in the right place, by the right person, in the right way – Improves system capacity, flexibility, and resiliency – Leverages community and government assets to reduce or remove obstacles to health and long-term wellness for individuals – Reduces costs to people and the practice – Prepares for the shift to pay for value and total cost of care
26	Mayo Practice	Patient-Centered Care Plan	A unified tool for patients, caregivers, and clinicians to see, make, and act on care decisions together.
27	Mayo Practice	Optimized Care Team: Primary Care	A co-located, multidisciplinary group of physicians, nurses, clinical assistants, and a new role of a navigator that works together to meet the needs of a shared team patient panel.
28	Mayo Practice	Optimized Care Team: Specialty Practice	Applying the Optimized Care Team in the specialty practice.
29	Mayo Practice	Wellness Navigators	A volunteer-provided, clinic-embedded service that connects patients with resources to address social determinants of health.
30	Mayo Practice	Project Mars	A major project reimagining the outpatient practice of the future. Focused on reducing outpatient practice costs by at least 30 percent while maintaining or improving patient experience and quality of care. The project is aiming to implement new models to greater than 40 percent of the outpatient practice by the end of 2014.

Count	Platform	Projects	Description
31	Mayo Practice	Project Mars: microConsult	A scheduled or unscheduled interaction between a provider and patient who connect with a specialist to answer a focused question. The connection occurs via information and communication technology, and the result allows the initiating providers to move forward with their treatment of the patient, eliminating the need for a separate referral.
32	Mayo Practice	Project Mars: SmartSpace	A project testing if automatically filling in clerical information (orders, clinical notes, billing, and surgical listings) will increase efficiencies and reduce redundancies. The hypothesis is that clerical resources can be reduced through situational awareness, real-time visual feedback of data, and condensed data entry streams involving natural user interfaces, including speech recognition and touch-enabled data entry.
33	Mayo Practice	Project Mars: Virtual Group Visit	The experimental family will test if group visits, also known as *shared medical appointments*, will lower costs, open access, and improve the patient experience and management of health for a subset of patients across different departments.
34	Mayo Practice	Cardiovascular Valve Clinic	The project is working to drive efficiencies in the Valve Clinic through the combination of workflow standardization, new communication strategies, and enabling tools to optimize the care team.
35	Mayo Practice	Phoenix Campus Advancement Project	The Phoenix Campus Advancement Project (PCAP) consists of a 217,000-square-foot, three-story expansion on top of the Proton Beam at Mayo Clinic Hospital–Arizona. The PCAP will provide space to create the comprehensive Cancer Center. CFI is helping to define what integrated cancer care is, understand what the patients desire to experience through their journey, and explore services and spaces for patients and providers.
36	Mayo Practice	Chemo Redesign	Designing a state-of-the-art chemotherapy facility connecting clinical care, research, and education while providing service, safety, and quality outcomes in a cost-effective manner.
37	Mayo Practice	Pediatrics Transitions	Gaining a greater understanding of the needs of patients, parents, and care team members to maintain or improve the overall health of patients 12 to 25 with chronic conditions as they transition from pediatric to adult care.
38	Mayo Practice	Hospital Patient Experience	Through focusing on a deep understanding of the patient journey in the hospital, we are working to create better experiences resulting in a competitive advantage in the marketplace.
39	Mayo Practice	Department of Medicine Practice Redesign	The Arizona Department of Medicine Practice Redesign is creating an outpatient practice that is more efficient and more satisfying for both patients and providers. A major component of this redesign is not only to find an ideal workflow for the current reimbursement climate but also to develop strong and flexible teamwork with effective tools to meet the changing health care landscape.

INDEX

ABOUT THE AUTHORS

Nicholas LaRusso, M.D., a physician scientist and practicing liver specialist, is the founding medical director of the Mayo Clinic Center for Innovation, the Charles H. Weinman Endowed Professor of Medicine and Biochemistry and Molecular Biology, and a Distinguished Investigator of Mayo Clinic.

Barbara Spurrier, MHA, is the founding and current administrative director of the Mayo Clinic Center for Innovation. She has advised senior leaders in the health care industry for over two decades, serving as a champion for innovation in large, complex environments.

Gianrico Farrugia, M.D., is the Carlson and Nelson Endowed Director of the Mayo Clinic Center for Individualized Medicine and the founding associate medical director of the Mayo Clinic Center for Innovation. He is a practicing gastroenterologist and a professor of medicine and physiology at Mayo Clinic.